That Affair Next Door

by

Anna Katharine Green

Double 9
BOOKS

That Affair Next Door
by Anna Katharine Green

ISBN: 978-93-58710-53-3

Published by

DOUBLE 9 BOOKS

2/13-B, Ansari Road
Daryaganj, New Delhi – 110002
info@double9books.com
www.double9books.com
Tel. 011-40042856

This book is under public domain

ABOUT THE AUTHOR

The American author Anna Katharine Green (1846–1955), who is recognized as one of the forerunners of detective fiction, was raised in a sophisticated and educated household and was born in Brooklyn, New York. Her debut book, "The Leavenworth Case," which was released in 1878, quickly rose to popularity. She produced countless short pieces in the genre in addition to almost 40 books. Intricate riddles, brilliant storytelling, and the use of forensic evidence were hallmarks of her books, which also often included characters like detective Ebenezer Gryce and the single sleuth Amelia Butterworth. Along with her contributions to the genre, Green pioneered the exploration of gender and social class issues in mysteries, often utilizing her characters to remark on societal injustices. She was on the executive committee of the New York State Suffrage Association and sponsored issues including public health and education, demonstrating her commitment to women's suffrage and charity. Her contributions to the detective fiction genre are still respected and recognized in modern times.

CONTENTS

BOOK I.
MISS BUTTERWORTH'S WINDOW.

I.
A DISCOVERY.

I am not an inquisitive woman, but when, in the middle of a certain warm night in September, I heard a carriage draw up at the adjoining house and stop, I could not resist the temptation of leaving my bed and taking a peep through the curtains of my window.

First: because the house was empty, or supposed to be so, the family still being, as I had every reason to believe, in Europe; and secondly: because, not being inquisitive, I often miss in my lonely and single life much that it would be both interesting and profitable for me to know.

Luckily I made no such mistake this evening. I rose and looked out, and though I was far from realizing it at the time, took, by so doing, my first step in a course of inquiry which has ended — —

But it is too soon to speak of the end. Rather let me tell you what I saw when I parted the curtains of my window in Gramercy Park, on the night of September 17, 1895.

Not much at first glance, only a common hack drawn up at the neighboring curb-stone. The lamp which is supposed to light our part of the block is some rods away on the opposite side of the street, so that I obtained but a shadowy glimpse of a young man and woman standing below me on the pavement. I could see, however, that the woman—and not the man—was putting money into the driver's hand. The next moment they were on the stoop of this long-closed house, and the coach rolled off.

It was dark, as I have said, and I did not recognize the young people,—at least their figures were not familiar to me; but when, in another instant, I heard the click of a night-key, and saw them, after a rather tedious fumbling at the lock, disappear from the stoop, I took it for granted that the gentleman was Mr. Van Burnam's eldest son Franklin, and the lady some relative of the family; though why this, its most punctilious member, should bring a guest at so late an hour into a house devoid of everything necessary to make the least exacting visitor comfortable, was a mystery that I retired to bed to meditate upon.

I did not succeed in solving it, however, and after some ten minutes had elapsed, I was settling myself again to sleep when I was re-aroused by a fresh sound from the quarter mentioned. The door I had so lately heard shut, opened again, and though I had to rush for it, I succeeded in getting to my window in time to catch a glimpse of the departing figure of the young man hurrying away towards Broadway. The young woman was not with him, and as I realized that he had left her behind him in the great, empty house, without apparent light and certainly without any companion, I began to question if this was like Franklin Van Burnam. Was it not more in keeping with the recklessness of his more easy-natured and less reliable brother, Howard, who, some two or three years back, had married a young wife of no very satisfactory antecedents, and who, as I had heard, had been ostracized by the family in consequence?

Whichever of the two it was, he had certainly shown but little consideration for his companion, and thus thinking, I fell off to sleep just as the clock struck the half hour after midnight.

Next morning as soon as modesty would permit me to approach the window, I surveyed the neighboring house minutely. Not a blind was open, nor a shutter displaced. As I am an early riser, this did not disturb me at the time, but when after breakfast I looked again and still failed to detect any evidences of life in the great barren front beside me, I began to feel uneasy. But I did nothing till noon, when going into my rear garden and observing that the back windows of the Van Burnam house were as closely shuttered as the front, I became so anxious that I stopped the next policeman I saw going by, and telling him my suspicions, urged him to ring the bell.

No answer followed the summons.

"There is no one here," said he.

"Ring again!" I begged.

And he rang again but with no better result.

"Don't you see that the house is shut up?" he grumbled. "We have had orders to watch the place, but none to take the watch off."

"There is a young woman inside," I insisted. "The more I think over last night's occurrence, the more I am convinced that the matter should be looked into."

He shrugged his shoulders and was moving away when we both observed a common-looking woman standing in front looking at us. She had a bundle in her hand, and her face, unnaturally ruddy though it was, had a scared look which was all the more remarkable from the fact that it was one of those wooden-like countenances which under ordinary circumstances are capable of but little expression. She was not a stranger to me; that is, I had seen her before in or about the house in which we were at that moment so interested; and not stopping to put any curb on my excitement, I rushed down to the pavement and accosted her.

"Who are you?" I asked. "Do you work for the Van Burnams, and do you know who the lady was who came here last night?"

The poor woman, either startled by my sudden address or by my manner which may have been a little sharp, gave a quick bound backward, and was only deterred by the near presence of the policeman from attempting flight. As it was, she stood her ground, though the fiery flush, which made her face so noticeable, deepened till her cheeks and brow were scarlet.

"I am the scrub-woman," she protested. "I have come to open the windows and air the house," —ignoring my last question.

"Is the family coming home?" the policeman asked.

"I don't know; I think so," was her weak reply.

"Have you the keys?" I now demanded, seeing her fumbling in her pocket.

She did not answer; a sly look displaced the anxious one she had hitherto displayed, and she turned away.

"I don't see what business it is of the neighbors," she muttered, throwing me a dissatisfied scowl over her shoulder.

"If you've got the keys, we will go in and see that things are all right," said the policeman, stopping her with a light touch.

She trembled; I saw that she trembled, and naturally became excited. Something was wrong in the Van Burnam mansion, and I was going to be present at its discovery. But her next words cut my hopes short.

"I have no objection to *your* going in," she said to the policeman, "but I will not give up my keys to *her*. What right has she in our house any way." And I thought I heard her murmur something about a meddlesome old maid.

The look which I received from the policeman convinced me that my ears had not played me false.

"The lady's right," he declared; and pushing by me quite disrespectfully, he led the way to the basement door, into which he and the so-called cleaner presently disappeared.

I waited in front. I felt it to be my duty to do so. The various passers-by stopped an instant to stare at me before proceeding on their way, but I did not flinch from my post. Not till I had heard that the young woman whom I had seen enter these doors at midnight was well, and that her delay in opening the windows was entirely due to fashionable laziness, would I feel justified in returning to my own home and its affairs. But it took patience and some courage to remain there. Several minutes elapsed before I perceived the shutters in the third story open, and a still longer time before a window on the second floor flew up and the policeman looked out, only to meet my inquiring gaze and rapidly disappear again.

Meantime three or four persons had stopped on the walk near me, the nucleus of a crowd which would not be long in collecting, and I was beginning to feel I was paying dearly for my virtuous resolution, when the front door burst violently open and we caught sight of the trembling form and shocked face of the scrub-woman.

"She's dead!" she cried, "she's dead! Murder!" and would have said more had not the policeman pulled her back, with a growl which sounded very much like a suppressed oath.

He would have shut the door upon me had I not been quicker than lightning. As it was, I got in before it slammed, and happily too; for just at that moment the house-cleaner, who had grown paler every instant, fell in a heap in the entry, and the policeman, who was not the man I would want about me in any trouble, seemed somewhat embarrassed by this new emergency, and let me lift the poor thing up and drag her farther into the hall.

She had fainted, and should have had something done for her, but anxious though I always am to be of help where help is needed, I had no sooner got within range of the parlor door with my burden, than I beheld a sight so terrifying that I involuntarily let the poor woman slip from my arms to the floor.

In the darkness of a dim corner (for the room had no light save that which came through the doorway where I stood) lay the form of a woman under a fallen piece of furniture. Her skirts and distended arms alone were visible; but no one who saw the rigid outlines of her limbs could doubt for a moment that she was dead.

At a sight so dreadful, and, in spite of all my apprehensions, so unexpected, I felt a sensation of sickness which in another moment might have ended in my fainting also, if I had not realized that it would never do for me to lose my wits in the presence of a man who had none too many of his own. So I shook off my momentary weakness, and turning to the policeman, who was hesitating between the unconscious figure of the woman outside the door and the dead form of the one within I cried sharply:

"Come, man, to business! The woman inside there is dead, but this one is living. Fetch me a pitcher of water from below if you can, and then go for whatever assistance you need. I'll wait here and bring this woman to. She is a strong one, and it won't take long."

"You'll stay here alone with that— —" he began.

But I stopped him with a look of disdain.

"Of course I will stay here; why not? Is there anything in the dead to be afraid of? Save me from the living, and I undertake to save myself from the dead."

But his face had grown very suspicious.

"You go for the water," he cried. "And see here! Just call out for some one to telephone to Police Headquarters for the Coroner and a detective. I don't quit this room till one or the other of them comes."

Smiling at a caution so very ill-timed, but abiding by my invariable rule of never arguing with a man unless I see some way of getting the better of him, I did what he bade me, though I hated dreadfully to leave the spot and its woful mystery, even for so short a time as was required.

"Run up to the second story," he called out, as I passed by the prostrate figure of the cleaner. "Tell them what you want from the window, or we will have the whole street in here."

So I ran up-stairs,—I had always wished to visit this house, but had never been encouraged to do so by the Misses Van Burnam,—and making my way into the front room, the door of which stood wide open, I rushed to the window and hailed the crowd, which by this time extended far out beyond the curb-stone.

"An officer!" I called out, "a police officer! An accident has occurred and the man in charge here wants the Coroner and a detective from Police Headquarters."

"Who's hurt?" "Is it a man?" "Is it a woman?" shouted up one or two; and "Let us in!" shouted others; but the sight of a boy rushing off to meet an advancing policeman satisfied me that help would soon be forthcoming, so I drew in my head and looked about me for the next necessity—water.

I was in a lady's bed-chamber, probably that of the eldest Miss Van Burnam; but it was a bed-chamber which had not been occupied for some months, and naturally it lacked the very articles which would have been of assistance to me in the present emergency. No *eau de Cologne* on the bureau, no camphor on the mantel-shelf. But there was water in the pipes (something I had hardly hoped for), and a mug on the wash-stand; so I filled the mug and ran with it to the door, stumbling, as I did so, over some small object which I presently perceived to be a little round pin-cushion. Picking it up, for I hate anything like disorder, I placed it on a table near by, and continued on my way.

The woman was still lying at the foot of the stairs. I dashed the water in her face and she immediately came to.

Sitting up, she was about to open her lips when she checked herself; a fact which struck me as odd, though I did not allow my surprise to become apparent.

Meantime I stole a glance into the parlor. The officer was standing where I had left him, looking down on the prostrate figure before him.

There was no sign of feeling in his heavy countenance, and he had not opened a shutter, nor, so far as I could see, disarranged an object in the room.

The mysterious character of the whole affair fascinated me in spite of myself, and leaving the now fully aroused woman in the hall, I was half-way across the parlor floor when the latter stopped me with a shrill cry:

"Don't leave me! I have never seen anything before so horrible. The poor dear! The poor dear! Why don't he take those dreadful things off her?"

She alluded not only to the piece of furniture which had fallen upon the prostrate woman, and which can best be described as a cabinet with closets below and shelves above, but to the various articles of *bric-à-brac* which had tumbled from the shelves, and which now lay in broken pieces about her.

"He will do so; they will do so very soon," I replied. "He is waiting for some one with more authority than himself; for the Coroner, if you know what that means."

"But what if she's alive! Those things will crush her. Let us take them off. I'll help. I'm not too weak to help."

"Do you know who this person is?" I asked, for her voice had more feeling in it than I thought natural to the occasion, dreadful as it was.

"I?" she repeated, her weak eyelids quivering for a moment as she tried to sustain my scrutiny. "How should I know? I came in with the policeman and haven't been any nearer than I now be. What makes you think I know anything about her? I'm only the scrub-woman, and don't even know the names of the family."

"I thought you seemed so very anxious," I explained, suspicious of her suspiciousness, which was of so sly and emphatic a character that it changed her whole bearing from one of fear to one of cunning in a moment.

"And who wouldn't feel the like of that for a poor creature lying crushed under a heap of broken crockery!"

Crockery! those Japanese vases worth hundreds of dollars! that ormulu clock and those Dresden figures which must have been more than a couple of centuries old!

"It's a poor sense of duty that keeps a man standing dumb and staring like that, when with a lift of his hand he could show us the like of her pretty face, and if it's dead she be or alive."

As this burst of indignation was natural enough and not altogether uncalled for from the standpoint of humanity, I gave the woman a nod of approval, and wished I were a man myself that I might lift the heavy cabinet or whatever it was that lay upon the poor creature before us. But not being a man, and not judging it wise to irritate the one representative of that sex then present, I made no remark, but only took a few steps farther into the room, followed, as it afterwards appeared, by the scrub-woman.

The Van Burnam parlors are separated by an open arch. It was to the right of this arch and in the corner opposite the doorway that the dead woman lay. Using my eyes, now that I was somewhat accustomed to the semi-darkness enveloping us, I noticed two or three facts which had hitherto escaped me. One was, that she lay on her back with her feet pointing towards the hall door, and another, that nowhere in the room, save in her immediate vicinity, were there to be seen any signs of struggle or disorder. All was as set and proper as in my own parlor when it has been undisturbed for any length of time by guests; and though I could not see far into the rooms beyond, they were to all appearance in an equally orderly condition.

Meanwhile the cleaner was trying to account for the overturned cabinet.

"Poor dear! poor dear! she must have pulled it over on herself! But however did she get into the house? And what was she doing in this great empty place?"

The policeman, to whom these remarks had evidently been addressed, growled out some unintelligible reply, and in her perplexity the woman turned towards me.

But what could I say to her? I had my own private knowledge of the matter, but she was not one to confide in, so I stoically shook my head. Doubly disappointed, the poor thing shrank back, after looking first at the policeman and then at me in an odd, appealing way, difficult to understand. Then her eyes fell again on the dead girl at her feet, and being nearer now than before, she evidently saw something that startled her, for she sank on her knees with a little cry and began examining the girl's skirts.

"What are you looking at there?" growled the policeman. "Get up, can't you! No one but the Coroner has right to lay hand on anything here."

"I'm doing no harm," the woman protested, in an odd, shaking voice. "I only wanted to see what the poor thing had on. Some blue stuff, isn't it?" she asked me.

"Blue serge," I answered; "store-made, but very good; must have come from Altman's or Stern's."

"I—I'm not used to sights like this," stammered the scrub-woman, stumbling awkwardly to her feet, and looking as if her few remaining wits had followed the rest on an endless vacation. "I—I think I shall have to go home." But she did not move.

"The poor dear's young, isn't she?" she presently insinuated, with an odd catch in her voice that gave to the question an air of hesitation and doubt.

"I think she is younger than either you or myself," I deigned to reply. "Her narrow pointed shoes show she has not reached the years of discretion."

"Yes, yes, so they do!" ejaculated the cleaner, eagerly—too eagerly for perfect ingenuousness. "That's why I said 'Poor dear!' and spoke of her pretty face. I am sorry for young folks when they get into trouble, aint you? You and me might lie here and no one be much the worse for it, but a sweet lady like this——"

This was not very flattering to me, but I was prevented from rebuking her by a prolonged shout from the stoop without, as a rush was made against the front door, followed by a shrill peal of the bell.

"Man from Headquarters," stolidly announced the policeman. "Open the door, ma'am; or step back into the further hall if you want me to do it."

Such rudeness was uncalled for; but considering myself too important a witness to show feeling, I swallowed my indignation and proceeded with all my native dignity to the front door.

II.
QUESTIONS.

As I did so, I could catch the murmur of the crowd outside as it seethed forward at the first intimation of the door being opened; but my attention was not so distracted by it, loud as it sounded after the quiet of the shut-up house, that I failed to notice that the door had not been locked by the gentleman leaving the night before, and that, consequently, only the night latch was on. With a turn of the knob it opened, showing me the mob of shouting boys and the forms of two gentlemen awaiting admittance on the door-step. I frowned at the mob and smiled on the gentlemen, one of whom was portly and easy-going in appearance, and the other spare, with a touch of severity in his aspect. But for some reason these gentlemen did not seem to appreciate the honor I had done them, for they both gave me a displeased glance, which was so odd and unsympathetic in its character that I bridled a little, though I soon returned to my natural manner. Did they realize at the first glance that I was destined to prove a thorn in the sides of every one connected with this matter, for days to come?

"Are you the woman who called from the window?" asked the larger of the two, whose business here I found it difficult at first to determine.

"I am," was my perfectly self-possessed reply. "I live next door and my presence here is due to the anxious interest I always take in my neighbors. I had reason to think that all was not as it should be in this house, and I was right. Look in the parlor, sirs."

They were already as far as the threshold of that room and needed no further encouragement to enter. The heavier man went first and the other followed, and you may be sure I was not far behind. The sight meeting our eyes was ghastly enough, as you know; but these men were evidently accustomed to ghastly sights, for they showed but little emotion.

"I thought this house was empty," observed the second gentleman, who was evidently a doctor.

"So it was till last night," I put in; and was about to tell my story, when I felt my skirts jerked.

Turning, I found that this warning had come from the cleaner who stood close beside me.

"What do you want?" I asked, not understanding her and having nothing to conceal.

"I?" she faltered, with a frightened air. "Nothing, ma'am, nothing."

"Then don't interrupt me," I harshly admonished her, annoyed at an interference that tended to throw suspicion upon my candor. "This woman came here to scrub and clean," I now explained; "it was by means of the key she carried that we were enabled to get into the house. I never spoke to her till a half hour ago."

At which, with a display of subtlety I was far from expecting in one of her appearance, she let her emotions take a fresh direction, and pointing towards the dead woman, she impetuously cried:

"But the poor child there! Aint you going to take those things off of her? It's wicked to leave her under all that stuff. Suppose there was life in her!"

"Oh! there's no hope of that," muttered the doctor, lifting one of the hands, and letting it fall again.

"Still—" he cast a side look at his companion, who gave him a meaning nod—"it might be well enough to lift this cabinet sufficiently for me to lay my hand on her heart."

They accordingly did this; and the doctor, leaning down, placed his hand over the poor bruised breast.

"No life," he murmured. "She has been dead some hours. Do you think we had better release the head?" he went on, glancing up at the portly man at his side.

But the latter, who was rapidly growing serious, made a slight protest with his finger, and turning to me, inquired, with sudden authority:

"What did you mean when you said that the house had been empty till last night?"

"Just what I said, sir. It was empty till about midnight, when two persons——" Again I felt my dress twitched, this time very cautiously. What did the woman want? Not daring to give her a look, for these men were only too ready to detect harm in everything I did, I gently drew my skirt away and took a step aside, going on as if no interruption had occurred. "Did I say persons? I should have said a man and a woman drove up to the house and entered. I saw them from my window."

"You did?" murmured my interlocutor, whom I had by this time decided to be a detective. "And this is the woman, I suppose?" he proceeded, pointing to the poor creature lying before us.

"Why, yes, of course. Who else can she be? I did not see the lady's face last night, but she was young and light on her feet, and ran up the stoop gaily."

"And the man? Where is the man? I don't see him here."

"I am not surprised at that. He went very soon after he came, not ten minutes after, I should say. That is what alarmed me and caused me to have the house investigated. It did not seem natural or like any of the Van Burnams to leave a woman to spend the night in so large a house alone."

"You know the Van Burnams?"

"Not well. But that don't signify. I know what report says of them; they are gentlemen."

"But Mr. Van Burnam is in Europe."

"He has two sons."

"Living here?"

"No; the unmarried one spends his nights at Long Branch, and the other is with his wife somewhere in Connecticut."

"How did the young couple you saw get in last night? Was there any one here to admit them?"

"No; the gentleman had a key."

"Ah, he had a key."

The tone in which this was said recurred to me afterwards, but at the moment I was much more impressed by a peculiar sound I heard behind me, something between a gasp and a click in the throat, which came I knew from the scrub-woman, and which, odd and contradictory as it may appear, struck me as an expression of satisfaction, though what there was in my admission to give satisfaction to this poor creature I could not conjecture. Moving so as to get a glimpse of her face, I went on with the grim self-possession natural to my character:

"And when he came out he walked briskly away. The carriage had not waited for him."

"Ah!" again muttered the gentleman, picking up one of the broken pieces of china which lay haphazard about the floor, while I studied the cleaner's face, which, to my amazement, gave evidences of a confusion of emotions most unaccountable to me.

Mr. Gryce may have noticed this too, for he immediately addressed her, though he continued to look at the broken piece of china in his hand.

"And how come you to be cleaning the house?" he asked. "Is the family coming home?"

"They are, sir," she answered, hiding her emotion with great skill the moment she perceived attention directed to herself, and speaking with a sudden volubility that made us all stare. "They are expected any day. I didn't know it till yesterday—was it yesterday? No, the day before—when young Mr. Franklin—he is the oldest son, sir, and a very nice man, a *very* nice man— sent me word by letter that I was to get the house ready. It isn't the first time I have done it for them, sir, and as soon as I could get the basement key from the agent, I came here, and worked all day yesterday, washing up the floors and dusting. I should have been at them again this morning if my husband hadn't been sick. But I had to go to the infirmary for medicine, and it was noon when I got here, and then I found this lady standing outside with a policeman, a very nice lady, a very *nice* lady indeed, sir, I pay my respects to her"—and she actually dropped me a curtsey like a peasant woman in a play—"and they took my key from me, and the policeman opens the door, and he and me go upstairs and into all the rooms, and when we come to this one— —"

She was getting so excited as to be hardly intelligible. Stopping herself with a jerk, she fumbled nervously with her apron, while I asked myself how she could have been at work in this house the day before without my knowing it. Suddenly I remembered that I was ill in the morning and busy in the afternoon at the Orphan Asylum, and somewhat relieved at finding so excellent an excuse for my ignorance, I looked up to see if the detective had noticed anything odd in this woman's behavior. Presumably he had, but having more experience than myself with the susceptibility of ignorant persons in the presence of danger and distress, he attached less importance to it than I did, for which I was secretly glad, without exactly knowing my reasons for being so.

"You will be wanted as a witness by the Coroner's jury," he now remarked to her, looking as if he were addressing the piece of china he was turning over in his hand. "Now, no nonsense!" he protested, as she commenced to tremble and plead. "You were the first one to see this dead woman, and you must be on hand to say so. As I cannot tell you when the inquest will be held, you had better stay around till the Coroner comes. He'll be here soon. You, and this other woman too."

By other woman he meant *me*, Miss Butterworth, of Colonial ancestry and no inconsiderable importance in the social world. But though I did not relish this careless association of myself with this poor scrub-woman, I was careful to show no displeasure, for I reasoned that as witnesses we were equal before the law, and that it was solely in this light he regarded us.

There was something in the manner of both these gentlemen which convinced me that while my presence was considered desirable in the house, it was not especially wanted in the room. I was therefore moving reluctantly away, when I felt a slight but peremptory touch on the arm, and turning, saw the detective at my side, still studying his piece of china.

He was, as I have said, of portly build and benevolent aspect; a fatherly-looking man, and not at all the person one would be likely to associate with the police. Yet he could take the lead very naturally, and when he spoke, I felt bound to answer him.

"Will you be so good, madam, as to relate over again, what you saw from your window last night? I am likely to have charge of this matter, and would be pleased to hear all you may have to say concerning it."

"My name is Butterworth," I politely intimated.

"And my name is Gryce."

"A detective?"

"The same."

"You must think this matter very serious," I ventured.

"Death by violence is always serious."

"You must regard this death as something more than an accident, I mean."

His smile seemed to say: "You will not know to-day how I regard it."

"And you will not know to-day what I think of it either," was my inward rejoinder, but I said nothing aloud, for the man was seventy-five if he was a day, and I have been taught respect for age, and have practised the same for fifty years and more.

I must have shown what was passing in my mind, and he must have seen it reflected on the polished surface of the porcelain he was contemplating, for his lips showed the shadow of a smile sufficiently sarcastic for me to see that he was far from being as easy-natured as his countenance indicated.

"Come, come," said he, "there is the Coroner now. Say what you have to say, like the straightforward, honest woman you appear."

"I don't like compliments," I snapped out. Indeed, they have always been obnoxious to me. As if there was any merit in being honest and straightforward, or any distinction in being told so!

"I am Miss Butterworth, and not in the habit of being spoken to as if I were a simple countrywoman," I objected. "But I will repeat what I saw last night, as it is no secret, and the telling of it won't hurt me and may help you."

Accordingly I went over the whole story, and was much more loquacious than I had intended to be, his manner was so insinuating and his inquiries so pertinent. But one topic we both failed to broach, and that was the peculiar manner of the scrub-woman. Perhaps it had not struck him as peculiar and perhaps it should not have struck me so, but in the silence which was preserved on the subject I felt I had acquired an advantage over him, which might lead to consequences of no small importance. Would I have felt thus or congratulated myself quite so much upon my fancied superiority, if I had known he was the man who managed the Leavenworth case, and who in his early years had experienced that very wonderful adventure on the staircase of the Heart's Delight? Perhaps I would; for though I have had no adventures, I feel capable of them, and as for any peculiar acumen he may have shown in his long and eventful career, why that is a quality which others may share with him, as I hope to be able to prove before finishing these pages.

III.
AMELIA DISCOVERS HERSELF.

There is a small room at the extremity of the Van Burnam mansion. In this I took refuge after my interview with Mr. Gryce. As I picked out the chair which best suited me and settled myself for a comfortable communion with my own thoughts, I was astonished to find how much I was enjoying myself, notwithstanding the thousand and one duties awaiting me on the other side of the party-wall.

Even this very solitude was welcome, for it gave me an opportunity to consider matters. I had not known up to this very hour that I had any special gifts. My father, who was a shrewd man of the old New England type, said more times than I am years old (which was not saying it as often as some may think) that Araminta (the name I was christened by, and the name you will find in the Bible record, though I sign myself Amelia, and insist upon being addressed as Amelia, being, as I hope, a sensible woman and not the piece of antiquated sentimentality suggested by the former cognomen)—that Araminta would live to make her mark; though in what capacity he never informed me, being, as I have observed, a shrewd man, and thus not likely to thoughtlessly commit himself.

I now know he was right; my pretensions dating from the moment I found that this affair, at first glance so simple, and at the next so complicated, had aroused in me a fever of investigation which no reasoning could allay. Though I had other and more personal matters on my mind, my thoughts would rest nowhere but on the details of this tragedy; and having, as I thought, noticed some few facts in connection with it, from which conclusions might be drawn, I amused myself with jotting them down on the back of a disputed grocer's bill I happened to find in my pocket.

Valueless as explaining this tragedy, being founded upon insufficient evidence, they may be interesting as showing the workings of my mind even at this early stage of the matter. They were drawn up under three heads.

First, was the death of this young woman an accident?

Second, was it a suicide?

Third, was it a murder?

Under the first head I wrote:

My reasons for not thinking it an accident.

1. If it had been an accident and she had pulled the cabinet over upon herself, she would have been found with her feet pointing towards the wall where the cabinet had stood.

(But her feet were towards the door and her head under the cabinet.)

2. The decent, even precise, arrangement of the clothing about her feet, which precludes any theory involving accident.

Under the second:

Reason for not thinking it suicide.

She could not have been found in the position observed without having lain down on the floor while living and then pulled the shelves down upon herself.

(A theory obviously too improbable to be considered.)

Under the third:

Reason for not thinking it murder.

She would need to have been held down on the floor while the cabinet was being pulled over on her; something which the quiet aspect of the hands and feet made appear impossible.

To this I added:

Reasons for accepting the theory of murder.

1. The fact that she did not go into the house alone; that a man entered with her, remained ten minutes, and then came out again and disappeared up the street with every appearance of haste and an anxious desire to leave the spot.

2. The front door, which he had unlocked on entering, was not locked by him on his departure, the catch doing the locking. Yet, though he could have re-entered so easily, he had shown no disposition to return.

3. The arrangement of the skirts, which show the touch of a careful hand after death.

Nothing clear, you see. I was doubtful of all; and yet my suspicions tended most toward murder.

I had eaten my luncheon before interfering in this matter, which was fortunate for me, as it was three o'clock before I was summoned to meet the Coroner, of whose arrival I had been conscious some time before.

He was in the front parlor where the dead girl lay, and as I took my way thither I felt the same sensations of faintness which had so nearly overcome me on the previous occasion. But I mastered them, and was quite myself before I crossed the threshold.

There were several gentlemen present, but of them all I only noticed two, one of whom I took to be the Coroner, while the other was my late interlocutor, Mr. Gryce. From the animation observable in the latter, I gathered that the case was growing in interest from the detective standpoint.

"Ah, and is this the witness?" asked the Coroner, as I stepped into the room.

"I am Miss Butterworth," was my calm reply. "*Amelia* Butterworth. Living next door and present at the discovery of this poor murdered body."

"Murdered," he repeated. "Why do you say murdered?"

For reply I drew from my pocket the bill on which I had scribbled my conclusions in regard to this matter.

"Read this," said I.

Evidently astonished, he took the paper from my hand, and, after some curious glances in my direction, condescended to do as I requested. The result was an odd but grudging look of admiration directed towards myself and a quick passing over of the paper to the detective.

The latter, who had exchanged his bit of broken china for a very much used and tooth-marked lead-pencil, frowned with a whimsical air at the latter before he put it in his pocket. Then he read my hurried scrawl.

"Two Richmonds in the field!" commented the Coroner, with a sly chuckle. "I am afraid I shall have to yield to their allied forces. Miss Butterworth, the cabinet is about to be raised; do you feel as if you could endure the sight?"

"I can stand anything where the cause of justice is involved," I replied.

"Very well, then, sit down, if you please. When the whole body is visible I will call you."

And stepping forward he gave orders to have the clock and broken china removed from about the body.

As the former was laid away on one end of the mantel some one observed:

"What a valuable witness that clock might have been had it been running when the shelves fell!"

But the fact was so patent that it had not been in motion for months that no one even answered; and Mr. Gryce did not so much as look towards it. But then we had all seen that the hands stood at three minutes to five.

I had been asked to sit down, but I found this impossible. Side by side with the detective, I viewed the replacing of that heavy piece of furniture against the wall, and the slow disclosure of the upper part of the body which had so long lain hidden.

That I did not give way is a proof that my father's prophecy was not without some reasonable foundation; for the sight was one to try the stoutest nerves, as well as to awaken the compassion of the hardest heart.

The Coroner, meeting my eye, pointed at the poor creature inquiringly.

"Is this the woman you saw enter here last night?"

I glanced down at her dress, noted the short summer cape tied to the neck with an elaborate bow of ribbon, and nodded my head.

"I remember the cape," said I. "But where is her hat? She wore one. Let me see if I can describe it." Closing my eyes I endeavored to recall the dim silhouette of her figure as she stood passing up the change to the driver; and was so far successful that I was ready to announce at the next moment that her hat presented the effect of a soft felt with one feather or one bow of ribbon standing upright from the side of the crown.

"Then the identity of this woman with the one you saw enter here last night is established," remarked the detective, stooping down and drawing from under the poor girl's body a hat, sufficiently like the one I had just described, to satisfy everybody that it was the same.

"As if there could be any doubt," I began.

But the Coroner, explaining that it was a mere formality, motioned me to stand aside in favor of the doctor, who seemed anxious to approach nearer the spot where the dead woman lay. This I was about to do when a sudden thought struck me, and I reached out my hand for the hat.

"Let me look at it for a moment," said I.

Mr. Gryce at once handed it over, and I took a good look at it inside and out.

"It is pretty badly crushed," I observed, "and does not present a very fresh appearance, but for all that it has been worn but once."

"How do you know?" questioned the Coroner.

"Let the other Richmond inform you," was my grimly uttered reply, as I gave it again into the detective's hand.

There was a murmur about me, whether of amusement or displeasure, I made no effort to decide. I was finding out something for myself, and I did not care what they thought of me.

"Neither has she worn this dress long," I continued; "but that is not true of the shoes. They are not old, but they have been acquainted with the pavement, and that is more than can be said of the hem of this gown. There are no gloves on her hands; a few minutes elapsed then before the assault; long enough for her to take them off."

"Smart woman!" whispered a voice in my ear; a half-admiring, half-sarcastic voice that I had no difficulty in ascribing to Mr. Gryce. "But are you sure she wore any? Did you notice that her hand was gloved when she came into the house?"

"No," I answered, frankly; "but so well-dressed a woman would not enter a house like this, without gloves."

"It was a warm night," some one suggested.

"I don't care. You will find her gloves as you have her hat; and you will find them with the fingers turned inside out, just as she drew them from her hand. So much I will concede to the warmth of the weather."

"Like these, for instance," broke in a quiet voice.

Startled, for a hand had appeared over my shoulder dangling a pair of gloves before my eyes, I cried out, somewhat too triumphantly I own:

"Yes, yes, just like those! Did you pick them up here? Are they hers?"

"You say that this is the way hers should look."

"And I repeat it."

"Then allow me to pay you my compliments. These were picked up here."

"But where?" I cried. "I thought I had looked this carpet well over."

He smiled, not at me but at the gloves, and the thought crossed me that he felt as if something more than the gloves was being turned inside out. I therefore pursed my mouth, and determined to stand more on my guard.

"It is of no consequence," I assured him; "all such matters will come out at the inquest."

Mr. Gryce nodded, and put the gloves back in his pocket. With them he seemed to pocket some of his geniality and patience.

"All these facts have been gone over before you came in," said he, which statement I beg to consider as open to doubt.

The doctor, who had hardly moved a muscle during all this colloquy, now rose from his kneeling position beside the girl's head.

"I shall have to ask the presence of another physician," said he. "Will you send for one from your office, Coroner Dahl?"

At which I stepped back and the Coroner stepped forward, saying, however, as he passed me:

"The inquest will be held day after to-morrow in my office. Hold yourself in readiness to be present. I regard you as one of my chief witnesses."

I assured him I would be on hand, and, obeying a gesture of his finger, retreated from the room; but I did not yet leave the house. A straight, slim man, with a very small head but a very bright eye, was leaning on the newel-post in the front hall, and when he saw me, started up so alertly I perceived that he had business with me, and so waited for him to speak.

"You are Miss Butterworth?" he inquired.

"I am, sir."

"And I am a reporter from the New York *World*. Will you allow me— —"

Why did he stop? I had merely looked at him. But he did stop, and that is saying considerable for a reporter from the New York *World*.

"I certainly am willing to tell you what I have told every one else," I interposed, considering it better not to make an enemy of so judicious a young man; and seeing him brighten up at this, I thereupon related all I considered desirable for the general public to know.

I was about passing on, when, reflecting that one good turn deserves another, I paused and asked him if he thought they would leave the dead girl in that house all night.

He answered that he did not think they would. That a telegram had been sent some time before to young Mr. Van Burnam, and that they were only awaiting his arrival to remove her.

"Do you mean Howard?" I asked.

"Is he the elder one?"

"No."

"It is the elder one they have summoned; the one who has been staying at Long Branch."

"How can they expect him then so soon?"

"Because he is in the city. It seems the old gentleman is going to return on the *New York*, and as she is due here to-day, Franklin Van Burnam has come to New York to meet him."

"Humph!" thought I, "lively times are in prospect," and for the first time I remembered my dinner and the orders which had not been given about some curtains which were to have been hung that day, and all the other reasons I had for being at home.

I must have shown my feelings, much as I pride myself upon my impassibility upon all occasions, for he immediately held out his arm, with an offer to pilot me through the crowd to my own house; and I was about to accept it when the door-bell rang so sharply that we involuntarily stopped.

"A fresh witness or a telegram for the Coroner," whispered the reporter in my ear.

I tried to look indifferent, and doubtless made out pretty well, for he added, after a sly look in my face:

"You do not care to stay any longer?"

I made no reply, but I think he was impressed by my dignity. Could he not see that it would be the height of ill-manners for me to rush out in the face of any one coming in?

An officer opened the door, and when we saw who stood there, I am sure that the reporter, as well as myself, was grateful that we listened to the dictates of politeness. It was young Mr. Van Burnam—Franklin; I mean the older and more respectable of the two sons.

He was flushed and agitated, and looked as if he would like to annihilate the crowd pushing him about on his own stoop. He gave an angry glance backward as he stepped in, and then I saw that a carriage covered with baggage stood on the other side of the street, and gathered that he had not returned to his father's house alone.

"What has happened? What does all this mean?" were the words he hurled at us as the door closed behind him and he found himself face to face with a half dozen strangers, among whom the reporter and myself stood conspicuous.

Mr. Gryce, coming suddenly from somewhere, was the one to answer him.

"A painful occurrence, sir. A young girl has been found here, dead, crushed under one of your parlor cabinets."

"A young girl!" he repeated. (Oh, how glad I was that I had been brought up never to transgress the principles of politeness.) "Here! in this shut-up house? What young girl? You mean old woman, do you not? the house-cleaner or some one——"

"No, Mr. Van Burnam, we mean what we say, though possibly I should call her a young lady. She is dressed quite fashionably."

"The ——" Really I cannot repeat in this public manner the word which Mr. Van Burnam used. I excused him at the time, but I will not perpetuate his forgetfulness in these pages.

"She is still lying as we found her," Mr. Gryce now proceeded in his quiet, almost fatherly way. "Will you not take a look at her? Perhaps you can tell us who she is?"

"I?" Mr. Van Burnam seemed quite shocked. "How should I know her! Some thief probably, killed while meddling with other people's property."

"Perhaps," quoth Mr. Gryce, laconically; at which I felt so angry, as tending to mislead my handsome young neighbor, that I irresistibly did what I had fully made up my mind not to do, that is, stepped into view and took a part in this conversation.

"How can you say that," I cried, "when her admittance here was due to a young man who let her in at midnight with a key, and then left her to eat out her heart in this great house all alone."

I have made sensations in my life, but never quite so marked a one as this. In an instant every eye was on me, with the exception of the detective's. His was on the figure crowning the newel-post, and bitterly severe his gaze was too, though it immediately grew wary as the young man started towards me and impetuously demanded:

"Who talks like that? Why, it's Miss Butterworth. Madam, I fear I did not fully understand what you said."

Whereupon I repeated my words, this time very quietly but clearly, while Mr. Gryce continued to frown at the bronze figure he had taken into his confidence. When I had finished, Mr. Van Burnam's countenance had changed, so had his manner. He held himself as erect as before, but not with as much bravado. He showed haste and impatience also, but not the same kind of haste and not quite the same kind of impatience. The corners of Mr. Gryce's mouth betrayed that he noted this change, but he did not turn away from the newel-post.

"This is a remarkable circumstance which you have just told me," observed Mr. Van Burnam, with the first bow I had ever received from him.

"I don't know what to think of it. But I still hold that it's some thief. Killed, did you say? Really dead? Well, I'd have given five hundred dollars not to have had it happen in this house."

He had been moving towards the parlor door, and he now entered it. Instantly Mr. Gryce was by his side.

"Are they going to close the door?" I whispered to the reporter, who was taking this all in equally with myself.

"I'm afraid so," he muttered.

And they did. Mr. Gryce had evidently had enough of my interference, and was resolved to shut me out, but I heard one word and caught one glimpse of Mr. Van Burnam's face before the heavy door fell to. The word was: "Oh, so bad as that! How can any one recognize her——" And the glimpse—well, the glimpse proved to me that he was much more profoundly agitated than he wished to appear, and any extraordinary agitation on his part was certainly in direct contradiction to the very sentence he was at that moment uttering.

IV.
SILAS VAN BURNAM.

"However much I may be needed at home, I cannot reconcile it with my sense of duty to leave just yet," I confided to the reporter, with what I meant to be a proper show of reason and self-restraint; "Mr. Van Burnam may wish to ask me some questions."

"Of course, of course," acquiesced the other. "You are very right; always are very right, I should judge."

As I did not know what he meant by this, I frowned, always a wise thing to do in an uncertainty; that is,—if one wishes to maintain an air of independence and aversion to flattery.

"Will you not sit down?" he suggested. "There is a chair at the end of the hall."

But I had no need to sit. The front door-bell again rang, and simultaneously with its opening, the parlor door unclosed and Mr. Franklin Van Burnam appeared in the hall, just as Mr. Silas Van Burnam, his father, stepped into the vestibule.

"Father!" he remonstrated, with a troubled air; "could you not wait?"

The elder gentleman, who had evidently just been driven up from the steamer, wiped his forehead with an irascible air, that I will say I had noticed in him before and on much less provocation.

"Wait, with a yelling crowd screaming murder in my ear, and Isabella on one side of me calling for salts, and Caroline on the opposite seat getting that blue look about the mouth we have learned to dread so in a hot day like this? No, sir, when there is anything wrong going on I want to know it, and evidently there is something wrong going on here. What is it? Some of Howard's——"

But the son, seizing me by the hand and drawing me forward, put a quick stop to the old gentleman's sentence. "Miss Butterworth, father! Our next-door neighbor, you know."

"Ah! hum! ha! Miss Butterworth. How do you do, ma'am? What the — — is she doing here?" he grumbled, not so low but that I heard both the profanity and the none too complimentary allusion to myself.

"If you will come into the parlor, I will tell you," urged the son. "But what have you done with Isabella and Caroline? Left them in the carriage with that hooting mob about them?"

"I told the coachman to drive on. They are probably half-way around the block by this time."

"Then come in here. But don't allow yourself to be too much affected by what you will see. A sad accident has occurred here, and you must expect the sight of blood."

"Blood! Oh, I can stand that, if Howard — — "

The rest was lost in the sound of the closing door.

And now, you will say, I ought to have gone. And you are right, but would you have gone yourself, especially as the hall was full of people who did not belong there?

If you would, then condemn me for lingering just a few minutes longer.

The voices in the parlor were loud, but they presently subsided; and when the owner of the house came out again, he had a subdued look which was as great a contrast to his angry aspect on entering, as was the change I had observed in his son. He was so absorbed indeed that he did not notice me, though I stood directly in his way.

"Don't let Howard come," he was saying in a thick, low voice to his son. "Keep Howard away till we are sure — — "

I am confident that his son pressed his arm at this point, for he stopped short and looked about him in a blind and dazed way.

"Oh!" he ejaculated, in a tone of great displeasure. "This is the woman who saw — — "

"Miss Butterworth, father," the anxious voice of his son broke in. "Don't try to talk; such a sight is enough to unnerve any man."

"Yes, yes," blustered the old gentleman, evidently taking some hint from the other's tone or manner. "But where are the girls? They will be dead with terror, if we don't relieve their minds. They got the idea it was their brother Howard who was hurt; and so did I, but it's only some wandering waif— some— — "

It seemed as if he was not to be allowed to finish any of his sentences, for Franklin interrupted him at this point to ask him what he was going to do with the girls. Certainly he could not bring them in here.

"No," answered the father, but in the dreamy, inconsequential way of one whose thoughts were elsewhere. "I suppose I shall have to take them to some hotel."

Ah, an idea! I flushed as I realized the opportunity which had come to me and had to wait a moment not to speak with too much eagerness.

"Let me play the part of a neighbor," I prayed, "and accommodate the young ladies for the night. My house is near and quiet."

"But the trouble it will involve," protested Mr. Franklin.

"Is just what I need to allay my excitement," I responded. "I shall be glad to offer them rooms for the night. If they are equally glad to accept them — —"

"They must be!" the old gentleman declared. "I can't go running round with them hunting up rooms to-night. Miss Butterworth is very good; go find the girls, Franklin; let me have them off my mind, at least."

The young man bowed. I bowed, and was slipping at last from my place by the stairs when, for the third time, I felt my dress twitched.

"Are you going to keep to that story?" a voice whispered in my ear. "About the young man and woman coming in the night, you know."

"Keep to it!" I whispered back, recognizing the scrub-woman, who had sidled up to me from some unknown quarter in the semi-darkness. "Why, it's true. Why shouldn't I keep to it."

A chuckle, difficult to describe but full of meaning, shook the arm of the woman as she pressed close to my side.

"Oh, you are a good one," she said. "I didn't know they made 'em so good!" And with another chuckle full of satisfaction and an odd sort of admiration I had certainly not earned, she slid away again into the darkness.

Certainly there was something in this woman's attitude towards this affair which merited attention.

V.
"THIS IS NO ONE I KNOW."

I welcomed the Misses Van Burnam with just enough good-will to show that I had not been influenced by any unworthy motives in asking them to my house.

I gave them my guest-chamber, but I invited them to sit in my front room as long as there was anything interesting going on in the street. I knew they would like to look out, and as this chamber boasts of a bay with two windows, we could all be accommodated. From where I sat I could now and then hear what they said, and I considered this but just, for if the young woman who had suffered so untimely an end was in any way connected with them, it was certainly best that the fact should not lie concealed; and one of them, that is Isabella, is such a chatterbox.

Mr. Van Burnam and his son had returned next door, and so far as we could observe from our vantage-point, preparations were being made for the body's removal. As the crowd below, driven away by the policemen one minute, only to collect again in another, swayed and grumbled in a continual expectation that was as continually disappointed, I heard Caroline's voice rise in two or three short sentences.

"They can't find Howard, or he would have been here before now. Did you see her that time when we were coming out of Clark's? Fanny Preston did, and said she was pretty."

"No, I didn't get a glimpse— —" A shout from the street below.

"I can't believe it," were the next words I heard, "but Franklin is awfully afraid— —"

"Hush! or the ogress— —" I am sure I heard her say ogress; but what followed was drowned in another loud murmur, and I caught nothing further till these sentences were uttered by the trembling and over-excited Caroline: "If it is she, pa will never be the same man again. To have her die in our house! O, there's Howard now!"

The interruption came quick and sharp, and it was followed by a double cry and an anxious rustle, as the two girls sprang to their feet in their anxiety to attract their brother's attention or possibly to convey him some warning.

But I did not give much heed to them. My eyes were on the carriage in which Howard had arrived, and which, owing to the ambulance in front, had stopped on the other side of the way. I was anxious to see him descend that I might judge if his figure recalled that of the man I had seen cross the pavement the night before. But he did not descend. Just as his hand was on the carriage door, a half dozen men appeared on the adjoining stoop carrying a burden which they hastened to deposit in the ambulance. He sank back when he saw it, and when his face became visible again, it was so white it seemed to be the only face in the street, though fifty people stood about staring at the house, at the ambulance, and at him.

Franklin Van Burnam had evidently come to the door with the rest; for Howard no sooner showed his face the second time than we saw the former dash down the steps and try to part the crowd in a vain attempt to reach his brother's side. Mr. Gryce was more successful. He had no difficulty in winning his way across the street, and presently I perceived him standing near the carriage exchanging a few words with its occupant. A moment later he drew back, and addressing the driver, jumped into the carriage with Howard, and was speedily driven off. The ambulance followed and some of the crowd, and as soon as a hack could be obtained, Mr. Van Burnam and his son took the same road, leaving us three women in a state of suspense, which as far as one of us was concerned, ended in a nervous attack that was not unlike heart failure. I allude, of course, to Caroline, and it took Isabella and myself a good half hour to bring her back to a normal condition, and when this was done, Isabella thought it incumbent upon her to go off into hysterics, which, being but a weak simulation of the other's state, I met with severity and cured with a frown. When both were in trim again I allowed myself one remark.

"One would think," said I, "that you knew the young woman who has fallen victim to her folly next door."

At which Isabella violently shook her head and Caroline observed:

"It is the excitement which has been too much for me. I am never strong, and this is such a dreadful home-welcoming. When will father and Franklin come back? It was very unkind of them to go off without one word of encouragement."

"They probably did not consider the fate of this unknown woman a matter of any importance to you."

The Van Burnam girls were unlike in appearance and character, but they showed an equal embarrassment at this, casting down their eyes and behaving so strangely that I was driven to wonder, without any show of hysterics I am happy to say, what would be the upshot of this matter, and how far I would become involved in it before the truth came to light.

At dinner they displayed what I should call their best society manner. Seeing this, I assumed my society manner also. It is formed on a different pattern from theirs, but is fully as impressive, I judge.

A most formal meal was the result. My best china was in use, but I had added nothing to my usual course of viands. Indeed, I had abstracted something. An *entrée*, upon which my cook prides herself, was omitted. Was I going to allow these proud young misses to think I had exerted myself to please them? No; rather would I have them consider me niggardly and an enemy to good living; so the *entrée* was, as the French say, suppressed.

In the evening their father came in. He was looking very dejected, and half his bluster was gone. He held a telegram crushed in his hand, and he talked very rapidly. But he confided none of his secrets to me, and I was obliged to say good-night to these young ladies without knowing much more about the matter engrossing us than when I left their house in the afternoon.

But others were not as ignorant as myself. A dramatic and highly exciting scene had taken place that evening at the undertaker's to which the unknown's body had been removed, and as I have more than once heard it minutely described, I will endeavor to transcribe it here with all the impartiality of an outsider.

When Mr. Gryce entered the carriage in which Howard sat, he noted first, that the young man was frightened; and secondly, that he made no effort to hide it. He had heard almost nothing from the detective. He knew that there had been a hue and cry for him ever since noon, and that he was wanted to identify a young woman who had been found dead in his father's house, but beyond these facts he had been told little, and yet he seemed to have no curiosity nor did he venture to express any surprise. He merely accepted the situation and was troubled by it, showing no inclination to talk till very near the end of his destination, when he suddenly pulled himself together and ventured this question:

"How did she—the young woman as you call her—kill herself?"

The detective, who in his long career among criminals and suspected persons, had seen many men and encountered many conditions, roused at this query with much of his old spirit. Turning from the man rather than toward him, he allowed himself a slight shrug of the shoulders as he calmly replied:

"She was found under a heavy piece of furniture; the cabinet with the vases on it, which you must remember stood at the left of the mantel-piece. It had crushed her head and breast. Quite a remarkable means of death, don't you think? There has been but one occurrence like it in my long experience."

"I don't believe what you tell me," was the young man's astonishing reply. "You are trying to frighten me or to make game of me. No lady would make use of any such means of death as that."

"I did not say she was a lady," returned Mr. Gryce, scoring one in his mind against his unwary companion.

A quiver passed down the young man's side where he came in contact with the detective.

"No," he muttered; "but I gathered from what you said, she was no common person; or why," he flashed out in sudden heat, "do you require me to go with you to see her? Have I the name of associating with any persons of the sex who are not ladies?"

"Pardon me," said Mr. Gryce, in grim delight at the prospect he saw slowly unfolding before him of one of those complicated affairs in which minds like his unconsciously revel; "I meant no insinuations. We have requested you, as we have requested your father and brother, to accompany us to the undertaker's, because the identification of the corpse is a most important point, and every formality likely to insure it must be observed."

"And did not they—my father and brother, I mean—recognize her?"

"It would be difficult for any one to recognize her who was not well acquainted with her."

A horrified look crossed the features of Howard Van Burnam, which, if a part of his acting, showed him to have genius for his *rôle*. His head sank back on the cushions of the carriage, and for a moment he closed his eyes. When he opened them again, the carriage had stopped, and Mr. Gryce, who had not noticed his emotion, of course, was looking out of the window with his hand on the handle of the door.

"Are we there already?" asked the young man, with a shudder. "I wish you had not considered it necessary for me to see her. I shall detect nothing familiar in her, I know."

Mr. Gryce bowed, repeated that it was a mere formality, and followed the young gentleman into the building and afterwards into the room where the dead body lay. A couple of doctors and one or two officials stood about, in whose faces the young man sought for something like encouragement before casting his eyes in the direction indicated by the detective. But there was little in any of these faces to calm him, and turning shortly away, he walked manfully across the room and took his stand by the detective.

"I am positive," he began, "that it is not my wife— —" At this moment the cloth that covered the body was removed, and he gave a great start of relief. "I said so," he remarked, coldly. "This is no one I know."

His sigh was echoed in double chorus from the doorway. Glancing that way he encountered the faces of his father and elder brother, and moved towards them with a relieved air that made quite another man of him in appearance.

"I have had my say," he remarked. "Shall I wait outside till you have had yours?"

"We have already said all that we had to," Franklin returned. "We declared that we did not recognize this person."

"Of course, of course," assented the other. "I don't see why they should have expected us to know her. Some common suicide who thought the house empty—But how did she get in?"

"Don't you know?" said Mr. Gryce. "Can it be that I forgot to tell you? Why, she was let in at night by a young man of medium height"—his eye ran up and down the graceful figure of the young *élégant* before him as he spoke—"who left her inside and then went away. A young man who had a key— —"

"A *key*? Franklin, I— —"

Was it a look from Franklin which made him stop? It is possible, for he turned on his heel as he reached this point, and tossing his head with quite a gay air, exclaimed: "But it is of no consequence! The girl is a stranger, and we have satisfied, I believe, all the requirements of the law in saying so, and may now drop the matter. Are you going to the club, Franklin?"

"Yes, but— —" Here the elder brother drew nearer and whispered something into the other's ear, who at that whisper turned again towards the place where the dead woman lay. Seeing this movement, his anxious father wiped the moisture from his forehead. Silas Van Burnam had been silent up to this moment and seemed inclined to continue so, but he watched his younger son with painful intentness.

"Nonsense!" broke from Howard's lips as his brother ceased his communication; but he took a step nearer the body, notwithstanding, and then another and another till he was at its side again.

The hands had not been injured, as we have said, and upon these his eyes now fell.

"They are like hers! O God! they are like hers!" he muttered, growing gloomy at once. "But where are the rings? There are no rings to be seen on these fingers, and she wore five, including her wedding-ring."

"Is it of your wife you are speaking?" inquired Mr. Gryce, who had edged up close to his side.

The young man was caught unawares.

He flushed deeply, but answered up boldly and with great appearance of candor:

"Yes; my wife left Haddam yesterday to come to New York, and I have not seen her since. Naturally I have felt some doubts lest this unhappy victim should be she. But I do not recognize her clothing; I do not recognize her form; only the hands look familiar."

"And the hair?"

"Is of the same color as hers, but it's a very ordinary color. I do not dare to say from anything I see that this is my wife."

"We will call you again after the doctor has finished his autopsy," said Mr. Gryce. "Perhaps you will hear from Mrs. Van Burnam before then."

But this intimation did not seem to bring comfort with it. Mr. Van Burnam walked away, white and sick, for which display of emotion there was certainly some cause, and rejoining his father tried to carry off the moment with the *aplomb* of a man of the world.

But that father's eye was fixed too steadily upon him; he faltered as he sat down, and finally spoke up, with feverish energy:

"If it is she, so help me, God, her death is a mystery to me! We have quarrelled more than once lately, and I have sometimes lost my patience with her, but she had no reason to wish for death, and I am ready to swear in defiance of those hands, which are certainly like hers, and the nameless something which Franklin calls a likeness, that it is a stranger who lies there, and that her death in our house is a coincidence."

"Well, well, we will wait," was the detective's soothing reply. "Sit down in the room opposite there, and give me your orders for supper, and I will see that a good meal is served you."

The three gentlemen, seeing no way of refusing, followed the discreet official who preceded them, and the door of the doctor's room closed upon him and the inquiries he was about to make.

VI.
NEW FACTS.

Mr. Van Burnam and his sons had gone through the formality of a supper and were conversing in the haphazard way natural to men filled with a subject they dare not discuss, when the door opened and Mr. Gryce came in.

Advancing very calmly, he addressed himself to the father:

"I am sorry," said he, "to be obliged to inform you that this affair is much more serious than we anticipated. This young woman was dead before the shelves laden with *bric-à-brac* fell upon her. It is a case of murder; obviously so, or I should not presume to forestall the Coroner's jury in their verdict."

Murder! it is a word to shake the stoutest heart!

The older gentleman reeled as he half rose, and Franklin, his son, betrayed in his own way an almost equal amount of emotion. But Howard, shrugging his shoulders as if relieved of an immense weight, looked about with a cheerful air, and briskly cried:

"Then it is not the body of my wife you have there. No one would murder Louise. I shall go away and prove the truth of my words by hunting her up at once."

The detective opened the door, beckoned in the doctor, who whispered two or three words into Howard's ear.

They failed to awake the emotion he evidently expected. Howard looked surprised, but answered without any change of voice:

"Yes, Louise had such a scar; and if it is true that this woman is similarly marked, then it is a mere coincidence. Nothing will convince me that my wife has been the victim of murder."

"Had you not better take a look at the scar just mentioned?"

"No. I am so sure of what I say that I will not even consider the possibility of my being mistaken. I have examined the clothing on this body you have shown me, and not one article of it came from my wife's wardrobe; nor would my wife go, as you have informed me this woman did, into a dark house at night with any other man than her husband."

"And so you absolutely refuse to acknowledge her."

"Most certainly."

The detective paused, glanced at the troubled faces of the other two gentlemen, faces that had not perceptibly altered during these declarations, and suggestively remarked:

"You have not asked by what means she was killed."

"And I don't care," shouted Howard.

"It was by very peculiar means, also new in my experience."

"It does not interest me," the other retorted.

Mr. Gryce turned to his father and brother.

"Does it interest *you*?" he asked.

The old gentleman, ordinarily so testy and so peremptory, silently nodded his head, while Franklin cried:

"Speak up quick. You detectives hesitate so over the disagreeables. Was she throttled or stabbed with a knife?"

"I have said the means were peculiar. She was stabbed, but not—with a knife."

I know Mr. Gryce well enough now to be sure that he did not glance towards Howard while saying this, and yet at the same time that he did not miss the quiver of a muscle on his part or the motion of an eyelash. But Howard's assumed *sang froid* remained undisturbed and his countenance imperturbable.

"The wound was so small," the detective went on, "that it is a miracle it did not escape notice. It was made by the thrust of some very slender instrument through——"

"The heart?" put in Franklin.

"Of course, of course," assented the detective; "what other spot is vulnerable enough to cause death?"

"Is there any reason why we should not go?" demanded Howard, ignoring the extreme interest manifested by the other two, with a determination that showed great doggedness of character.

The detective ignored *him*.

"A quick stroke, a sure stroke, a fatal stroke. The girl never breathed after."

"But what of those things under which she lay crushed?"

"Ah, in them lies the mystery! Her assailant must have been as subtle as he was sure."

And still Howard showed no interest.

"I wish to telegraph to Haddam," he declared, as no one answered the last remark. Haddam was the place where he and his wife had been spending the summer.

"We have already telegraphed there," observed Mr. Gryce. "Your wife has not yet returned."

"There are other places," defiantly insisted the other. "I can find her if you give me the opportunity."

Mr. Gryce bowed.

"I am to give orders, then, for this body to be removed to the Morgue."

It was an unexpected suggestion, and for an instant Howard showed that he had feelings with the best. But he quickly recovered himself, and avoiding the anxious glances of his father and brother, answered with offensive lightness:

"I have nothing to do with that. You must do as you think proper."

And Mr. Gryce felt that he had received a check, and did not know whether to admire the young man for his nerve or to execrate him for his brutality. That the woman whom he had thus carelessly dismissed to the ignominy of the public gaze was his wife, the detective did not doubt.

VII.
MR. GRYCE DISCOVERS MISS AMELIA.

To return to my own observations. I was almost as ignorant of what I wanted to know at ten o'clock on that memorable night as I was at five, but I was determined not to remain so. When the two Misses Van Burnam had retired to their room, I slipped away to the neighboring house and boldly rang the bell. I had observed Mr. Gryce enter it a few minutes before, and I was resolved to have some talk with him.

The hall-lamp was lit, and we could discern each other's faces as he opened the door. Mine may have been a study, but I am sure his was. He had not expected to be confronted by an elderly lady at that hour of night.

"Well!" he dryly ejaculated, "I am sensible of the honor, Miss Butterworth." But he did not ask me in.

"I expected no less," said I. "I saw you come in, and I followed as soon after as I could. I have something to say to you."

He admitted me then and carefully closed the door. Feeling free to be myself, I threw off the veil I had tied under my chin and confronted him with what I call the true spirit.

"Mr. Gryce," I began, "let us make an exchange of civilities. Tell me what you have done with Howard Van Burnam, and I will tell you what I have observed in the course of this afternoon's investigation."

This aged detective is used to women, I have no doubt, but he is not used to *me*. I saw it by the way he turned over and over the spectacles he held in his hand. I made an effort to help him out.

"I have noted something to-day which I think has escaped *you*. It is so slight a clue that most women would not speak of it. But being interested in the case, I will mention it, if in return you will acquaint me with what will appear in the papers to-morrow."

He seemed to like it. He peered through his glasses and at them with the smile of a discoverer. "I am your very humble servant," he declared; and I felt as if my father's daughter had received her first recognition.

But he did not overwhelm me with confidences. O, no, he is very sly, this old and well-seasoned detective; and while appearing to be very communicative, really parted with but little information. He said enough, however, for me to gather that matters looked grim for Howard, and if this was so, it must have become apparent that the death they were investigating was neither an accident nor a suicide.

I hinted as much, and he, for his own ends no doubt, admitted at last that a wound had been found on the young woman which could not have been inflicted by herself; at which I felt such increased interest in this remarkable murder that I must have made some foolish display of it, for the wary old gentleman chuckled and ogled his spectacles quite lovingly before shutting them up and putting them into his pocket.

"And now what have you to tell me?" he inquired, sliding softly between me and the parlor door.

"Nothing but this. Question that queer-acting house-cleaner closely. She has something to tell which it is your business to know."

I think he was disappointed. He looked as if he regretted the spectacles he had pocketed, and when he spoke there was an edge to his tone I had not noticed in it before.

"Do you know what that something is?" he asked.

"No, or I should tell you myself."

"And what makes you think she is hiding anything from us?"

"Her manner. Did you not notice her manner?"

He shrugged his shoulders.

"It conveyed much to me," I insisted. "If I were a detective I would have the secret out of that woman or die in the attempt."

He laughed; this sly, old, almost decrepit man laughed outright. Then he looked severely at his old friend on the newel-post, and drawing himself up with some show of dignity, made this remark:

"It is my very good fortune to have made your acquaintance, Miss Butterworth. You and I ought to be able to work out this case in a way that will be satisfactory to all parties."

He meant it for sarcasm, but I took it quite seriously, that is to all appearance. I am as sly as he, and though not quite as old—now *I* am sarcastic—have some of his wits, if but little of his experience.

"Then let us to work," said I. "You have your theories about this murder, and I have mine; let us see how they compare."

If the image he had under his eye had not been made of bronze, I am sure it would have become petrified by the look he now gave it. What to me seemed but the natural proposition of an energetic woman with a special genius for his particular calling, evidently struck him as audacity of the grossest kind. But he confined his display of astonishment to the figure he was eying, and returned me nothing but this most gentlemanly retort:

"I am sure I am obliged to you, madam, and possibly I may be willing to consider your very thoughtful proposition later, but now I am busy, very busy, and if you will await my presence in your house for a half hour——"

"Why not let me wait here," I interposed. "The atmosphere of the place may sharpen my faculties. I already feel that another sharp look into that parlor would lead to the forming of some valuable theory."

"You—" Well, he did not say what I was, or rather, what the image he was apostrophizing, was. But he must have meant to utter a compliment of no common order.

The prim courtesy I made in acknowledgment of his good intention satisfied him that I had understood him fully; and changing his whole manner to one more in accordance with business, he observed after a moment's reflection:

"You came to a conclusion this afternoon, Miss Butterworth, for which I should like some explanation. In investigating the hat which had been drawn from under the murdered girl's remains, you made the remark that it had been worn but once. I had already come to the same conclusion, but by other means, doubtless. Will you tell me what it was that gave point to your assertion?"

"There was but one prick of a hat-pin in it," I observed. "If you have been in the habit of looking into young women's hats, you will appreciate the force of my remark."

"The deuce!" was his certainly uncalled for exclamation. "Women's eyes for women's matters! I am greatly indebted to you, ma'am. You have solved a very important problem for us. A hat-pin! humph!" he muttered to himself. "The devil in a man is not easily balked; even such an innocent article as that can be made to serve, when all other means are lacking."

It is perhaps a proof that Mr. Gryce is getting old, that he allowed these words to escape him. But having once given vent to them, he made no effort to retract them, but proceeded to take me into his confidence so far as to explain:

"The woman who was killed in that room owed her death to the stab of a thin, long pin. We had not thought of a hat-pin, but upon your mentioning it, I am ready to accept it as the instrument of death. There was no pin to be seen in the hat when you looked at it?"

"None. I examined it most carefully."

He shook his head and seemed to be meditating. As I had plenty of time I waited, expecting him to speak again. My patience seemed to impress him. Alternately raising and lowering his hands like one in the act of weighing something, he soon addressed me again, this time in a tone of banter:

"This pin—if pin it was—was found broken in the wound. We have been searching for the end that was left in the murderer's hand, and we have not found it. It is not on the floors of the parlors nor in this hallway. What do you think the ingenious user of such an instrument would do with it?"

This was said, I am now sure, out of a spirit of sarcasm. He was amusing himself with me, but I did not realize it then. I was too full of my subject.

"He would not have carried it away," I reasoned shortly, "at least not far. He did not throw it aside on reaching the street, for I watched his movements so closely that I would have observed him had he done this. It is in the house then, and presumably in the parlor, even if you do not find it on the floor."

"Would you like to look for it?" he impressively asked. I had no means of knowing at that time that when he was impressive he was his least candid and trustworthy self.

"Would I," I repeated; and being spare in figure and much more active in my movements that one would suppose from my age and dignified deportment, I ducked under his arms and was in Mr. Van Burnam's parlor before he had recovered from his surprise.

That a man like him could look foolish I would not have you for a moment suppose. But he did not look very well satisfied, and I had a chance to throw more than one glance around me before he found his tongue again.

"An unfair advantage, ma'am; an unfair advantage! I am old and I am rheumatic; you are young and sound as a nut. I acknowledge my folly in endeavoring to compete with you and must make the best of the situation. And now, madam, where is that pin?"

It was lightly said, but for all that I saw that my opportunity had come. If I could find this instrument of murder, what might I not expect from his gratitude. Nerving myself for the task thus set me, I peered hither and thither, taking in every article in the room before I made a step forward. There had been some attempt to rectify its disorder. The broken pieces of china had been lifted and laid carefully away on newspapers upon the shelves from which they had fallen. The cabinet stood upright in its place, and the clock which had tumbled face upward, had been placed upon the mantel shelf in the same position. The carpet was therefore free, save for the stains which told such a woful story of past tragedy and crime.

"You have moved the tables and searched behind the sofas," I suggested.

"Not an inch of the floor has escaped our attention, madam."

My eyes fell on the register, which my skirts half covered. It was closed; I stooped and opened it. A square box of tin was visible below, at the bottom of which I perceived the round head of a broken hat-pin.

Never in my life had I felt as I did at that minute. Rising up, I pointed at the register and let some of my triumph become apparent; but not all, for I was by no means sure at that moment, nor am I by any means sure now, that he had not made the discovery before I did and was simply testing my pretensions.

However that may be, he came forward quickly and after some little effort drew out the broken pin and examined it curiously.

"I should say that this is what we want," he declared, and from that moment on showed me a suitable deference.

"I account for its being there in this way," I argued. "The room was dark; for whether he lighted it or not to commit his crime, he certainly did not leave it lighted long. Coming out, his foot came in contact with the iron of the register and he was struck by a sudden thought. He had not dared to leave the head of the pin lying on the floor, for he hoped that he had covered up his crime by pulling the heavy cabinet over upon his victim; nor did he wish to carry away such a memento of his cruel deed. So he dropped it down the register, where he doubtless expected it would fall into the furnace pipes out of sight. But the tin box retained it. Is not that plausible, sir?"

"I could not have reasoned better myself, madam. We shall have you on the force, yet."

But at the familiarity shown by this suggestion, I bridled angrily. "I am Miss Butterworth," was my sharp retort, "and any interest I may take in this matter is due to my sense of justice."

Seeing that he had offended me, the astute detective turned the conversation back to business.

"By the way," said he, "your woman's knowledge can help me out at another point. If you are not afraid to remain in this room alone for a moment, I will bring an article in regard to which I should like your opinion."

I assured him I was not in the least bit afraid, at which he made me another of his anomalous bows and passed into the adjoining parlor. He did not stop there. Opening the sliding-doors communicating with the dining-room beyond, he disappeared in the latter room, shutting the doors behind him. Being now alone for a moment on the scene of crime, I crossed over to the mantel-shelf, and lifted the clock that lay there.

Why I did this I scarcely know. I am naturally very orderly (some people call me precise) and it probably fretted me to see so valuable an object out of its natural position. However that was, I lifted it up and set it upright, when to my amazement it began to tick. Had the hands not stood as they did when my eyes first fell on the clock lying face up on the floor at the dead girl's side, I should have thought the works had been started since that time by Mr. Gryce or some other officious person. But they pointed now as then to a few minutes before five and the only conclusion I could arrive at was, that the clock had been in running order when it fell, startling as this fact appeared in a house which had not been inhabited for months.

But if it had been in running order and was only stopped by its fall upon the floor, why did the hands point at five instead of twelve which was the hour at which the accident was supposed to have happened? Here was matter for thought, and that I might be undisturbed in my use of it, I hastened to lay the clock down again, even taking the precaution to restore the hands to the exact position they had occupied before I had started up the works. If Mr. Gryce did not know their secret, why so much the worse for Mr. Gryce.

I was back in my old place by the register before the folding-doors unclosed again. I was conscious of a slight flush on my cheek, so I took from my pocket that perplexing grocer-bill and was laboriously going down its long line of figures, when Mr. Gryce reappeared.

He had to my surprise a woman's hat in his hand.

"Well!" thought I, "what does this mean!"

It was an elegant specimen of millinery, and was in the latest style. It had ribbons and flowers and bird wings upon it, and presented, as it was turned about by Mr. Gryce's deft hand, an appearance which some might have called charming, but to me was simply grotesque and absurd.

"Is that a last spring's hat?" he inquired.

"I don't know, but I should say it had come fresh from the milliner's."

"I found it lying with a pair of gloves tucked inside it on an otherwise empty shelf in the dining-room closet. It struck me as looking too new for a discarded hat of either of the Misses Van Burnam. What do you think?"

"Let me take it," said I.

"O, it's been worn," he smiled, "several times. And the hat-pin is in it, too."

"There is something else I wish to see."

He handed it over.

"I think it belongs to one of them," I declared. "It was made by La Mole of Fifth Avenue, whose prices are simply—wicked."

"But the young ladies have been gone—let me see—five months. Could this have been bought before then?"

"Possibly, for this is an imported hat. But why should it have been left lying about in that careless way? It cost twenty dollars, if not thirty, and if for any reason its owner decided not to take it with her, why didn't she pack it away properly? I have no patience with the modern girl; she is made up of recklessness and extravagance."

"I hear that the young ladies are staying with you," was his suggestive remark.

"They are."

"Then you can make some inquiries about this hat; also about the gloves, which are an ordinary street pair."

"Of what color?"

"Grey; they are quite fresh, size six."

"Very well; I will ask the young ladies about them."

"This third room is used as a dining-room, and the closet where I found them is one in which glass is kept. The presence of this hat there is a mystery, but I presume the Misses Van Burnam can solve it. At all events, it is very improbable that it has anything to do with the crime which has been committed here."

"Very," I coincided.

"So improbable," he went on, "that on second thoughts I advise you not to disturb the young ladies with questions concerning it unless further reasons for doing so become apparent."

"Very well," I returned. But I was not deceived by his second thoughts.

As he was holding open the parlor door before me in a very significant way, I tied my veil under my chin, and was about to leave when he stopped me.

"I have another favor to ask," said he, and this time with his most benignant smile. "Miss Butterworth, do you object to sitting up for a few nights till twelve o'clock?"

"Not at all," I returned, "if there is any good reason for it."

"At twelve o'clock to-night a gentleman will enter this house. If you will note him from your window I will be obliged."

"To see whether he is the same one I saw last night? Certainly I will take a look, but— —"

"To-morrow night," he went on, imperturbably, "the test will be repeated, and I should like to have you take another look; without prejudice, madam; remember, without prejudice."

"I have no prejudices— —" I began.

"The test may not be concluded in two nights," he proceeded, without any notice of my words. "So do not be in haste to spot your man, as the vulgar expression is. And now good-night—we shall meet again to-morrow."

"Wait!" I called peremptorily, for he was on the point of closing the door. "I saw the man but faintly; it is an impression only that I received. I would not wish a man to hang through any identification I could make."

"No man hangs on simple identification. We shall have to prove the crime, madam, but identification is important; even such as you can make."

There was no more to be said; I uttered a calm good-night and hastened away. By a judicious use of my opportunities I had become much less ignorant on the all-important topic than when I entered the house.

It was half past eleven when I returned home, a late hour for me to enter my respectable front door alone. But circumstances had warranted my escapade, and it was with quite an easy conscience and a cheerful sense of accomplishment that I went up to my room and prepared to sit out the half hour before midnight.

I am a comfortable sort of person when alone, and found no difficulty in passing this time profitably. Being very orderly, as you must have remarked, I have everything at hand for making myself a cup of tea at any time of day or night; so feeling some need of refreshment, I set out the little table I reserve for such purposes and made the tea and sat down to sip it.

While doing so, I turned over the subject occupying my mind, and endeavored to reconcile the story told by the clock with my preconceived theory of this murder; but no reconcilement was possible. The woman had been killed at twelve, and the clock had fallen at five. How could the two be made to agree, and which, since agreement was impossible, should be made to give way, the theory or the testimony of the clock? Both seemed incontrovertible, and yet one must be false. Which?

I was inclined to think that the trouble lay with the clock; that I had been deceived in my conclusions, and that it was not running at the time of the crime. Mr. Gryce may have ordered it wound, and then have had it laid on its back to prevent the hands from shifting past the point where they had stood at the time of the crime's discovery. It was an unexplainable act, but a possible one; while to suppose that it was going when the shelves fell, stretched improbability to the utmost, there having been, so far as we could learn, no one in the house for months sufficiently dexterous to set so valuable a timepiece; for who could imagine the scrub-woman engaging in a task requiring such delicate manipulation.

No! some meddlesome official had amused himself by starting up the works, and the clue I had thought so important would probably prove valueless.

There was humiliation in the thought, and it was a relief to me to hear an approaching carriage just as the clock on my mantel struck twelve. Springing from my chair, I put out my light and flew to the window.

The coach drew up and stopped next door. I saw a gentleman descend and step briskly across the pavement to the neighboring stoop. The figure he presented was not that of the man I had seen enter the night before.

VIII.
THE MISSES VAN BURNAM.

Late as it was when I retired, I was up betimes in the morning—as soon, in fact, as the papers were distributed. The *Tribune* lay on the stoop. Eagerly I seized it; eagerly I read it. From its headlines you may judge what it had to say about this murder:

A STARTLING DISCOVERY IN THE VAN BURNAM MANSION IN GRAMERCY PARK.

A Young Girl Found there, Lying Dead under an Overturned Cabinet.

Evidences that she was Murdered before it was Pulled down upon her.

Thought by Some to be Mrs. Howard Van Burnam.

A Fearful Crime Involved in an Impenetrable Mystery.

What Mr. Van Burnam Says about it: He does not Recognize the Woman as his Wife.

So, so, it was his wife they were talking about. I had not expected that. Well! well! no wonder the girls looked startled and concerned. And I paused to recall what I had heard about Howard Van Burnam's marriage.

It had not been a fortunate one. His chosen bride was pretty enough, but she had not been bred in the ways of fashionable society, and the other members of the family had never recognized her. The father, especially, had cut his son dead since his marriage, and had even gone so far as to threaten to dissolve the partnership in which they were all involved. Worse than this, there had been rumors of a disagreement between Howard and his wife. They were not always on good terms, and opinions differed as to which was most in fault. So much for what I knew of these two mentioned parties.

Reading the article at length, I learned that Mrs. Van Burnam was missing; that she had left Haddam for New York the day before her husband, and had not since been heard from. Howard was confident, however, that the publicity given to her disappearance by the papers would bring immediate news of her.

The effect of the whole article was to raise grave doubts as to the candor of Mr. Van Burnam's assertions, and I am told that in some of the less scrupulous papers these doubts were not only expressed, but actual surmises ventured upon as to the identity between the person whom I had seen enter the house with the young girl. As for my own name, it was blazoned forth in anything but a gratifying manner. I was spoken of in one paper—a kind friend told me this—as the prying Miss Amelia. As if my prying had not given the police their only clue to the identification of the criminal.

The New York *World* was the only paper that treated me with any consideration. That young man with the small head and beady eyes was not awed by me for nothing. He mentioned me as the clever Miss Butterworth whose testimony is likely to be of so much value in this very interesting case.

It was the *World* I handed the Misses Van Burnam when they came down-stairs to breakfast. It did justice to me and not too much injustice to him. They read it together, their two heads plunged deeply into the paper so that I could not watch their faces. But I could see the sheet shake, and I noticed that their social veneer was not as yet laid on so thickly that they could hide their real terror and heart-ache when they finally confronted me again.

"Did you read—have you seen this horrible account?" quavered Caroline, as she met my eye.

"Yes, and I now understand why you felt such anxiety yesterday. Did you know your sister-in-law, and do you think she could have been beguiled into your father's house in that way?"

It was Isabella who answered.

"We never have seen her and know little of her, but there is no telling what such an uncultivated person as she might do. But that our good brother Howard ever went in there with her is a lie, isn't it, Caroline?—a base and malicious lie?"

"Of course it is, of course, of course. You don't think the man you saw was Howard, do you, dear Miss Butterworth?"

Dear? O dear!

"I am not acquainted with your brother," I returned. "I have never seen him but a few times in my life. You know he has not been a very frequent visitor at your father's house lately."

They looked at me wistfully, *so* wistfully.

"Say it was not Howard," whispered Caroline, stealing up a little nearer to my side.

"And we will never forget it," murmured Isabella, in what I am obliged to say was not her society manner.

"I hope to be able to say it," was my short rejoinder, made difficult by the prejudices I had formed. "When I see your brother, I may be able to decide at a glance that the person I saw entering your house was not he."

"Yes, oh, yes. Do you hear that, Isabella? Miss Butterworth will save Howard yet. O you dear old soul. I could almost love you!"

This was not agreeable to me. I a dear old soul! A term to be applied to a butter-woman not to a Butterworth. I drew back and their sentimentalities came to an end. I hope their brother Howard is not the guilty man the papers make him out to be, but if he is, the Misses Van Burnam's fine phrase, *We could almost love you*, will not deter me from being honest in the matter.

Mr. Gryce called early, and I was glad to be able to tell him that the gentleman who visited him the night before did not recall the impression made upon me by the other. He received the communication quietly, and from his manner I judged that it was more or less expected. But who can be a correct judge of a detective's manner, especially one so foxy and imperturbable as this one? I longed to ask who his visitor was, but I did not dare, or rather—to be candid in little things that you may believe me in great—I was confident he would not tell me, so I would not compromise my dignity by a useless question.

He went after a five minutes' stay, and I was about to turn my attention to household affairs, when Franklin came in.

His sisters jumped like puppets to meet him.

"O," they cried, for once thinking and speaking alike, "have you found her?"

His silence was so eloquent that he did not need to shake his head.

"But you will before the day is out?" protested Caroline.

"It is too early yet," added Isabella.

"I never thought I would be glad to see that woman under any circumstances," continued the former, "but I believe now that if I saw her coming up the street on Howard's arm, I should be happy enough to rush out and—and——"

"Give her a hug," finished the more impetuous Isabella.

It was not what Caroline meant to say, but she accepted the emendation, with just the slightest air of deprecation. They were both evidently much attached to Howard, and ready in his trouble to forget and forgive everything. I began to like them again.

"Have you read the horrid papers?" and "How is papa this morning?" and "What shall we do to save Howard?" now flew in rapid questions from their lips; and feeling that it was but natural they should have their little say, I sat down in my most uncomfortable chair and waited for these first ebullitions to exhaust themselves.

Instantly Mr. Van Burnam took them by the arm, and led them away to a distant sofa.

"Are you happy here?" he asked, in what he meant for a very confidential tone. But I can hear as readily as a deaf person anything which is not meant for my ears.

"O she's kind enough," whispered Caroline, "but so stingy. Do take us where we can get something to eat."

"She puts all her money into china! Such plates!—*and so little on them!*"

At these expressions, uttered with all the emphasis a whisper will allow, I just hugged myself in my quiet corner. The dear, giddy things! But they should see, they should see.

"I fear"—it was Mr. Van Burnam who now spoke—"I shall have to take my sisters from under your kind care to-day. Their father needs them, and has, I believe, already engaged rooms for them at the Plaza."

"I am sorry," I replied, "but surely they will not leave till they have had another meal with me. Postpone your departure, young ladies, till after luncheon, and you will greatly oblige me. We may never meet so agreeably again."

They fidgeted (which I had expected), and cast secret looks of almost comic appeal at their brother, but he pretended not to see them, being disposed for some reason to grant my request. Taking advantage of the momentary hesitation that ensued, I made them all three my most conciliatory bow, and said as I retreated behind the portière:

"I shall give my orders for luncheon now. Meanwhile, I hope the young ladies will feel perfectly free in my house. All that I have is at their command." And was gone before they could protest.

When I next saw them, they were upstairs in my front room. They were seated together in the window and looked miserable enough to have a little diversion. Going to my closet, I brought out a band-box. It contained my best bonnet.

"Young ladies, what do you think of this?" I inquired, taking the bonnet out and carefully placing it on my head.

I myself consider it a very becoming article of headgear, but their eyebrows went up in a scarcely complimentary fashion.

"You don't like it?" I remarked. "Well, I think a great deal of young girls' taste; I shall send it back to Madame More's to-morrow."

"I don't think much of Madame More," observed Isabella, "and after Paris— —"

"Do you like La Mole better?" I inquired, bobbing my head to and fro before the mirror, the better to conceal my interest in the venture I was making.

"I don't like any of them but D'Aubigny," returned Isabella. "She charges twice what La Mole does— —"

Twice! What are these girls' purses made of, or rather their father's!

"But she has the *chic* we are accustomed to see in French millinery. I shall *never* go anywhere else."

"We were recommended to her in Paris," put in Caroline, more languidly. Her interest was only half engaged by this frivolous topic.

"But did you never have one of La Mole's hats?" I pursued, taking down a hand-mirror, ostensibly to get the effect of my bonnet in the back, but really to hide my interest in their unconscious faces.

"Never!" retorted Isabella. "I would not patronize the thing."

"Nor you?" I urged, carelessly, turning towards Caroline.

"No; I have never been inside her shop."

"Then whose is— —" I began and stopped. A detective doing the work I was, would not give away the object of his questions so recklessly.

"Then who is," I corrected, "the best person after D'Aubigny? I never can pay *her* prices. I should think it wicked."

"O don't ask us," protested Isabella. "We have never made a study of the best bonnet-maker. At present we wear hats."

And having thus thrown their youth in my face, they turned away to the window again, not realizing that the middle-aged lady they regarded with such disdain had just succeeded in making them dance to her music most successfully.

The luncheon I ordered was elaborate, for I was determined that the Misses Van Burnam should see that I knew how to serve a fine meal, and that my plates were not always better than my viands.

I had invited in a couple of other guests so that I should not seem to have put myself out for two young girls, and as they were quiet people like myself, the meal passed most decorously. When it was finished, the Misses Caroline and Isabella had lost some of their consequential airs, and I really think the deference they have since showed me is due more to the surprise they felt at the perfection of this dainty luncheon, than to any considerate appreciation of my character and abilities.

They left at three o'clock, still without news of Mrs. Van Burnam; and being positive by this time that the shadows were thickening about this family, I saw them depart with some regret and a positive feeling of commiseration. Had they been reared to a proper reverence for their elders, how much more easy it would have been to see earnestness in Caroline and affectionate impulses in Isabella.

The evening papers added but little to my knowledge. Great disclosures were promised, but no hint given of their nature. The body at the Morgue had not been identified by any of the hundreds who had viewed it, and Howard still refused to acknowledge it as that of his wife. The morrow was awaited with anxiety.

So much for the public press!

At twelve o'clock at night, I was again seated in my window. The house next door had been lighted since ten, and I was in momentary expectation of its nocturnal visitor. He came promptly at the hour set, alighted from the carriage with a bound, shut the carriage-door with a slam, and crossed the pavement with cheerful celerity. His figure was not so positively like, nor yet so positively unlike, that of the supposed murderer that I could definitely say, "This is he," or, "This is not he," and I went to bed puzzled, and not a little burdened by a sense of the responsibility imposed upon me in this matter.

And so passed the day between the murder and the inquest.

IX.
DEVELOPMENTS.

Mr. Gryce called about nine o'clock next morning.

"Well," said he, "what about the visitor who came to see me last night?"

"Like and unlike," I answered. "Nothing could induce me to say he is the man we want, and yet I would not dare to swear he was not."

"You are in doubt, then, concerning him?"

"I am."

Mr. Gryce bowed, reminded me of the inquest, and left. Nothing was said about the hat.

At ten o'clock I prepared to go to the place designated by him. I had never attended an inquest in my life, and felt a little flurried in consequence, but by the time I had tied the strings of my bonnet (the despised bonnet, which, by the way, I did not return to More's), I had conquered this weakness, and acquired a demeanor more in keeping with my very important position as chief witness in a serious police investigation.

I had sent for a carriage to take me, and I rode away from my house amid the shouts of some half dozen boys collected on the curb-stone. But I did not allow myself to feel dashed by this publicity. On the contrary, I held my head as erect as nature intended, and my back kept the line my good health warrants. The path of duty has its thorny passages, but it is for strong minds like mine to ignore them.

Promptly at ten o'clock I entered the room reserved for the inquest, and was ushered to the seat appointed me. Though never a self-conscious woman, I could not but be aware of the many eyes that followed me, and endeavored so to demean myself that there should be no question as to my respectable standing in the community. This I considered due to the memory of my father, who was very much in my thoughts that day.

The Coroner was already in his seat when I entered, and though I did not perceive the good face of Mr. Gryce anywhere in his vicinity, I had no doubt he was within ear-shot. Of the other people I took small note, save of the honest scrub-woman, of whose red face and anxious eyes under a preposterous bonnet (which did *not come* from La Mole's), I caught vague glimpses as the crowd between us surged to and fro.

None of the Van Burnams were visible, but this did not necessarily mean that they were absent. Indeed, I was very sure, from certain indications, that more than one member of the family could be seen in the small room connecting with the large one in which we witnesses sat with the jury.

The policeman, Carroll, was the first man to talk. He told of my stopping him on his beat and of his entrance into Mr. Van Burnam's house with the scrub-woman. He gave the details of his discovery of the dead woman's body on the parlor floor, and insisted that no one—here he looked very hard at me—had been allowed to touch the body till relief had come to him from Headquarters.

Mrs. Boppert, the scrub-woman, followed him; and if she was watched by no one else in that room, she was watched by me. Her manner before the Coroner was no more satisfactory, according to my notion, than it had been in Mr. Van Burnam's parlor. She gave a very perceptible start when they spoke her name, and looked quite scared when the Bible was held out towards her. But she took the oath notwithstanding, and with her testimony the inquiry began in earnest.

"What is your name?" asked the Coroner.

As this was something she could not help knowing, she uttered the necessary words glibly, though in a way that showed she resented his impertinence in asking her what he already knew.

"Where do you live? And what do you do for a living?" rapidly followed.

She replied that she was a scrub-woman and cleaned people's houses, and having said this, she assumed a very dogged air, which I thought strange enough to raise a question in the minds of those who watched her. But no one else seemed to regard it as anything but the embarrassment of ignorance.

"How long have you known the Van Burnam family?" the Coroner went on.

"Two years, sir, come next Christmas."

"Have you often done work for them?"

"I clean the house twice a year, fall and spring."

"Why were you at this house two days ago?"

"To scrub the kitchen floors, sir, and put the pantries in order."

"Had you received notice to do so?"

"Yes, sir, through Mr. Franklin Van Burnam."

"And was that the first day of your work there?"

"No, sir; I had been there all the day before."

"You don't speak loud enough," objected the Coroner; "remember that every one in this room wants to hear you."

She looked up, and with a frightened air surveyed the crowd about her. Publicity evidently made her most uncomfortable, and her voice sank rather than rose.

"Where did you get the key of the house, and by what door did you enter?"

"I went in at the basement, sir, and I got the key at Mr. Van Burnam's agent in Dey Street. I had to go for it; sometimes they send it to me; but not this time."

"And now relate your meeting with the policeman on Wednesday morning, in front of Mr. Van Burnam's house."

She tried to tell her story, but she made awkward work of it, and they had to ply her with questions to get at the smallest fact. But finally she managed to repeat what we already knew, how she went with the policeman into the house, and how they stumbled upon the dead woman in the parlor.

Further than this they did not question her, and I, Amelia Butterworth, had to sit in silence and see her go back to her seat, redder than before, but with a strangely satisfied air that told me she had escaped more easily than she had expected. And yet Mr. Gryce had been warned that she knew more than appeared, and by one in whom he seemed to have placed some confidence!

The doctor was called next. His testimony was most important, and contained a surprise for me and more than one surprise for the others. After a short preliminary examination, he was requested to state how long the woman had been dead when he was called in to examine her.

"More than twelve and less than eighteen hours," was his quiet reply.

"Had the rigor mortis set in?"

"No; but it began very soon after."

"Did you examine the wounds made by the falling shelves and the vases that tumbled with them?"

"I did."

"Will you describe them?"

He did so.

"And now"—there was a pause in the Coroner's question which roused us all to its importance, "which of these many serious wounds was in your opinion the cause of her death?"

The witness was accustomed to such scenes, and was perfectly at home in them. Surveying the Coroner with a respectful air, he turned slowly towards the jury and answered in a slow and impressive manner:

"I feel ready to declare, sirs, that none of them did. She was not killed by the falling of the cabinet upon her."

"Not killed by the falling shelves! Why not? Were they not sufficiently heavy, or did they not strike her in a vital place?"

"They were heavy enough, and they struck her in a way to kill her if she had not been already dead when they fell upon her. As it was, they simply bruised a body from which life had already departed."

As this was putting it very plainly, many of the crowd who had not been acquainted with these facts previously, showed their interest in a very unmistakable manner; but the Coroner, ignoring these symptoms of growing excitement, hastened to say:

"This is a very serious statement you are making, doctor. If she did not die from the wounds inflicted by the objects which fell upon her, from what cause did she die? Can you say that her death was a natural one, and that the falling of the shelves was merely an unhappy accident following it?"

"No, sir; her death was not natural. She was killed, but not by the falling cabinet."

"Killed, and not by the cabinet? How then? Was there any other wound upon her which you regard as mortal?"

"Yes, sir. Suspecting that she had perished from other means than appeared, I made a most rigid examination of her body, when I discovered under the hair in the nape of the neck, a minute spot, which, upon probing, I found to be the end of a small, thin point of steel. It had been thrust by a careful hand into the most vulnerable part of the body, and death must have ensued at once."

This was too much for certain excitable persons present, and a momentary disturbance arose, which, however, was nothing to that in my own breast.

So! so! it was her neck that had been pierced, and not her heart. Mr. Gryce had allowed us to think it was the latter, but it was not this fact which stupefied me, but the skill and diabolical coolness of the man who had inflicted this death-thrust.

After order had been restored, which I will say was very soon, the Coroner, with an added gravity of tone, went on with his questions:

"Did you recognize this bit of steel as belonging to any instrument in the medical profession?"

"No; it was of too untempered steel to have been manufactured for any thrusting or cutting purposes. It was of the commonest kind, and had broken short off in the wound. It was the end only that I found."

"Have you this end with you,—the point, I mean, which you found imbedded at the base of the dead woman's brain?"

"I have, sir"; and he handed it over to the jury. As they passed it along, the Coroner remarked:

"Later we will show you the remaining portion of this instrument of death," which did not tend to allay the general excitement. Seeing this, the Coroner humored the growing interest by pushing on his inquiries.

"Doctor," he asked, "are you prepared to say how long a time elapsed between the infliction of this fatal wound and those which disfigured her?"

"No, sir, not exactly; but some little time."

Some little time, when the murderer was in the house only ten minutes! All looked their surprise, and, as if the Coroner had divined this feeling of general curiosity, he leaned forward and emphatically repeated:

"More than ten minutes?"

The doctor, who had every appearance of realizing the importance of his reply, did not hesitate. Evidently his mind was quite made up.

"Yes; more than ten minutes."

This was the shock *I* received from his testimony.

I remembered what the clock had revealed to me, but I did not move a muscle of my face. I was learning self-control under these repeated surprises.

"This is an unexpected statement," remarked the Coroner. "What reasons have you to urge in explanation of it?"

"Very simple and very well known ones; at least, among the profession. There was too little blood seen, for the wounds to have been inflicted before death or within a few minutes after it. Had the woman been living when they were made, or even had she been but a short time dead, the floor would have been deluged with the blood gushing from so many and such serious injuries. But the effusion was slight, so slight that I noticed it at once, and came to the conclusions mentioned before I found the mark of the stab that occasioned death."

"I see, I see! And was that the reason you called in two neighboring physicians to view the body before it was removed from the house?"

"Yes, sir; in so important a matter, I wished to have my judgment confirmed."

"And these physicians were— —"

"Dr. Campbell, of 110 East — — Street, and Dr. Jacobs, of — — Lexington Avenue."

"Are these gentlemen here?" inquired the Coroner of an officer who stood near.

"They are, sir."

"Very good; we will now proceed to ask one or two more questions of this witness. You told us that even had the woman been but a few minutes dead when she received these contusions, the floor would have been more or less deluged by her blood. What reason have you for this statement?"

"This; that in a few minutes, let us say ten, since that number has been used, the body has not had time to cool, nor have the blood-vessels had sufficient opportunity to stiffen so as to prevent the free effusion of blood."

"Is a body still warm at ten minutes after death?"

"It is."

"So that your conclusions are logical deductions from well-known facts?"

"Certainly, sir."

A pause of some duration followed.

When the Coroner again proceeded, it was to remark:

"The case is complicated by these discoveries; but we must not allow ourselves to be daunted by them. Let me ask you, if you found any marks upon this body which might aid in its identification?"

"One; a slight scar on the left ankle."

"What kind of a scar? Describe it."

"It was such as a burn might leave. In shape it was long and narrow, and it ran up the limb from the ankle-bone."

"Was it on the right foot?"

"No; on the left."

"Did you call the attention of any one to this mark during or after your examination?"

"Yes; I showed it to Mr. Gryce the detective, and to my two coadjutors; and I spoke of it to Mr. Howard Van Burnam, son of the gentleman in whose house the body was found."

It was the first time this young gentleman's name had been mentioned, and it made my blood run cold to see how many side-long looks and expressive shrugs it caused in the motley assemblage. But I had no time for sentiment; the inquiry was growing too interesting.

"And why," asked the Coroner, "did you mention it to this young man in preference to others?"

"Because Mr. Gryce requested me to. Because the family as well as the young man himself had evinced some apprehension lest the deceased might prove to be his missing wife, and this seemed a likely way to settle the question."

"And did it? Did he acknowledge it to be a mark he remembered to have seen on his wife?"

"He said she had such a scar, but he would not acknowledge the deceased to be his wife."

"Did he see the scar?"

"No; he would not look at it."

"Did you invite him to?"

"I did; but he showed no curiosity."

Doubtless thinking that silence would best emphasize this fact, which certainly was an astonishing one, the Coroner waited a minute. But there was no silence. An indescribable murmur from a great many lips filled up the gap. I felt a movement of pity for the proud family whose good name was thus threatened in the person of this young gentleman.

"Doctor," continued the Coroner, as soon as the murmur had subsided, "did you notice the color of the woman's hair?"

"It was a light brown."

"Did you sever a lock? Have you a sample of this hair here to show us?"

"I have, sir. At Mr. Gryce's suggestion I cut off two small locks. One I gave him and the other I brought here."

"Let me see it."

The doctor passed it up, and in sight of every one present the Coroner tied a string around it and attached a ticket to it.

"That is to prevent all mistake," explained this very methodical functionary, laying the lock aside on the table in front of him. Then he turned again to the witness.

"Doctor, we are indebted to you for your valuable testimony, and as you are a busy man, we will now excuse you. Let Dr. Jacobs be called."

As this gentleman, as well as the witness who followed him, merely corroborated the statements of the other, and made it an accepted fact that the shelves had fallen upon the body of the girl some time after the first wound had been inflicted, I will not attempt to repeat their testimony. The question now agitating me was whether they would endeavor to fix the time at which the shelves fell by the evidence furnished by the clock.

X.
IMPORTANT EVIDENCE.

Evidently not; for the next words I heard were: "Miss Amelia Butterworth!"

I had not expected to be called so soon, and was somewhat flustered by the suddenness of the summons, for I am only human. But I rose with suitable composure, and passed to the place indicated by the Coroner, in my usual straightforward manner, heightened only by a sense of the importance of my position, both as a witness and a woman whom the once famous Mr. Gryce had taken more or less into his confidence.

My appearance seemed to awaken an interest for which I was not prepared. I was just thinking how well my name had sounded uttered in the sonorous tones of the Coroner, and how grateful I ought to be for the courage I had displayed in substituting the genteel name of Amelia for the weak and sentimental one of Araminta, when I became conscious that the eyes directed towards me were filled with an expression not easy to understand. I should not like to call it admiration and will not call it amusement, and yet it seemed to be made up of both. While I was puzzling myself over it, the first question came.

As my examination before the Coroner only brought out the facts already related, I will not burden you with a detailed account of it. One portion alone may be of interest. I was being questioned in regard to the appearance of the couple I had seen entering the Van Burnam mansion, when the Coroner asked if the young woman's step was light, or if it betrayed hesitation.

I replied: "No hesitation; she moved quickly, almost gaily."

"And he?"

"Was more moderate; but there is no signification in that; he may have been older."

"No theories, Miss Butterworth; it is facts we are after. Now, do you know that he was older?"

"No, sir."

"Did you get any idea as to his age?"

"The impression he made was that of being a young man."

"And his height?"

"Was medium, and his figure slight and elegant. He moved as a gentleman moves; of this I can speak with great positiveness."

"Do you think you could identify him, Miss Butterworth, if you should see him?"

I hesitated, as I perceived that the whole swaying mass eagerly awaited my reply. I even turned my head because I saw others doing so; but I regretted this when I found that I, as well as others, was glancing towards the door beyond which the Van Burnams were supposed to sit. To cover up the false move I had made—for I had no wish as yet to centre suspicion upon anybody—I turned my face quickly back to the crowd and declared in as emphatic a tone as I could command:

"I have thought I could do so if I saw him under the same circumstances as those in which my first impression was made. But lately I have begun to doubt even that. I should never dare trust to my memory in this regard."

The Coroner looked disappointed, and so did the people around me.

"It is a pity," remarked the Coroner, "that you did not see more plainly. And, now, how did these persons gain an entrance into the house?"

I answered in the most succinct way possible.

I told them how he had used a door-key in entering, of the length of time the man stayed inside, and of his appearance on going away. I also related how I came to call a policeman to investigate the matter next day, and corroborated the statements of this official as to the appearance of the deceased at time of discovery.

And there my examination stopped. I was not asked any questions tending to bring out the cause of the suspicion I entertained against the scrub-woman, nor were the discoveries I had made in conjunction with Mr. Gryce inquired into. It was just as well, perhaps, but I would never approve of a piece of work done for me in this slipshod fashion.

A recess now followed. Why it was thought necessary, I cannot imagine, unless the gentlemen wished to smoke. Had they felt as much interest in this murder as I did, they would not have wanted bite or sup till the dreadful question was settled. There being a recess, I improved the opportunity by going into a restaurant near by where one can get very good buns and coffee at a reasonable price. But I could have done without them.

The next witness, to my astonishment, was Mr. Gryce. As he stepped forward, heads were craned and many women rose in their seats to get a glimpse of the noted detective. I showed no curiosity myself, for by this time I knew his features well, but I did feel a great satisfaction in seeing him before the Coroner, for now, thought I, we shall hear something worth our attention.

But his examination, though interesting, was not complete. The Coroner, remembering his promise to show us the other end of the steel point which had been broken off in the dead girl's brain, limited himself to such inquiries as brought out the discovery of the broken hat-pin in Mr. Van Burnam's parlor register. No mention was made by the witness of any assistance which he may have received in making this discovery; a fact which caused me to smile: men are so jealous of any interference in their affairs.

The end found in the register and the end which the Coroner's physician had drawn from the poor woman's head were both handed to the jury, and it was interesting to note how each man made his little effort to fit the two ends together, and the looks they interchanged as they found themselves successful. Without doubt, and in the eyes of all, the instrument of death had been found. But what an instrument!

The felt hat which had been discovered under the body was now produced and the one hole made by a similar pin examined. Then Mr. Gryce was asked if any other pin had been picked up from the floor of the room, and he replied, no; and the fact was established in the minds of all present that the young woman had been killed by a pin taken from her own hat.

"A subtle and cruel crime; the work of a calculating intellect," was the Coroner's comment as he allowed the detective to sit down. Which expression of opinion I thought reprehensible, as tending to prejudice the jury against the only person at present suspected.

The inquiry now took a turn. The name of Miss Ferguson was called. Who was Miss Ferguson? It was a new name to most of us, and her face when she rose only added to the general curiosity. It was the plainest face imaginable, yet it was neither a bad nor unintelligent one. As I studied it and noted the nervous contraction that disfigured her lip, I could not but be sensible of my blessings. I am not handsome myself, though there have been persons who have called me so, but neither am I ugly, and in contrast to this woman—well, I will say nothing. I only know that, after seeing her, I felt profoundly grateful to a kind Providence.

As for the poor woman herself, she knew she was no beauty, but she had become so accustomed to seeing the eyes of other people turn away from her face, that beyond the nervous twitching of which I have spoken, she showed no feeling.

"What is your full name, and where do you live?" asked the Coroner.

"My name is Susan Ferguson, and I live in Haddam, Connecticut," was her reply, uttered in such soft and beautiful tones that every one was astonished. It was like a stream of limpid water flowing from a most unsightly-looking rock. Excuse the metaphor; I do not often indulge.

"Do you keep boarders?"

"I do; a few, sir; such as my house will accommodate."

"Whom have you had with you this summer?"

I knew what her answer would be before she uttered it; so did a hundred others, but they showed their knowledge in different ways. I did not show mine at all.

"I have had with me," said she, "a Mr. and Mrs. Van Burnam from New York. Mr. Howard Van Burnam is his full name, if you wish me to be explicit."

"Any one else?"

"A Mr. Hull, also from New York, and a young couple from Hartford. My house accommodates no more."

"How long have the first mentioned couple been with you?"

"Three months. They came in June."

"Are they with you still?"

"Virtually, sir. They have not moved their trunks; but neither of them is in Haddam at present. Mrs. Van Burnam came to New York last Monday morning, and in the afternoon her husband also left, presumably for New York. I have seen nothing of either of them since."

(It was on Tuesday night the murder occurred.)

"Did either of them take a trunk?"

"No, sir."

"A hand-bag?"

"Yes; Mrs. Van Burnam carried a bag, but it was a very small one."

"Large enough to hold a dress?"

"O no, sir."

"And Mr. Van Burnam?"

"He carried an umbrella; I saw nothing else."

"Why did they not leave together? Did you hear any one say?"

"Yes; I heard them say Mrs. Van Burnam came against her husband's wishes. He did not want her to leave Haddam, but she would, and he was none too pleased at it. Indeed they had words about it, and as both our rooms overlook the same veranda, I could not help hearing some of their talk."

"Will you tell us what you heard?"

"It does not seem right" (thus this honest woman spoke), "but if it's the law, I must not go against it. I heard him say these words: 'I have changed my mind, Louise. The more I think of it, the more disinclined I am to have you meddle in the matter. Besides, it will do no good. You will only add to the prejudice against you, and our life will become more unbearable than it is now.'"

"Of what were they speaking?"

"I do not know."

"And what did she reply?"

"O, she uttered a torrent of words that had less sense in them than feeling. She wanted to go, she would go, *she* had not changed *her* mind, and considered that her impulses were as well worth following as his cool judgment. She was not happy, had never been happy, and meant there should be a change, even if it were for the worse. But she did not believe it would be for the worse. Was she not pretty? Was she not very pretty when in distress and looking up thus? And I heard her fall on her knees, a movement which called out a grunt from her husband, but whether this was an expression of approval or disapproval I cannot say. A silence followed, during which I caught the sound of his steady tramping up and down the room. Then she spoke again in a petulant way. 'It may seem foolish to *you*' she cried, 'knowing me as you do, and being used to seeing me in all my moods. But to him it will be a surprise, and I will so manage it that it will effect all we want, and more, too, perhaps. I—I have a genius for some things, Howard; and my better angel tells me I shall succeed.'"

"And what did he reply to that?"

"That the name of her better angel was Vanity; that his father would see through her blandishments; that he forbade her to prosecute her schemes; and much more to the same effect. To all of which she answered by a vigorous stamp of her foot, and the declaration that she was going to do what she thought best in spite of all opposition; that it was a lover, and not a tyrant that she had married, and that if he did not know what was good for himself, she did, and that when he received an intimation from his father that the breach in the family was closed, then he would acknowledge that if she had no fortune and no connections, she had at least a plentiful supply of wit. Upon which he remarked: 'A poor qualification when it verges upon folly!' which seemed to close the conversation, for I heard no more till the sound of her skirts rustling past my door assured me she had carried her point and was leaving the house. But this was not done without great discomfiture to her husband, if one may judge from the few brief but emphatic words that escaped him before he closed his own door and followed her down the hall."

"Do you remember those words?"

"They were swear words, sir; I am sorry to say it, but he certainly cursed her and his own folly. Yet I always thought he loved her."

"Did you see her after she passed your door?"

"Yes, sir, on the walk outside."

"Was she then on the way to the train?"

"Yes, sir."

"Carrying the bag of which you have spoken?"

"Yes, sir; another proof of the state of feeling between them, for he was very considerate in his treatment of ladies, and I never saw him do anything ungallant before."

"You say you watched her as she went down the walk?"

"Yes, sir; it is human nature, sir; I have no other excuse to offer."

It was an apology I myself might have made. I conceived a liking for this homely matter-of-fact woman.

"Did you note her dress?"

"Yes, sir; that is human nature also, or, rather, woman's nature."

"Particularly, madam; so that you can describe it to the jury before you?"

"I think so."

"Will you, then, be good enough to tell us what sort of a dress Mrs. Van Burnam wore when she left your house for the city?"

"It was a black and white plaid silk, very rich— —"

Why, what did this mean? We had all expected a very different description.

"It was made fashionably, and the sleeves—well, it is impossible to describe the sleeves. She wore no wrap, which seemed foolish to me, for we have very sudden changes sometimes in September."

"A plaid dress! And did you notice her hat?"

"O, I have seen the hat often. It was of every conceivable color. It would have been called bad taste at one time, but now-a-days— —"

The pause was significant. More than one man in the room chuckled, but the women kept a discreet silence.

"Would you know that hat if you saw it?"

"I should think I would!"

The emphasis was that of a countrywoman, and amused some people notwithstanding the melodious tone in which it was uttered. But it did not amuse me; my thoughts had flown to the hat which Mr. Gryce had found in the third room of Mr. Van Burnam's house, and which was of every color of the rainbow.

The Coroner asked two other questions, one in regard to the gloves worn by Mrs. Van Burnam, and the other in regard to her shoes. To the first, Miss Ferguson replied that she did not notice her gloves, and to the other, that Mrs. Van Burnam was very fashionable, and as pointed shoes were the fashion, in cities at least, she probably wore pointed shoes.

The discovery that Mrs. Van Burnam had been differently dressed on that day from the young woman found dead in the Van Burnam parlors, had acted as a shock upon most of the spectators. They were just beginning to recover from it when Miss Ferguson sat down. The Coroner was the only one who had not seemed at a loss. Why, we were soon destined to know.

XI.
THE ORDER CLERK.

A lady well known in New York society was the next person summoned. She was a friend of the Van Burnam family, and had known Howard from childhood. She had not liked his marriage; indeed, she rather participated in the family feeling against it, but when young Mrs. Van Burnam came to her house on the preceding Monday, and begged the privilege of remaining with her for one night, she had not had the heart to refuse her. Mrs. Van Burnam had therefore slept in her house on Monday night.

Questioned in regard to that lady's appearance and manner, she answered that her guest was unnaturally cheerful, laughing much and showing a great vivacity; that she gave no reason for her good spirits, nor did she mention her own affairs in any way,—rather took pains not to do so.

"How long did she stay?"

"Till the next morning."

"And how was she dressed?"

"Just as Miss Ferguson has described."

"Did she bring her hand-bag to your house?"

"Yes, and left it there. We found it in her room after she was gone."

"Indeed! And how do you account for that?"

"She was preoccupied. I saw it in her cheerfulness, which was forced and not always well timed."

"And where is that bag now?"

"Mr. Van Burnam has it. We kept it for a day and as she did not call for it, sent it down to the office on Wednesday morning."

"Before you had heard of the murder?"

"O yes, before I had heard anything about the murder."

"As she was your guest, you probably accompanied her to the door?"

"I did, sir."

"Did you notice her hands? Can you say what was the colcr of her gloves?"

"I do not think she wore any gloves on leaving; it was very warm, and she held them in her hand. I remembered this, for I noticed the sparkle of her rings as she turned to say good-bye."

"Ah, you saw her rings!"

"Distinctly."

"So that when she left you she was dressed in a black and white plaid silk, had a large hat covered with flowers on her head, and wore rings?"

"Yes, sir."

And with these words ringing in the ears of the jury, the witness sat down.

What was coming? Something important, or the Coroner would not look so satisfied, or the faces of the officials about him so expectant. I waited with great but subdued eagerness for the testimony of the next witness, who was a young man by the name of Callahan.

I don't like young men in general. They are either over-suave and polite, as if they condescended to remember that you are elderly and that it is their duty to make you forget it, or else they are pert and shallow and disgust you with their egotism. But this young man looked sensible and business-like, and I took to him at once, though what connection he could have with this affair I could not imagine.

His first words, however, settled all questions as to his personality: He was the order clerk at Altman's.

As he acknowledged this, I seemed to have some faint premonition of what was coming. Perhaps I had not been without some vague idea of the truth ever since I had put my mind to work on this matter; perhaps my wits only received their real spur then; but certainly I knew what he was going to say as soon as he opened his lips, which gave me quite a good opinion of myself, whether rightfully or not, I leave you to judge.

His evidence was short, but very much to the point. On the seventeenth of September, as could be verified by the books, the firm had received an order for a woman's complete outfit, to be sent, C.O.D., to Mrs. James Pope at the Hotel D— —, on Broadway. Sizes and measures and some particulars were stated, and as the order bore the words *In haste* underlined upon it, several clerks had assisted him in filling this order, which when filled had been sent by special messenger to the place designated.

Had he this order with him?

He had.

And could he identify the articles sent to fill it?

He could.

At which the Coroner motioned to an officer and a pile of clothing was brought forward from some mysterious corner and laid before the witness.

Immediately expectation rose to a high pitch, for every one recognized, or thought he did, the apparel which had been taken from the victim.

The young man, who was of the alert, nervous type, took up the articles one by one and examined them closely.

As he did so, the whole assembled crowd surged forward and lightning-like glances from a hundred eyes followed his every movement and expression.

"Are they the same?" inquired the Coroner.

The witness did not hesitate. With one quick glance at the blue serge dress, black cape, and battered hat, he answered in a firm tone:

"They are."

And a clue was given at last to the dreadful mystery absorbing us.

The deep-drawn sigh which swept through the room testified to the universal satisfaction; then our attention became fixed again, for the Coroner, pointing to the undergarments accompanying the articles already mentioned, demanded if they had been included in the order.

There was as little hesitation in the reply given to this question as to the former. He recognized each piece as having come from his establishment. "You will note," said he, "that they have never been washed, and that the pencil marks are still on them."

"Very good," observed the Coroner, "and you will note that one article there is torn down the back. Was it in that condition when sent?"

"It was not, sir."

"All were in perfect order?"

"Most assuredly, sir."

"Very good, again. The jury will take cognizance of this fact, which may be useful to them in their future conclusions. And now, Mr. Callahan, do you notice anything lacking here from the list of articles forwarded by you?"

"No, sir."

"Yet there is one very necessary adjunct to a woman's outfit which is not to be found here."

"Yes, sir, the shoes; but I am not surprised at that. We sent shoes, but they were not satisfactory, and they were returned."

"Ah, I see. Officer, show the witness the shoes that were taken from the deceased."

This was done, and when Mr. Callahan had examined them, the Coroner inquired if they came from his store. He replied no.

Whereupon they were held up to the jury, and attention called to the fact that, while rather new than old, they gave signs of having been worn more than once; which was not true of anything else taken from the victim.

This matter settled, the Coroner proceeded with his questions.

"Who carried the articles ordered, to the address given?"

"A man in our employ, named Clapp."

"Did he bring back the amount of the bill?"

"Yes, sir; less the five dollars charged for the shoes."

"What was the amount, may I ask?"

"Here is our cash-book, sir. The amount received from Mrs. James Pope, Hotel D— —, on the seventeenth of September, is, as you see, seventy-five dollars and fifty-eight cents."

"Let the jury see the book; also the order."

They were both handed to the jury, and if ever I wished myself in any one's shoes, save my own very substantial ones, it was at that moment. I did so want a peep at that order.

It seemed to interest the jury also, for their heads drew together very eagerly over it, and some whispers and a few knowing looks passed between them. Finally one of them spoke:

"It is written in a very odd hand. Do you call this a woman's writing or a man's?"

"I have no opinion to give on the subject," rejoined the witness. "It is intelligible writing, and that is all that comes within my province."

The twelve men shifted on their seats and surveyed the Coroner eagerly. Why did he not proceed? Evidently he was not quick enough to suit them.

"Have you any further questions for this witness?" asked that gentleman after a short delay.

Their nervousness increased, but no one ventured to follow the Coroner's suggestion. A poor lot, I call them, a very poor lot! I would have found plenty of questions to put to him.

I expected to see the man Clapp called next, but I was disappointed in this. The name uttered was Henshaw, and the person who rose in answer to it was a tall, burly man with a shock of curly black hair. He was the clerk of the Hotel D— —, and we all forgot Clapp in our eagerness to hear what this man had to say.

His testimony amounted to this:

That a person by the name of Pope was registered on his books. That she came to his house on the seventeenth of September, some time near noon. That she was not alone; that a person she called her husband accompanied her, and that they had been given a room, at her request, on the second floor overlooking Broadway.

"Did you see the husband? Was it his handwriting we see in your register?"

"No, sir. He came into the office, but he did not approach the desk. It was she who registered for them both, and who did all the business in fact. I thought it queer, but took it for granted he was ill, for he held his head very much down, and acted as if he felt disturbed or anxious."

"Did you notice him closely? Would you be able to identify him on sight?"

"No, sir, I should not. He looked like a hundred other men I see every day: medium in height and build, with brown hair and brown moustache. Not noticeable in any way, sir, except for his hang-dog air and evident desire not to be noticed."

"But you saw him later?"

"No, sir. After he went to his room he stayed there, and no one saw him. I did not even see him when he left the house. His wife paid the bill and he did not come into the office."

"But you saw her well; you would know her again?"

"Perhaps, sir; but I doubt it. She wore a thick veil when she came in, and though I might remember her voice, I have no recollection of her features for I did not see them."

"You can give a description of her dress, though; surely you must have looked long enough at a woman who wrote her own and her husband's name in your register, for you to remember her clothes."

"Yes, for they were very simple. She had on what is called a gossamer, which covered her from neck to toe, and on her head a hat wrapped all about with a blue veil."

"So that she might have worn any dress under that gossamer?"

"Yes, sir."

"And any hat under that veil?"

"Any one that was large enough, sir."

"*Very* good. Now, did you see her hands?"

"Not to remember them."

"Did she have gloves on?"

"I cannot say. I did not stand and watch her, sir."

"That is a pity. But you say you heard her voice."

"Yes, sir."

"Was it a lady's voice? Was her tone refined and her language good?"

"They were, sir."

"When did they leave? How long did they remain in your house?"

"They left in the evening; after tea, I should say."

"How? On foot or in a carriage?"

"In a carriage; one of the hacks that stand in front of the door."

"Did they bring any baggage with them?"

"No, sir."

"Did they take any away?"

"The lady carried a parcel."

"What kind of a parcel?"

"A brown-paper parcel, like clothing done up."

"And the gentleman?"

"I did not see him."

"Was she dressed the same in going as in coming?"

"To all appearance, except her hat. That was smaller."

"She had the gossamer on still, then?"

"Yes, sir."

"And a veil?"

"Yes, sir."

"Only that the hat it covered was smaller?"

"Yes, sir."

"And now, how did you account to yourself for the parcel and the change of hat?"

"I didn't account for them. I didn't think anything about them at the time; but, since I have had the subject brought to my mind, I find it easy enough. She had a package delivered to her while she was in our house, or rather packages; they were quite numerous, I believe."

"Can you recall the circumstances of their delivery?"

"Yes, sir; the man who brought the packages said that they had not been paid for, so I allowed him to carry them to Mrs. James Pope's room. When he went away, he had but one small parcel with him; the rest he had left."

"And this is all you can tell us about this singular couple? Had they no meals in your house?"

"No, sir; the gentleman—or I suppose I should say the lady, sir, for the order was given in her voice—sent for two dozen oysters and a bottle of ale, which were furnished to them in their rooms; but they didn't come to the dining-room."

"Is the boy here who carried up those articles?"

"He is, sir."

"And the chambermaid who attended to their rooms?"

"Yes, sir."

"Then you may answer this question, and we will excuse you. How was the gentleman dressed when you saw him?"

"In a linen duster and a felt hat."

"Let the jury remember that. And now let us hear from Richard Clapp. Is Richard Clapp in the room?"

"I am, sir," answered a cheery voice; and a lively young man with a shrewd eye and a wide-awake manner popped up from behind a portly woman on a side seat and rapidly came forward.

He was asked several questions before the leading one which we all expected; but I will not record them here. The question which brought the reply most eagerly anticipated was this:

"Do you remember being sent to the Hotel D——with several packages for a Mrs. James Pope?"

"I do, sir."

"Did you deliver them in person? Did you see the lady?"

A peculiar look crossed his face and we all leaned forward. But his answer brought a shock of disappointment with it.

"No, I didn't, sir. She wouldn't let me in. She bade me lay the things down by the door and wait in the rear hall till she called me."

"And you did this?"

"Yes, sir."

"But you kept your eye on the door, of course?"

"Naturally, sir."

"And saw——"

"A hand steal out and take in the things."

"A woman's hand?"

"No; a man's. I saw the white cuff."

"And how long was it before they called you?"

"Fifteen minutes, I should say. I heard a voice cry 'Here!' and seeing their door open, I went toward it. But by the time I reached it, it was shut again, and I only heard the lady say that all the articles but the shoes were satisfactory, and would I thrust the bill in under the door. I did so, and they were some minutes counting out the change, but presently the door opened slightly, and I saw a man's hand holding out the money, which was correct to the cent. 'You need not receipt the bill,' cried the lady from somewhere in the room. 'Give him the shoes and let him go.' So I received the shoes in the same mysterious way I had the money, and seeing no reason for waiting longer, pocketed the bills and returned to the store."

"Has the jury any further questions to ask the witness?"

Of course not. They were ninnies, all of them, and——But, contrary to my expectation, one of them did perk up courage, and, wriggling very much on his seat, ventured to ask if the cuff he had seen on the man's hand when it was thrust through the doorway had a button in it.

The answer was disappointing. The witness had not noticed any.

The juror, somewhat abashed, sank into silence, at which another of the precious twelve, inspired no doubt by the other's example, blurted out:

"Then what was the color of the coat sleeve? You surely can remember that."

But another disappointment awaited us.

"He did not wear any coat. It was a shirt sleeve I saw."

A shirt sleeve! There was no clue in that. A visible look of dejection spread through the room, which was not dissipated till another witness stood up.

This time it was the bell-boy of the hotel who had been on duty that day. His testimony was brief, and added but little to the general knowledge. He had been summoned more than once by these mysterious parties, but only to receive his orders through a closed door. He had not entered the room at all.

He was followed by the chambermaid, who testified that she was in the room once while they were there; that she saw them both then, but did not catch a glimpse of their faces; Mr. Pope was standing in the window almost entirely shielded by the curtains, and Mrs. Pope was busy hanging up something in the wardrobe. The gentleman had on his duster and the lady her gossamer; it was but a few minutes after their arrival.

Questioned in regard to the state of the room after they left it, she said that there was a lot of brown paper lying about, marked B. Altman, but nothing else that did not belong there.

"Not a tag, nor a hat-pin, nor a bit of memorandum, lying on bureau or table?"

"Nothing, sir, so far as I mind. I wasn't on the look-out for anything, sir. They were a queer couple, but we have lots of queer couples at our house, and the most I notices, sir, is those what remember the chambermaid and those what don't. This couple was of the kind what don't."

"Did you sweep the room after their departure?"

"I always does. They went late, so I swept the room the next morning."

"And threw the sweepings away, of course?"

"Of course; would you have me keep them for treasures?"

"It might have been well if you had," muttered the Coroner. "The combings from the lady's hair might have been very useful in establishing her identity."

The porter who has charge of the lady's entrance was the last witness from this house. He had been on duty on the evening in question and had noticed this couple leaving. They both carried packages, and had attracted his attention first, by the long, old-fashioned duster which the gentleman wore, and secondly, by the pains they both took not to be observed by any one. The woman was veiled, as had already been said, and the man held his package in such a way as to shield his face entirely from observation.

"So that you would not know him if you saw him again?" asked the Coroner.

"Exactly, sir," was the uncomprising answer.

As he sat down, the Coroner observed: "You will note from this testimony, gentlemen, that this couple, signing themselves Mr. and Mrs. James Pope of Philadelphia, left this house dressed each in a long garment eminently fitted for purposes of concealment,—he in a linen duster, and she in a gossamer. Let us now follow this couple a little farther and see what became of these disguising articles of apparel. Is Seth Brown here?"

A man, who was so evidently a hackman that it seemed superfluous to ask him what his occupation was, shuffled forward at this.

It was in his hack that this couple had left the D——. He remembered them very well as he had good reason to. First, because the man paid him before entering the carriage, saying that he was to let them out at the northwest corner of Madison Square, and secondly——But here the Coroner interrupted him to ask if he had seen the gentleman's face when he paid him. The answer was, as might have been expected, No. It was dark, and he had not turned his head.

"Didn't you think it queer to be paid before you reached your destination?"

"Yes, but the rest was queerer. After I had taken the money—I never refuses money, sir—and was expecting him to get into the hack, he steps up to me again and says in a lower tone than before: 'My wife is very nervous. Drive slow, if you please, and when you reach the place I have named, watch your horses carefully, for if they should move while she is getting out, the shock would throw her into a spasm.' As she had looked very pert and lively, I thought this mighty queer, and I tried to get a peep at his face, but he was too smart for me, and was in the carriage before I could clap my eye on him."

"But you were more fortunate when they got out? You surely saw one or both of them then?"

"No, sir, I didn't. I had to watch the horses' heads, you know. I shouldn't like to be the cause of a young lady having a spasm."

"Do you know in what direction they went?"

"East, I should say. I heard them laughing long after I had whipped up my horses. A queer couple, sir, that puzzled me some, though I should not have thought of them twice if I had not found next day——"

"Well?"

"The gentleman's linen duster and the neat brown gossamer which the lady had worn, lying folded under the two back cushions of my hack; a present for which I was very much obliged to them, but which I was not long allowed to enjoy, for yesterday the police——"

"Well, well, no matter about that. Here is a duster and here is a brown gossamer. Are these the articles you found under your cushions?"

"If you will examine the neck of the lady's gossamer, you can soon tell, sir. There was a small hole in the one I found, as if something had been snipped out of it; the owner's name, most likely."

"Or the name of the place where it was bought," suggested the Coroner, holding the garment up to view so as to reveal a square hole under the collar.

"That's it!" cried the hackman. "That's the very one. Shame, I say, to spoil a new garment that way."

"Why do you call it new?" asked the Coroner.

"Because it hasn't a mud spot or even a mark of dust upon it. We looked it all over, my wife and I, and decided it had not been long off the shelf. A pretty good haul for a poor man like me, and if the police——"

But here he was cut short again by an important question:

"There is a clock but a short distance from the place where you stopped. Did you notice what time it was when you drove away?"

"Yes, sir. I don't know why I remember it, but I do. As I turned to go back to the hotel, I looked up at this clock. It was half-past eleven."

XII.
THE KEYS.

We were all by this time greatly interested in the proceedings; and when another hackman was called we recognized at once that an effort was about to be made to connect this couple with the one who had alighted at Mr. Van Burnam's door.

The witness, who was a melancholy chap, kept his stand on the east side of the Square. At about twenty minutes to twelve, he was awakened from a nap he had been taking on the top of his coach, by a sharp rap on his whip arm, and looking down, he saw a lady and gentleman standing at the door of his vehicle.

"We want to go to Gramercy Park," said the lady. "Drive us there at once."

"I nodded, for what is the use of wasting words when it can be avoided; and they stepped at once into the coach."

"Can you describe them—tell us how they looked?"

"I never notice people; besides, it was dark; but he had a swell air, and she was pert and merry, for she laughed as she closed the door."

"Can't you remember how they were dressed?"

"No, sir; she had on something that flapped about her shoulders, and he had a dark hat on his head, but that was all I saw."

"Didn't you see his face?"

"Not a bit of it; he kept it turned away. He didn't want nobody looking at *him*. She did all the business."

"Then you saw *her* face?"

"Yes, for a minute. But I wouldn't know it again. She was young and purty, and her hand which dropped the money into mine was small, but I couldn't say no more, not if you was to give me the town."

"Did you know that the house you stopped at was Mr. Van Burnam's, and that it was supposed to be empty?"

"No, sir, I'm not one of the swell ones. My acquaintances live in another part of the town."

"But you noticed that the house was dark?"

"I may have. I don't know."

"And that is all you have to tell us about them?"

"No, sir; the next morning, which was yesterday, sir, as I was a-dusting out the coach I found under the cushions a large blue veil, folded and lying very flat. But it had been slit with a knife and could not be worn."

This was strange too, and while more than one person about me ventured an opinion, I muttered to myself, "James Pope, his mark!" astonished at a coincidence which so completely connected the occupants of the two coaches.

But the Coroner was able to produce a witness whose evidence carried the matter on still farther. A policeman in full uniform testified next, and after explaining that his beat led him from Madison Avenue to Third on Twenty-seventh Street, went on to say that as he was coming up this street on Tuesday evening some few minutes before midnight, he encountered, somewhere between Lexington Avenue and Third, a man and woman walking rapidly towards the latter avenue, each carrying a parcel of some dimensions; that he noted them because they seemed so merry, but would have thought nothing of it, if he had not presently perceived them coming back without the parcels. They were chatting more gaily than ever. The lady wore a short cape, and the gentleman a dark coat, but he could give no other description of their appearance, for they went by rapidly, and he was more interested in wondering what they had done with such large parcels in such a short time at that hour of night, than in noting how they looked or whither they were going. He did observe, however, that they proceeded towards Madison Square, and remembers now that he heard a carriage suddenly drive away from that direction.

The Coroner asked him but one question:

"Had the lady no parcel when you saw her last?"

"I saw none."

"Could she not have carried one under her cape?"

"Perhaps, if it was small enough."

"As small as a lady's hat, say?"

"Well, it would have to be smaller than some of them are now, sir."

And so terminated this portion of the inquiry.

A short delay followed the withdrawal of this witness. The Coroner, who was a somewhat portly man, and who had felt the heat of the day very much, leaned back and looked anxious, while the jury, always restless, moved in their seats like a set of school-boys, and seemed to long for the hour of adjournment, notwithstanding the interest which everybody but themselves seemed to take in this exciting investigation.

Finally an officer, who had been sent into the adjoining room, came back with a gentleman, who was no sooner recognized as Mr. Franklin Van Burnam than a great change took place in the countenances of all present. The Coroner sat forward and dropped the large palm-leaf fan he had been industriously using for the last few minutes, the jury settled down, and the whispering of the many curious ones about me grew less audible and finally ceased altogether. A gentleman of the family was about to be interrogated, and such a gentleman!

I have purposely refrained from describing this best known and best reputed member of the Van Burnam family, foreseeing this hour when he would attract the attention of a hundred eyes and when his appearance would require our special notice. I will therefore endeavor to picture him to you as he looked on this memorable morning, with just the simple warning that you must not expect me to see with the eyes of a young girl or even with those of a fashionable society woman. I know a man when I see him, and I had always regarded Mr. Franklin as an exceptionally fine-looking and prepossessing gentleman, but I shall not go into raptures, as I heard a girl behind me doing, nor do I feel like acknowledging him as a paragon of all the virtues—as Mrs. Cunningham did that evening in my parlor.

He is a medium-sized man, with a shape not unlike his brother's. His hair is dark and so are his eyes, but his moustache is brown and his complexion quite fair. He carries himself with distinction, and though his countenance in repose has a precise air that is not perfectly agreeable, it has, when he speaks or smiles, an expression at once keen and amiable.

On this occasion he failed to smile, and though his elegance was sufficiently apparent, his worth was not so much so. Yet the impression generally made was favorable, as one could perceive from the air of respect with which his testimony was received.

He was asked many questions. Some were germane to the matter in hand and some seemed to strike wide of all mark. He answered them all courteously, showing a manly composure in doing so, that served to calm the fever-heat into which many had been thrown by the stories of the two hackmen. But as his evidence up to this point related merely to minor concerns, this was neither strange nor conclusive. The real test began when the Coroner, with a certain bluster, which may have been meant to attract the attention of the jury, now visibly waning, or, as was more likely, may have been the unconscious expression of a secret if hitherto well concealed embarrassment, asked the witness whether the keys to his father's front door had any duplicates.

The answer came in a decidedly changed tone. "No. The key used by our agent opens the basement door only."

The Coroner showed his satisfaction. "No duplicates," he repeated; "then you will have no difficulty in telling us where the keys to your father's front door were kept during the family's absence."

Did the young man hesitate, or was it but imagination on my part—"They were usually in my possession."

"Usually!" There was irony in the tone; evidently the Coroner was getting the better of his embarrassment, if he had felt any. "And where were they on the seventeenth of this month? Were they in your possession then?"

"No, sir." The young man tried to look calm and at his ease, but the difficulty he felt in doing so was apparent. "On the morning of that day," he continued, "I passed them over to my brother."

Ah! here was something tangible as well as important. I began to fear the police understood themselves only too well; and so did the whole crowd of persons there assembled. A groan in one direction was answered by a sigh in another, and it needed all the Coroner's authority to prevent an outbreak.

Meanwhile Mr. Van Burnam stood erect and unwavering, though his eye showed the suffering which these demonstrations awakened. He did not turn in the direction of the room where we felt sure his family was gathered, but it was evident that his thoughts did, and that most painfully. The Coroner, on the contrary, showed little or no feeling; he had brought the investigation up to this critical point and felt fully competent to carry it farther.

"May I ask," said he, "where the transference of these keys took place?"

"I gave them to him in our office last Tuesday morning. He said he might want to go into the house before his father came home."

"Did he say why he wanted to go into the house?"

"No."

"Was he in the habit of going into it alone and during the family's absence?"

"No."

"Had he any clothes there? or any articles belonging to himself or his wife which he would be likely to wish to carry away?"

"No."

"Yet he wanted to go in?"

"He said so."

"And you gave him the keys without question?"

"Certainly, sir."

"Was that not opposed to your usual principles—to your way of doing things, I should say?"

"Perhaps; but principles, by which I suppose you mean my usual business methods, do not govern me in my relations with my brother. He asked me a favor, and I granted it. It would have to have been a much larger one for me to have asked an explanation from him before doing so."

"Yet you are not on good terms with your brother; at least you have not had the name of being, for some time?"

"We have had no quarrel."

"Did he return the keys you lent him?"

"No."

"Have you seen them since?"

"No."

"Would you know them if they were shown you?"

"I would know them if they unlocked our front door."

"But you would not know them on sight?"

"I don't think so."

"Mr. Van Burnam, it is disagreeable for me to go into family matters, but if you have had no quarrel with your brother, how comes it that you and he have had so little intercourse of late?"

"He has been in Connecticut and I at Long Branch. Is not that a good answer, sir?"

"Good, but not good enough. You have a common office in New York, have you not?"

"Certainly, the firm's office."

"And you sometimes meet there, even while residing in different localities?"

"Yes, our business calls us in at times and then we meet, of course."

"Do you talk when you meet?"

"Talk?"

"Of other matters besides business, I mean. Are your relations friendly? Do you show the same spirit towards each other as you did three years ago, say?"

"We are older; perhaps we are not quite so voluble."

"But do you feel the same?"

"No. I see you will have it, and so I will no longer hold back the truth. We are not as brotherly in our intercourse as we used to be; but there is no animosity between us. I have a decided regard for my brother."

This was said quite nobly, and I liked him for it, but I began to feel that perhaps it had been for the best after all that I had never been intimate with the family. But I must not forestall either events or my opinions.

"Is there any reason"—it is the Coroner, of course, who is speaking—"why there should be any falling off in your mutual confidence? Has your brother done anything to displease you?"

"We did not like his marriage."

"Was it an unhappy one?"

"It was not a suitable one."

"Did you know Mrs. Van Burnam well, that you say this?"

"Yes, I knew her, but the rest of the family did not."

"Yet they shared in your disapprobation?"

"They felt the marriage more than I did. The lady—excuse me, I never like to speak ill of the sex—was not lacking in good sense or virtue, but she was not the person we had a right to expect Howard to marry."

"And you let him see that you thought so?"

"How could we do otherwise?"

"Even after she had been his wife for some months?"

"We could not like her."

"Did your brother—I am sorry to press this matter—ever show that he felt your change of conduct towards him?"

"I find it equally hard to answer," was the quick reply. "My brother is of an affectionate nature, and he has some, if not all, of the family's pride. I think he did feel it, though he never said so. He is not without loyalty to his wife."

"Mr. Van Burnam, of whom does the firm doing business under the name of Van Burnam & Sons consist?"

"Of the three persons mentioned."

"No others?"

"No."

"Has there ever been in your hearing any threat made by the senior partner of dissolving this firm as it stands?"

"I have heard"—I felt sorry for this strong but far from heartless man, but I would not have stopped the inquiry at this point if I could; I was far too curious—"I have heard my father say that he would withdraw if Howard did not. Whether he would have done so, I consider open to doubt. My father is a just man and never fails to do the right thing, though he sometimes speaks with unnecessary harshness."

"He made the threat, however?"

"Yes."

"And Howard heard it?"

"Or of it; I cannot say which."

"Mr. Van Burnam, have you noticed any change in your brother since this threat was uttered?"

"How, sir; what change?"

"In his treatment of his wife, or in his attitude towards yourself?"

"I have not seen him in the company of his wife since they went to Haddam. As for his conduct towards myself, I can say no more than I have already. We have never forgotten that we are children of one mother."

"Mr. Van Burnam, how many times have you seen Mrs. Howard Van Burnam?"

"Several. More frequently before they were married than since."

"You were in your brother's confidence, then, at that time; knew he was contemplating marriage?"

"It was in my endeavors to prevent the match that I saw so much of Miss Louise Stapleton."

"Ah! I am glad of the explanation! I was just going to inquire why you, of all members of the family, were the only one to know your brother's wife by sight."

The witness, considering this question answered, made no reply. But the next suggestion could not be passed over.

"If you saw Mrs. Van Burnam so often, you are acquainted with her personal appearance?"

"Sufficiently so; as well as I know that of my ordinary calling-acquaintance."

"Was she light or dark?"

"She had brown hair."

"Similar to this?"

The lock held up was the one which had been cut from the head of the dead girl.

"Yes, somewhat similar to that." The tone was cold; but he could not hide his distress.

"Mr. Van Burnam, have you looked well at the woman who was found murdered in your father's house?"

"I have, sir."

"Is there anything in her general outline or in such features as have escaped disfigurement to remind you of Mrs. Howard Van Burnam?"

"I may have thought so—at first glance," he replied, with decided effort.

"And did you change your mind at the second?"

He looked troubled, but answered firmly: "No, I cannot say that I did. But you must not regard my opinion as conclusive," he hastily added. "My knowledge of the lady was comparatively slight."

"The jury will take that into account. All we want to know now is whether you can assert from any knowledge you have or from anything to be noted in the body itself, that it is not Mrs. Howard Van Burnam?"

"I cannot."

And with this solemn assertion his examination closed.

The remainder of the day was taken up in trying to prove a similarity between Mrs. Van Burnam's handwriting and that of Mrs. James Pope as seen in the register of the Hotel D—— and on the order sent to Altman's. But the only conclusion reached was that the latter might be the former disguised, and even on this point the experts differed.

XIII.
HOWARD VAN BURNAM.

The gentleman who stepped from the carriage and entered Mr. Van Burnam's house at twelve o'clock that night produced so little impression upon me that I went to bed satisfied that no result would follow these efforts at identification.

And so I told Mr. Gryce when he arrived next morning. But he seemed by no means disconcerted, and merely requested that I would submit to one more trial. To which I gave my consent, and he departed.

I could have asked him a string of questions, but his manner did not invite them, and for some reason I was too wary to show an interest in this tragedy superior to that felt by every right-thinking person connected with it.

At ten o'clock I was in my old seat in the court-room. The same crowd with different faces confronted me, amid which the twelve stolid countenances of the jury looked like old friends. Howard Van Burnam was the witness called, and as he came forward and stood in full view of us all, the interest of the occasion reached its climax.

His countenance wore a reckless look that did not serve to prepossess him with the people at whose mercy he stood. But he did not seem to care, and waited for the Coroner's questions with an air of ease which was in direct contrast to the drawn and troubled faces of his father and brother just visible in the background.

Coroner Dahl surveyed him a few minutes before speaking, then he quietly asked if he had seen the dead body of the woman who had been found lying under a fallen piece of furniture in his father's house.

He replied that he had.

"Before she was removed from the house or after it?"

"After."

"Did you recognize it? Was it the body of any one you know?"

"I do not think so."

"Has your wife, who was missing yesterday, been heard from yet, Mr. Van Burnam?"

"Not to my knowledge, sir."

"Had she not—that is, your wife—a complexion similar to that of the dead woman just alluded to?"

"She had a fair skin and brown hair, if that is what you mean. But these attributes are common to too many women for me to give them any weight in an attempted identification of this importance."

"Had they no other similar points of a less general character? Was not your wife of a slight and graceful build, such as is attributed to the subject of this inquiry?"

"My wife was slight and she was graceful, common attributes also."

"And your wife had a scar?"

"Yes."

"On the left ankle?"

"Yes."

"Which the deceased also has?"

"That I do not know. They say so, but I had no interest in looking."

"Why, may I ask? Did you not think it a remarkable coincidence?"

The young man frowned. It was the first token of feeling he had given.

"I was not on the look-out for coincidences," was his cold reply. "I had no reason to think this unhappy victim of an unknown man's brutality my wife, and so did not allow myself to be moved by even such a fact as this."

"You had no reason," repeated the Coroner, "to think this woman your wife. Had you any reason to think she was not?"

"Yes."

"Will you give us that reason?"

"I had more than one. First, my wife would never wear the clothes I saw on the girl whose dead body was shown to me. Secondly, she would never go to any house alone with a man at the hour testified to by one of your witnesses."[A]

"Not with any man?"

"I did not mean to include her husband in my remark, cf course. But as I did not take her to Gramercy Park, the fact that the deceased woman entered an empty house accompanied by a man, is proof enough to me that she was not Louise Van Burnam."

"When did you part with your wife?"

"On Monday morning at the depot in Haddam."

"Did you know where she was going?"

"I knew where she said she was going."

"And where was that, may I ask?"

"To New York, to interview my father."

"But your father was not in New York?"

"He was daily expected here. The steamer on which he had sailed from Southampton was due on Tuesday."

"Had she an interest in seeing your father? Was there any special reason why she should leave you for doing so?"

"She thought so; she thought he would become reconciled to her entrance into our family if he should see her suddenly and without prejudiced persons standing by."

"And did you fear to mar the effect of this meeting if you accompanied her?"

"No, for I doubted if the meeting would ever take place. I had no sympathy with her schemes, and did not wish to give her the sanction of my presence."

"Was that the reason you let her go to New York alone?"

"Yes."

"Had you no other?"

"No."

"Why did you follow her, then, in less than five hours?"

"Because I was uneasy; because I also wanted to see my father; because I am a man accustomed to carry out every impulse; and impulse led me that day in the direction of my somewhat headstrong wife."

"Did you know where your wife intended to spend the night?"

"I did not. She has many friends, or at least I have, in the city, and I concluded she would go to one of them—as she did."

"When did you arrive in the city? before ten o'clock?"

"Yes, a few minutes before."

"Did you try to find your wife?"

"No. I went directly to the club."

"Did you try to find her the next morning?"

"No; I had heard that the steamer had not yet been sighted off Fire Island, so considered the effort unnecessary."

"Why? What connection is there between this fact and an endeavor on your part to find your wife?"

"A very close one. She had come to New York to throw herself at my father's feet. Now she could only do this at the steamer or in——"

"Why do you not proceed, Mr. Van Burnam?"

"I will. I do not know why I stopped,—or in his own house."

"In his own house? In the house in Gramercy Park, do you mean?"

"Yes, he has no other."

"The house in which this dead girl was found?"

"Yes,"—impatiently.

"Did you think she might throw herself at his feet there?"

"She said she might; and as she is romantic, foolishly romantic, I thought her fully capable of doing so."

"And so you did not seek her in the morning?"

"No, sir."

"How about the afternoon?"

This was a close question; we saw that he was affected by it though he tried to carry it off bravely.

"I did not see her in the afternoon. I was in a restless frame of mind, and did not remain in the city."

"Ah! indeed! and where did you go?"

"Unless necessary, I prefer not to say."

"It is necessary."

"I went to Coney Island."

"Alone?"

"Yes."

"Did you see anybody there you know?"

"No."

"And when did you return?"

"At midnight."

"When did you reach your rooms?"

"Later."

"How much later?"

"Two or three hours."

"And where were you during those hours?"

"I was walking the streets."

The ease, the quietness with which he made these acknowledgments were remarkable. The jury to a man honored him with a prolonged stare, and the awe-struck crowd scarcely breathed during their utterance. At the last sentence a murmur broke out, at which he raised his head and with an air of surprise surveyed the people before him. Though he must have known what their astonishment meant, he neither quailed nor blanched, and while not in reality a handsome man, he certainly looked handsome at this moment.

I did not know what to think; so forbore to think anything. Meanwhile the examination went on.

"Mr. Van Burnam, I have been told that the locket I see there dangling from your watch-chain contains a lock of your wife's hair. Is it so?"

"I have a lock of her hair in this; yes."

"Here is a lock clipped from the head of the unknown woman whose identity we seek. Have you any objection to comparing the two?"

"It is not an agreeable task you have set me," was the imperturbable response; "but I have no objection to doing what you ask." And calmly lifting the chain, he took off the locket, opened it, and held it out courteously toward the Coroner. "May I ask you to make the first comparison," he said.

The Coroner, taking the locket, laid the two locks of brown hair together, and after a moment's contemplation of them both, surveyed the young man seriously, and remarked:

"They are of the same shade. Shall I pass them down to the jury?"

Howard bowed. You would have thought he was in a drawing-room, and in the act of bestowing a favor. But his brother Franklin showed a very different countenance, and as for their father, one could not even see his face, he so persistently held up his hand before it.

The jury, wide-awake now, passed the locket along, with many sly nods and a few whispered words. When it came back to the Coroner, he took it and handed it to Mr. Van Burnam, saying:

"I wish you would observe the similarity for yourself. I can hardly detect any difference between them."

"Thank you! I am willing to take your word for it," replied the young man, with most astonishing *aplomb*. And Coroner and jury for a moment looked baffled, and even Mr. Gryce, of whose face I caught a passing glimpse at this instant, stared at the head of his cane, as if it were of thicker wood than he expected and had more knotty points on it than even his accustomed hand liked to encounter.

Another effort was not out of place, however; and the Coroner, summoning up some of the pompous severity he found useful at times, asked the witness if his attention had been drawn to the dead woman's hands.

He acknowledged that it had. "The physician who made the autopsy urged me to look at them, and I did; they were certainly very like my wife's."

"Only like."

"I cannot say that they were my wife's. Do you wish me to perjure myself?"

"A man should know his wife's hands as well as he knows her face."

"Very likely."

"And you are ready to swear these were not the hands of your wife?"

"I am ready to swear I did not so consider them."

"And that is all?"

"That is all."

The Coroner frowned and cast a glance at the jury. They needed prodding now and then, and this is the way he prodded them. As soon as they gave signs of recognizing the hint he gave them, he turned back, and renewed his examination in these words:

"Mr. Van Burnam, did your brother at your request hand you the keys of your father's house on the morning of the day on which this tragedy occurred?"

"He did."

"Have you those keys now?"

"I have not."

"What have you done with them? Did you return them to your brother?"

"No; I see where your inquiries are tending, and I do not suppose you will believe my simple word; but I lost the keys on the day I received them; that is why——"

"Well, you may continue, Mr. Van Burnam."

"I have no more to say; my sentence was not worth completing."

The murmur which rose about him seemed to show dissatisfaction; but he remained imperturbable, or rather like a man who did not hear. I began to feel a most painful interest in the inquiry, and dreaded, while I anxiously anticipated, his further examination.

"You lost the keys; may I ask when and where?"

"That I do not know; they were missing when I searched for them; missing from my pocket, I mean."

"Ah! and when did you search for them?"

"The next day—after I had heard—of—of what had taken place in my father's house."

The hesitations were those of a man weighing his reply. They told on the jury, as all such hesitations do; and made the Coroner lose an atom of the respect he had hitherto shown this easy-going witness.

"And you do not know what became of them?"

"No."

"Or into whose hands they fell?"

"No, but probably into the hands of the wretch——"

To the astonishment of everybody he was on the verge of vehemence; but becoming sensible of it, he controlled himself with a suddenness that was almost shocking.

"Find the murderer of this poor girl," said he, with a quiet air that was more thrilling than any display of passion, "and ask *him* where he got the keys with which he opened the door of my father's house at midnight."

Was this a challenge, or just the natural outburst of an innocent man. Neither the jury nor the Coroner seemed to know, the former looking startled and the latter nonplussed. But Mr. Gryce, who had moved now into view, smoothed the head of his cane with quite a loving touch, and did not seem at this moment to feel its inequalities objectionable.

"We will certainly try to follow your advice," the Coroner assured him. "Meanwhile we must ask how many rings your wife is in the habit of wearing?"

"Five. Two on the left hand and three on the right."

"Do you know these rings?"

"I do."

"Better than you know her hands?"

"As well, sir."

"Were they on her hands when you parted from her in Haddam?"

"They were."

"Did she always wear them?"

"Almost always. Indeed I do not ever remember seeing her take off more than one of them."

"Which one?"

"The ruby with the diamond setting."

"Had the dead girl any rings on when you saw her?"

"No, sir."

"Did you look to see?"

"I think I did in the first shock of the discovery."

"And you saw none?"

"No, sir."

"And from this you concluded she was not your wife?"

"From this and other things."

"Yet you must have seen that the woman was in the habit of wearing rings, even if they were not on her hands at that moment?"

"Why, sir? What should I know about her habits?"

"Is not that a ring I see now on your little finger?"

"It is; my seal ring which I always wear."

"Will you pull it off?"

"Pull it off!"

"If you please; it is a simple test I am requiring of you, sir."

The witness looked astonished, but pulled off the ring at once.

"Here it is," said he.

"Thank you, but I do not want it. I merely want you to look at your finger."

The witness complied, evidently more nonplussed than disturbed by this command.

"Do you see any difference between that finger and the one next it?"

"Yes; there is a mark about my little finger showing where the ring has pressed."

"Very good; there were such marks on the fingers of the dead girl, who, as you say, had no rings on. I saw them, and perhaps you did yourself?"

"I did not; I did not look closely enough."

"They were on the little finger of the right hand, on the marriage finger of the left, and on the forefinger of the same. On which fingers did your wife wear rings?"

"On those same fingers, sir, but I will not accept this fact as proving her identity with the deceased. Most women do wear rings, and on those very fingers."

The Coroner was nettled, but he was not discouraged. He exchanged looks with Mr. Gryce, but nothing further passed between them and we were left to conjecture what this interchange of glances meant.

The witness, who did not seem to be affected either by the character of this examination or by the conjectures to which it gave rise, preserved his *sang-froid*, and eyed the Coroner as he might any other questioner, with suitable respect, but with no fear and but little impatience. And yet he must have known the horrible suspicion darkening the minds of many people present, and suspected, even if against his will, that this examination, significant as it was, was but the forerunner of another and yet more serious one.

"You are very determined," remarked the Coroner in beginning again, "not to accept the very substantial proofs presented you of the identity between the object of this inquiry and your missing wife. But we are not yet ready to give up the struggle, and so I must ask if you heard the description given by Miss Ferguson of the manner in which your wife was dressed on leaving Haddam?

"I have."

"Was it a correct account? Did she wear a black and white plaid silk and a hat trimmed with various colored ribbons and flowers?"

"She did."

"Do you remember the hat? Were you with her when she bought it, or did you ever have your attention drawn to it in any particular way?"

"I remember the hat."

"Is this it, Mr. Van Burnam?"

I was watching Howard, and the start he gave was so pronounced and the emotion he displayed was in such violent contrast to the self-possession he had maintained up to this point, that I was held spell-bound by the shock I received, and forebore to look at the object which the Coroner had suddenly held up for inspection. But when I did turn my head towards it, I recognized at once the multi-colored hat which Mr. Gryce had brought in from the third room of Mr. Van Burnam's house on the evening I was there, and realized almost in the same breath that great as this mystery had hitherto seemed it was likely to prove yet greater before its proper elucidation was arrived at.

"Was that found in my father's house? Where—where was that hat found?" stammered the witness, so far forgetting himself as to point towards the object in question.

"It was found by Mr. Gryce in a closet off your father's dining-room, a short time after the dead girl was carried out."

"I don't believe it," vociferated the young man, paling with something more than anger, and shaking from head to foot.

"Shall I put Mr. Gryce on his oath again?" asked the Coroner, mildly.

The young man stared; evidently these words failed to reach his understanding.

"*Is* it your wife's hat?" persisted the Coroner with very little mercy. "Do you recognize it for the one in which she left Haddam?"

"Would to God I did not!" burst in vehement distress from the witness, who at the next moment broke down altogether and looked about for the support of his brother's arm.

Franklin came forward, and the two brothers stood for a moment in the face of the whole surging mass of curiosity-mongers before them, arm in arm, but with very different expressions on their two proud faces. Howard was the first to speak.

"If that was found in the parlors of my father's house," he cried, "then the woman who was killed there was my wife." And he started away with a wild air towards the door.

"Where are you going?" asked the Coroner, quietly, while an officer stepped softly before him, and his brother compassionately drew him back by the arm.

"I am going to take her from that horrible place; she is my wife. Father, you would not wish her to remain in that spot for another moment, would you, while we have a house we call our own?"

Mr. Van Burnam the senior, who had shrunk as far from sight as possible through these painful demonstrations, rose up at these words from his agonized son, and making him an encouraging gesture, walked hastily out of the room; seeing which, the young man became calmer, and though he did not cease to shudder, tried to restrain his first grief, which to those who looked closely at him was evidently very sincere.

"I would not believe it was she," he cried, in total disregard of the presence he was in, "I *would not* believe it; but now——" A certain pitiful gesture finished the sentence, and neither Coroner nor jury seemed to know just how to proceed, the conduct of the young man being so markedly different from what they had expected. After a short pause, painful enough to all concerned, the Coroner, perceiving that very little could be done with the witness under the circumstances, adjourned the sitting till afternoon.

FOOTNOTES:

[A] Why could he not have said Miss Butterworth? These Van Burnams are proud, most vilely proud as the poet has it.—A. B.

XIV.
A SERIOUS ADMISSION.

I went at once to a restaurant. I ate because it was time to eat, and because any occupation was welcome that would pass away the hours of waiting. I was troubled; and I did not know what to make of myself. I was no friend to the Van Burnams; I did not like them, and certainly had never approved of any of them but Mr. Franklin, and yet I found myself altogether disturbed over the morning's developments, Howard's emotion having appealed to me in spite of my prejudices. I could not but think ill of him, his conduct not being such as I could honestly commend. But I found myself more ready to listen to the involuntary pleadings of my own heart in his behalf than I had been prior to his testimony and its somewhat startling termination.

But they were not through with him yet, and after the longest three hours I ever passed, we were again convened before the Coroner.

I saw Howard as soon as anybody did. He came in, arm in arm as before, with his faithful brother, and sat down in a retired corner behind the Coroner. But he was soon called forward.

His face when the light fell on it was startling to most of us. It was as much changed as if years, instead of hours, had elapsed since last we saw it. No longer reckless in its expression, nor easy, nor politely patient, it showed in its every lineament that he had not only passed through a hurricane of passion, but that the bitterness, which had been its worst feature, had not passed with the storm, but had settled into the core of his nature, disturbing its equilibrium forever. My emotions were not allayed by the sight; but I kept all expression of them out of view. I must be sure of his integrity before giving rein to my sympathies.

The jury moved and sat up quite alert when they saw him. I think that if these especial twelve men could have a murder case to investigate every day, they would grow quite wide-awake in time. Mr. Van Burnam made no demonstration. Evidently there was not likely to be a repetition of the morning's display of passion. He had been iron in his impassibility at that time, but he was steel now, and steel which had been through the fiercest of fires.

The opening question of the Coroner showed by what experience these fires had been kindled.

"Mr. Van Burnam, I have been told that you have visited the Morgue in the interim which has elapsed since I last questioned you. Is that true?"

"It is."

"Did you, in the opportunity thus afforded, examine the remains of the woman whose death we are investigating, attentively enough to enable you to say now whether they are those of your missing wife?"

"I have. The body is that of Louise Van Burnam; I crave your pardon and that of the jury for my former obstinacy in refusing to recognize it. I thought myself fully justified in the stand I took. I see now that I was not."

The Coroner made no answer. There was no sympathy between him and this young man. Yet he did not fail in a decent show of respect; perhaps because he did feel some sympathy for the witness's unhappy father and brother.

"You then acknowledge the victim to have been your wife?"

"I do."

"It is a point gained, and I compliment the jury upon it. We can now proceed to settle, if possible, the identity of the person who accompanied Mrs. Van Burnam into your father's house."

"Wait," cried Mr. Van Burnam, with a strange air, "*I acknowledge I was that person.*"

It was coolly, almost fiercely said, but it was an admission that wellnigh created a hubbub. Even the Coroner seemed moved, and cast a glance at Mr. Gryce which showed his surprise to be greater than his discretion.

"You acknowledge," he began—but the witness did not let him finish.

"I acknowledge that I was the person who accompanied her into that empty house; but I do not acknowledge that I killed her. She was alive and well when I left her, difficult as it is for me to prove it. It was the realization of this difficulty which made me perjure myself this morning."

"So," murmured the Coroner, with another glance at Mr. Gryce, "you acknowledge that you perjured yourself. Will the room be quiet!"

But the lull came slowly. The contrast between the appearance of this elegant young man and the significant admissions he had just made (admissions which to three quarters of the persons there meant more, much more, than he acknowledged), was certainly such as to provoke interest of the deepest kind. I felt like giving rein to my own feelings, and was not surprised at the patience shown by the Coroner. But order was restored at last, and the inquiry proceeded.

"We are then to consider the testimony given by you this morning as null and void?"

"Yes, so far as it contradicts what I have just stated."

"Ah, then you will no doubt be willing to give us your evidence again?"

"Certainly, if you will be so kind as to question me."

"Very well; where did your wife and yourself first meet after your arrival in New York?"

"In the street near my office. She was coming to see me, but I prevailed upon her to go uptown."

"What time was this?"

"After ten and before noon. I cannot give the exact hour."

"And where did you go?"

"To a hotel on Broadway; you have already heard of our visit there."

"You are, then, the Mr. James Pope, whose wife registered in the books of the Hotel D—— on the seventeenth of this month?"

"I have said so."

"And may I ask for what purpose you used this disguise, and allowed your wife to sign a wrong name?"

"To satisfy a freak. She considered it the best way of covering up a scheme she had formed; which was to awaken the interest of my father under the name and appearance of a stranger, and not to inform him who she was till he had given some evidence of partiality for her."

"Ah, but for such an end was it necessary for her to assume a strange name before she saw your father, and for you both to conduct yourselves in the mysterious way you did all that day and evening?"

"I do not know. She thought so, and I humored her. I was tired of working against her, and was willing she should have her own way for a time."

"And for this reason you let her fit herself out with clothes down to her very undergarments?"

"Yes; strange as it may seem, I was just such a fool. I had entered into her scheme, and the means she took to change her personality only amused me. She wished to present herself to my father as a girl obliged to work for her living, and was too shrewd to excite suspicion in the minds of any of the family by any undue luxury in her apparel. At least that was the excuse she gave me for the precautions she took, though I think the delight she experienced in anything romantic and unusual had as much to do with it as anything else. She enjoyed the game she was playing, and wished to make as much of it as possible."

"Were her own garments much richer than those she ordered from Altman's?"

"Undoubtedly. Mrs. Van Burnam wore nothing made by American seamstresses. Fine clothes were her weakness."

"I see, I see; but why such an attempt on your part to keep yourself in the background? Why let your wife write your assumed names in the hotel register, for instance, instead of doing it yourself?"

"It was easier for her; I know no other reason. She did not mind putting down the name Pope. I did."

It was an ungracious reflection upon his wife, and he seemed to feel it so; for he almost immediately added: "A man will sometimes lend himself to a scheme of which the details are obnoxious. It was so in this case; but she was too interested in her plans to be affected by so small a matter as this."

This explained more than one mysterious action on the part of this pair while they were at the Hotel D— —. The Coroner evidently considered it in this light, for he dwelt but little longer on this phase of the case, passing at once to a fact concerning which curiosity had hitherto been roused without receiving any satisfaction.

"In leaving the hotel," said he, "you and your wife were seen carrying certain packages, which were missing from your arms when you alighted at Mr. Van Burnam's house. What was in those packages, and where did you dispose of them before you entered the second carriage?"

Howard made no demur in answering.

"My wife's clothes were in them," said he, "and we dropped them somewhere on Twenty-seventh Street near Third Avenue, just as we saw an old woman coming along the sidewalk. We knew that she would stop and pick them up, and she did, for we slid into a dark shadow made by a projecting stoop and watched her. Is that too simple a method for disposing of certain encumbering bundles, to be believed, sir?"

"That is for the jury to decide," answered the Coroner, stiffly. "But why were you so anxious to dispose of these articles? Were they not worth some money, and would it not have been simpler and much more natural to have left them at the hotel till you chose to send for them? That is, if you were simply engaged in playing, as you say, a game upon your father, and not upon the whole community?"

"Yes," Mr. Van Burnam acknowledged, "that would have been the natural thing, no doubt; but we were not following natural instincts at the time, but a woman's *bizarre* caprices. We did as I said; and laughed long, I assure you, over its unqualified success; for the old woman not only grabbed the packages with avidity, but turned and fled away with them, just as if she had expected this opportunity and had prepared herself to make the most of it."

"It was very laughable, certainly," observed the Coroner, in a hard voice. "*You* must have found it very ridiculous"; and after giving the witness a look full of something deeper than sarcasm, he turned towards the jury as if to ask them what they thought of these very forced and suspicious explanations.

But they evidently did not know what to think, and the Coroner's looks flew back to the witness who of all the persons present seemed the least impressed by the position in which he stood.

"Mr. Van Burnam," said he, "you showed a great deal of feeling this morning at being confronted with your wife's hat. Why was this, and why did you wait till you saw this evidence of her presence on the scene of death to acknowledge the facts you have been good enough to give us this afternoon?"

"If I had a lawyer by my side, you would not ask me that question, or if you did, I would not be allowed to answer it. But I have no lawyer here, and so I will say that I was greatly shocked by the catastrophe which had happened to my wife, and under the stress of my first overpowering emotions had the impulse to hide the fact that the victim of so dreadful a mischance was my wife. I thought that if no connection was found between myself and this dead woman, I would stand in no danger of the suspicion which must cling to the man who came into the house with her. But like most first impulses, it was a foolish one and gave way under the strain of investigation. I, however, persisted in it as long as possible, partially because my disposition is an obstinate one, and partially because I hated to acknowledge myself a fool; but when I saw the hat, and recognized it as an indisputable proof of her presence in the Van Burnam house that night, my confidence in the attempt I was making broke down all at once. I could deny her shape, her hands, and even the scar, which she might have had in common with other women, but I could not deny her hat. Too many persons had seen her wear it."

But the Coroner was not to be so readily imposed upon.

"I see, I see," he repeated with great dryness, "and I hope the jury will be satisfied. And they probably will, unless they remember the anxiety which, according to your story, was displayed by your wife to have her whole outfit in keeping with her appearance as a working girl. If she was so particular as to think it necessary to dress herself in store-made undergarments, why make all these precautions void by carrying into the house a hat with the name of an expensive milliner inside it?"

"Women are inconsistent, sir. She liked the hat and hated to part with it. She thought she could hide it somewhere in the great house, at least that was what she said to me when she tucked it under her cape."

The Coroner, who evidently did not believe one word of this, stared at the witness as if curiosity was fast taking the place of indignation. And I did not wonder. Howard Van Burnam, as thus presented to our notice by his own testimony, was an anomaly, whether we were to believe what he was saying at the present time or what he had said during the morning session. But I wished I had had the questioning of him.

His next answer, however, opened up one dark place into which I had been peering for some time without any enlightenment. It was in reply to the following query:

"All this," said the Coroner, "is very interesting; but what explanation have you to give for taking your wife into your father's empty house at an hour so late, and then leaving her to spend the best part of the dark night alone?"

"None," said he, "that will strike you as sensible and judicious. But we were not sensible that night, neither were we judicious, or I would not be standing here trying to explain what is not explainable by any of the ordinary rules of conduct. She was set upon being the first to greet my father on his entrance into his own home, and her first plan had been to do so in her own proper character as my wife, but afterwards the freak took her, as I have said, to personify the housekeeper whom my father had cabled us to have in waiting at his house,—a cablegram which had reached us too late for any practical use, and which we had therefore ignored,—and fearing he might come early in the morning, before she could be on hand to make the favorable impression she intended, she wished to be left in the house that night; and I humored her. I did not foresee the suffering that my departure might cause her, or the fears that were likely to spring from her lonely position in so large and empty a dwelling. Or rather, I should say, *she* did not foresee them; for she begged me not to stay with her, when I hinted at the darkness and dreariness of the place, saying that she was too jolly to feel fear or think of anything but the surprise my father and sisters would experience in discovering that their very agreeable young housekeeper was the woman they had so long despised."

"And why," persisted the Coroner, edging forward in his interest and so allowing me to catch a glimpse of Mr. Gryce's face as he too leaned forward in his anxiety to hear every word that fell from this remarkable witness,— "why do you speak of her fear? What reason have you to think she suffered apprehension after your departure?"

"Why?" echoed the witness, as if astounded by the other's lack of perspicacity. "Did she not kill herself in a moment of terror and discouragement? Leaving her, as I did, in a condition of health and good spirits, can you expect me to attribute her death to any other cause than a sudden attack of frenzy caused by terror?"

"Ah!" exclaimed the Coroner in a suspicious tone, which no doubt voiced the feelings of most people present; "then you think your wife committed suicide?"

"Most certainly," replied the witness, avoiding but two pairs of eyes in the whole crowd, those of his father and brother.

"*With* a hat-pin," continued the Coroner, letting his hitherto scarcely suppressed irony become fully visible in voice and manner, "thrust into the back of her neck at a spot young ladies surely would have but little reason to know is peculiarly fatal! Suicide! when she was found crushed under a pile of *bric-à-brac*, which was thrown down or fell upon her hours after she received the fatal thrust!"

"I do not know how else she could have died," persisted the witness, calmly, "unless she opened the door to some burglar. And what burglar would kill a woman in that way, when he could pound her with his fists? No; she was frenzied and stabbed herself in desperation; or the thing was done by accident, God knows how! And as for the testimony of the experts—we all know how easily the wisest of them can be mistaken even in matters of as serious import as these. *If all the experts in the world"* —here his voice rose and his nostrils dilated till his aspect was actually commanding and impressed us all like a sudden transformation—"*If all the experts in the world were to swear that those shelves were thrown upon her after she had lain therefor four hours dead, I would not believe them. Appearances or no appearances, blood or no blood, I here declare that she pulled that cabinet over in her death-struggle; and upon the truth of this fact I am ready to rest my honor as a man and my integrity as her husband."*

An uproar immediately followed, amid which could be heard cries of "He lies!" "He's a fool!" The attitude taken by the witness was so unexpected that the most callous person present could not fail to be affected by it. But curiosity is as potent a passion as surprise, and in a few minutes all was still again and everybody intent to hear how the Coroner would answer these asseverations.

"I have heard of a blind man denying the existence of light," said that gentleman, "but never before of a sensible being like yourself urging the most untenable theories in face of such evidence as has been brought before us during this inquiry. If your wife committed suicide, or if the entrance of the point of a hat-pin into her spine was effected by accident, how comes the head of the pin to have been found so many feet away from her and in such a place as the parlor register?"

"It may have flown there when it broke, or, what is much more probable, been kicked there by some of the many people who passed in and out of the room between the time of her death and that of its discovery."

"But the register was found closed," urged the Coroner. "Was it not, Mr. Gryce?"

That person thus appealed to, rose for an instant.

"It was," said he, and deliberately sat down again.

The face of the witness, which had been singularly free from expression since his last vehement outbreak, clouded over for an instant and his eye fell as if he felt himself engaged in an unequal struggle. But he recovered his courage speedily, and quietly observed:

"The register may have been closed by a passing foot. I have known of stranger coincidences than that."

"Mr. Van Burnam," asked the Coroner, as if weary of subterfuges and argument, "have you considered the effect which this highly contradictory evidence of yours is likely to have on your reputation?"

"I have."

"And are you ready to accept the consequences?"

"If any especial consequences follow, I must accept them, sir."

"When did you lose the keys which you say you have not now in your possession? This morning you asserted that you did not know; but perhaps this afternoon you may like to modify that statement."

"I lost them after I left my wife shut up in my father's house."

"Soon?"

"Very soon."

"How soon?"

"Within an hour, I should judge."

"How do you know it was so soon?"

"I missed them at once."

"Where were you when you missed them?"

"I don't know; somewhere. I was walking the streets, as I have said. I don't remember just where I was when I thrust my hands into my pocket and found the keys gone."

"You do not?"

"No."

"But it was within an hour after leaving the house?"

"Yes."

"Very good; the keys have been found."

The witness started, started so violently that his teeth came together with a click loud enough to be heard over the whole room.

"Have they?" said he, with an effort at nonchalance which, however, failed to deceive any one who noticed his change of color. "*You* can tell me, then, where I lost them."

"They were found," said the Coroner, "in their usual place above your brother's desk in Duane Street."

"Oh!" murmured the witness, utterly taken aback or appearing so. "I cannot account for their being found in the office. I was so sure I dropped them in the street."

"I did not think you could account for it," quietly observed the Coroner. And without another word he dismissed the witness, who staggered to a seat as remote as possible from the one where he had previously been sitting between his father and brother.

XV.
A RELUCTANT WITNESS.

A pause of decided duration now followed; an exasperating pause which tried even me, much as I pride myself upon my patience. There seemed to be some hitch in regard to the next witness. The Coroner sent Mr. Gryce into the neighboring room more than once, and finally, when the general uneasiness seemed on the point of expressing itself by a loud murmur, a gentleman stepped forth, whose appearance, instead of allaying the excitement, renewed it in quite an unprecedented and remarkable way.

I did not know the person thus introduced.

He was a handsome man, a very handsome man, if the truth must be told, but it did not seem to be this fact which made half the people there crane their heads to catch a glimpse of him. Something else, something entirely disconnected with his appearance there as a witness, appeared to hold the people enthralled and waken a subdued enthusiasm which showed itself not only in smiles, but in whispers and significant nudges, chiefly among the women, though I noticed that the jurymen stared when somebody obliged them with the name of this new witness. At last it reached my ears, and though it awakened in me also a decided curiosity, I restrained all expression of it, being unwilling to add one jot to this ridiculous display of human weakness.

Randolph Stone, as the intended husband of the rich Miss Althorpe, was a figure of some importance in the city, and while I was very glad of this opportunity of seeing him, I did not propose to lose my head or forget, in the marked interest his person invoked, the very serious cause which had brought him before us. And yet I suppose no one in the room observed his figure more minutely.

He was elegantly made and possessed, as I have said, a face of peculiar beauty. But these were not his only claims to admiration. He was a man of undoubted intelligence and great distinction of manner. The intelligence did not surprise me, knowing, as I did, how he had raised himself to his present enviable position in society in the short space of five years. But the perfection of his manner astonished me, though how I could have expected anything less in a man honored by Miss Althorpe's regard, I cannot say. He had that clear pallor of complexion which in a smooth-shaven face is so impressive, and his voice when he spoke had that music in it which only comes from great cultivation and a deliberate intent to please.

He was a friend of Howard's, that I saw by the short look that passed between them when he first entered the room; but that it was not as a friend he stood there was apparent from the state of amazement with which the former recognized him, as well as from the regret to be seen underlying the polished manner of the witness himself. Though perfectly self-possessed and perfectly respectful, he showed by every means possible the pain he felt in adding one feather-weight to the evidence against a man with whom he was on terms of more or less intimacy.

But let me give his testimony. Having acknowledged that he knew the Van Burnam family well, and Howard in particular, he went on to state that on the night of the seventeenth he had been detained at his office by business of a more than usual pressing nature, and finding that he could expect no rest for that night, humored himself by getting off the cars at Twenty-first Street instead of proceeding on to Thirty-third Street, where his apartments were.

The smile which these words caused (Miss Althorpe lives in Twenty-first Street) woke no corresponding light on his face. Indeed, he frowned at it, as if he felt that the gravity of the situation admitted of nothing frivolous or humorsome. And this feeling was shared by Howard, for he started when the witness mentioned Twenty-first Street, and cast him a haggard look of dismay which happily no one saw but myself, for every one else was concerned with the witness. Or should I except Mr. Gryce?

"I had of course no intentions beyond a short stroll through this street previous to returning to my home," continued the witness, gravely; "and am sorry to be obliged to mention this freak of mine, but find it necessary in order to account for my presence there at so unusual an hour."

"You need make no apologies," returned the Coroner. "Will you state on what line of cars you came from your office?"

"I came up Third Avenue."

"Ah! and walked towards Broadway?"

"Yes."

"So that you necessarily passed very near the Van Burnam mansion?"

"Yes."

"At what time was this, can you say?"

"At four, or nearly four. It was half-past three when I left my office."

"Was it light at that hour? Could you distinguish objects readily?"

"I had no difficulty in seeing."

"And what did you see? Anything amiss at the Van Burnam mansion?"

"No, sir, nothing amiss. I merely saw Howard Van Burnam coming down the stoop as I went by the corner."

"You made no mistake. It was the gentleman you name, and no other whom you saw on this stoop at this hour?"

"I am very sure that it was he. I am sorry— —"

But the Coroner gave him no opportunity to finish.

"You and Mr. Van Burnam are friends, you say, and it was light enough for you to recognize each other; then you probably spoke?"

"No, we did not. I was thinking—well of other, things," and here he allowed the ghost of a smile to flit suggestively across his firm-set lips. "And Mr. Van Burnam seemed preoccupied also, for, as far as I know, he did not even look my way."

"And you did not stop?"

"No, he did not look like a man to be disturbed."

"And this was at four on the morning of the eighteenth?"

"At four."

"You are certain of the hour and of the day?"

"I am certain. I should not be standing here if I were not very sure of my memory. I am sorry," he began again, but he was stopped as peremptorily as before by the Coroner.

"Feeling has no place in an inquiry like this." And the witness was dismissed.

Mr. Stone, who had manifestly given his evidence under compulsion, looked relieved at its termination. As he passed back to the room from which he had come, many only noticed the extreme elegance of his form and the proud cast of his head, but I saw more than these. I saw the look of regret he cast at his friend Howard.

A painful silence followed his withdrawal, then the Coroner spoke to the jury:

"Gentlemen, I leave you to judge of the importance of this testimony. Mr. Stone is a well-known man of unquestionable integrity, but perhaps Mr. Van

Burnam can explain how he came to visit his father's house at four o'clock in the morning on that memorable night, when according to his latest testimony he left his wife there at twelve. We will give him the opportunity."

"There is no use," began the young man from the place where he sat. But gathering courage even while speaking, he came rapidly forward, and facing Coroner and jury once more, said with a false kind of energy that imposed upon no one:

"I can explain this fact, but I doubt if you will accept my explanation. I was at my father's house at that hour, but not in it. My restlessness drove me back to my wife, but not finding the keys in my pocket, I came down the stoop again and went away."

"Ah, I see now why you prevaricated this morning in regard to the time when you missed those keys."

"I know that my testimony is full of contradictions."

"You feared to have it known that you were on the stoop of your father's house for the second time that night?"

"Naturally, in face of the suspicion I perceived everywhere about me."

"And this time you did not go in?"

"No."

"Nor ring the bell?"

"No."

"Why not, if you left your wife within, alive and well?"

"I did not wish to disturb her. My purpose was not strong enough to surmount the least difficulty. I was easily deterred from going where I had little wish to be."

"So that you merely went up the stoop and down again at the time Mr. Stone saw you?"

"Yes, and if he had passed a minute sooner he would have seen this: seen me go up, I mean, as well as seen me come down. I did not linger long in the doorway."

"But you did linger there a moment?"

"Yes; long enough to hunt for the keys and get over my astonishment at not finding them."

"Did you notice Mr. Stone going by on Twenty-first Street?"

"No."

"Was it as light as Mr. Stone has said?"

"Yes, it was light."

"And you did not notice him?"

"No."

"Yet you must have followed very closely behind him?"

"Not necessarily. I went by the way of Twentieth Street, sir. Why, I do not know, for my rooms are uptown. I do not know why I did half the things I did that night."

"I can readily believe it," remarked the Coroner.

Mr. Van Burnam's indignation rose.

"You are trying," said he, "to connect me with the fearful death of my wife in my father's lonely house. You cannot do it, for I am as innocent of that death as you are, or any other person in this assemblage. Nor did I pull those shelves down upon her as you would have this jury think, in my last thoughtless visit to my father's door. She died according to God's will by her own hand or by means of some strange and unaccountable accident known only to Him. And so you will find, if justice has any place in these investigations and a manly intelligence be allowed to take the place of prejudice in the breasts of the twelve men now sitting before me."

And bowing to the Coroner, he waited for his dismissal, and receiving it, walked back not to his lonely corner, but to his former place between his father and brother, who received him with a wistful air and strange looks of mingled hope and disbelief.

"The jury will render their verdict on Monday morning," announced the Coroner, and adjourned the inquiry.

BOOK II.
THE WINDINGS OF A LABYRINTH.

XVI.
COGITATIONS.

My cook had prepared for me a most excellent dinner, thinking that I needed all the comfort possible after a day of such trying experiences. But I ate little of it; my thoughts were too busy, my mind too much exercised. What would be the verdict of the jury, and could this especial jury be relied upon to give a just verdict?

At seven I had left the table and was shut up in my own room. I could not rest till I had fathomed my own mind in regard to the events of the day.

The question—the great question, of course, now—was how much of Howard's testimony was to be believed, and whether he was, notwithstanding his asseverations to the contrary, the murderer of his wife. To most persons the answer seemed easy. From the expression of such people as I had jostled in leaving the court-room, I judged that his sentence had already been passed in the minds of most there present. But these hasty judgments did not influence me. I hope I look deeper than the surface, and my mind would not subscribe to his guilt, notwithstanding the bad impression made upon me by his falsehoods and contradictions.

Now why would not my mind subscribe to it? Had sentiment got the better of me, Amelia Butterworth, and was I no longer capable of looking a thing squarely in the face? Had the Van Burnams, of all people in the world, awakened my sympathies at the cost of my good sense, and was I disposed to see virtue in a man in whom every circumstance as it came to light revealed little but folly and weakness? The lies he had told—for there is no other word to describe his contradictions—would have been sufficient under most circumstances to condemn a man in my estimation. Why, then, did I secretly look for excuses to his conduct?

Probing the matter to the bottom, I reasoned in this way: The latter half of his evidence was a complete contradiction of the first, purposely so. In the first, he made himself out a cold-hearted egotist with not enough interest in his wife to make an effort to determine whether she and the murdered woman were identical; in the latter, he showed himself in the light of a man influenced to the point of folly by a woman to whom he had been utterly unyielding a few hours before.

Now, knowing human nature to be full of contradictions, I could not satisfy myself that I should be justified in accepting either half of his testimony as absolutely true. The man who is all firmness one minute may be all weakness the next, and in face of the calm assertions made by this one when driven to bay by the unexpected discoveries of the police, I dared not decide that his final assurances were altogether false, and that he was not the man I had seen enter the adjoining house with his wife.

Why, then, not carry the conclusion farther and admit, as reason and probability suggested, that he was also her murderer; that he had killed her during his first visit and drawn the shelves down upon her in the second? Would not this account for all the phenomena to be observed in connection with this otherwise unexplainable affair? Certainly, all but one—one that was perhaps known to nobody but myself, and that was the testimony given by the clock. It said that the shelves fell at five, whereas, according to Mr. Stone's evidence, it was four, or thereabouts, when Mr. Van Burnam left his father's house. But the clock might not have been a reliable witness. It might have been set wrong, or it might not have been running at all at the time of the accident. No, it would not do for me to rely too much upon anything so doubtful, nor did I; yet I could not rid myself of the conviction that Howard spoke the truth when he declared in face of Coroner and jury that they could not connect him with this crime; and whether this conclusion sprang from sentimentality or intuition, I was resolved to stick to it for the present night at least. The morrow might show its futility, but the morrow had not come.

Meanwhile, with this theory accepted, what explanation could be given of the very peculiar facts surrounding this woman's death? Could the supposition of suicide advanced by Howard before the Coroner be entertained for a moment, or that equally improbable suggestion of accident?

Going to my bureau drawer, I drew out the old grocer-bill which has already figured in these pages, and re-read the notes I had scribbled on its back early in the history of this affair. They related, if you will remember, to this very question, and seemed even now to answer it in a more or less convincing way. Will you pardon me if I transcribe these notes again, as I cannot imagine my first deliberations on this subject to have made a deep enough impression for you to recall them without help from me.

The question raised in these notes was threefold, and the answers, as you will recollect, were transcribed before the cause of death had been determined by the discovery of the broken pin in the dead woman's brain.

These are the queries:

First: was her death due to accident?

Second: was it effected by her own hand?

Third: was it a murder?

The replies given are in the form of reasons, as witness:

My reasons for not thinking it an accident.

1. If it had been an accident, and she had pulled the cabinet over upon herself,[B] she would have been found with her feet pointing towards the wall where the cabinet had stood. But her feet were towards the door and her head under the cabinet.

2. The precise arrangement of the clothing about her feet, which precluded any theory involving accident.

My reason for not thinking it a suicide.

She could not have been found in the position observed without having lain down on the floor while living, and then pulled the shelves down upon herself. (A theory obviously too improbable to be considered.)

My reason for not thinking it murder.

She would need to have been held down on the floor while the cabinet was being pulled over on her, a thing which the quiet aspect of the hands and feet make appear impossible. (Very good, but we know now that she was dead when the shelves fell over, so that my one excuse for not thinking it a murder is rendered null.)

My reasons for thinking it a murder.

----But I will not repeat these. My reasons for not thinking it an accident or a suicide remained as good as when they were written, and if her death had not been due to either of these causes, then it must have been due to some murderous hand. Was that hand the hand of her husband? I have already given it as my opinion that it was not.

Now, how to make that opinion good, and reconcile me again to myself; for I am not accustomed to have my instincts at war with my judgment. Is there any reason for my thinking as I do? Yes, the manliness of man. He only looked well when he was repelling the suspicion he saw in the surrounding faces. But that might have been assumed, just as his careless manner was assumed during the early part of the inquiry. I must have some stronger reason than this for my belief. The two hats? Well, he had explained how there came to be two hats on the scene of crime, but his explanation had not been very satisfactory. *I* had seen no hat in her hand when she crossed the pavement to her father's house. But then she might have carried it under her cape without my seeing it—perhaps. The discovery of two hats and of two pairs of gloves in Mr. Van Burnam's parlors was a fact worth further investigation, and mentally I made a note of it, though at the moment I saw no prospect of engaging in this matter further than my duties as a witness required.

And now what other clue was offered me, save the one I have already mentioned as being given by the clock? None that I could seize upon; and feeling the weakness of the cause I had so obstinately embraced, I rose from my seat at the tea-table and began making such alterations in my toilet as would prepare me for the evening and my inevitable callers.

"Amelia," said I to myself, as I encountered my anything but satisfied reflection in the glass, "can it be that you ought, after all, to have been called Araminta? Is a momentary display of spirit on the part of a young man of doubtful principles, enough to make you forget the dictates of good sense which have always governed you up to this time?"

The stern image which confronted me from the mirror made me no reply, and smitten with sudden disgust, I left the glass and went below to greet some friends who had just ridden up in their carriage.

They remained one hour, and they discussed one subject: Howard Van Burnam and his probable connection with the crime which had taken place next door. But though I talked some and listened more, as is proper for a woman in her own house, I said nothing and heard nothing which had not been already said and heard in numberless homes that night. Whatever thoughts I had which in any way differed from those generally expressed, I kept to myself, — whether guided by discretion or pride, I cannot say; probably by both, for I am not deficient in either quality.

Arrangements had already been made for the burial of Mrs. Van Burnam that night, and as the funeral ceremony was to take place next door, many of my guests came just to sit in my windows and watch the coming and going of the few people invited to the ceremony.

But I discouraged this. I have no patience with idle curiosity. Consequently by nine I was left alone to give the affair such real attention as it demanded; something which, of course, I could not have done with a half dozen gossiping friends leaning over my shoulder.

FOOTNOTES:

[B] As was asserted by her husband in his sworn examination.

XVII.
BUTTERWORTH VERSUS GRYCE.

The result of this attention can be best learned from the conversation I held with Mr. Gryce the next morning.

He came earlier than usual, but he found me up and stirring.

"Well," he cried, accosting me with a smile as I entered the parlor where he was seated, "it is all right this time, is it not? No trouble in identifying the gentleman who entered your neighbor's house last night at a quarter to twelve?"

Resolved to probe this man's mind to the bottom, I put on my sternest air.

"I had not expected any one to enter there so late last night," said I. "Mr. Van Burnam declared so positively at the inquest that he was the person we have been endeavoring to identify, that I did not suppose you would consider it necessary to bring him to the house for me to see."

"And so you were not in the window?"

"I did not say that; I am always where I have promised to be, Mr. Gryce."

"Well, then?" he inquired sharply.

I was purposely slow in answering him—I had all the longer time to search his face. But its calmness was impenetrable, and finally I declared:

"The man you brought with you last night—you were the person who accompanied him, were you not—was *not* the man I saw alight there four nights ago."

He may have expected it; it may have been the very assertion he desired from me, but his manner showed displeasure, and the quick "How?" he uttered was sharp and peremptory.

"I do not ask who it was," I went on, with a quiet wave of my hand that immediately restored him to himself, "for I know you will not tell me. But what I do hope to know is the name of the man who entered that same house at just ten minutes after nine. He was one of the funeral guests, and he arrived in a carriage that was immediately preceded by a coach from which four persons alighted, two ladies and two gentlemen."

"I do not know the gentleman, ma'am," was the detective's half-surprised and half-amused retort. "I did not keep track of every guest that attended the funeral."

"Then you didn't do your work as well as I did mine," was my rather dry reply. "For I noted every one who went in; and that gentleman, whoever he was, was more like the person I have been trying to identify than any one I have seen enter there during my four midnight vigils."

Mr. Gryce smiled, uttered a short "Indeed!" and looked more than ever like a sphinx. I began quietly to hate him, under my calm exterior.

"Was Howard at his wife's funeral?" I asked.

"He was, ma'am."

"And did he come in a carriage?"

"He did, ma'am."

"Alone?"

"He thought he was alone; yes, ma'am."

"Then may it not have been he?"

"I can't say, ma'am."

Mr. Gryce was so obviously out of his element under this cross-examination that I could not suppress a smile even while I experienced a very lively indignation at his reticence. He may have seen me smile and he may not, for his eyes, as I have intimated, were always busy with some object entirely removed from the person he addressed; but at all events he rose, leaving me no alternative but to do the same.

"And so you didn't recognize the gentleman I brought to the neighboring house just before twelve o'clock," he quietly remarked, with a calm ignoring of my last question which was a trifle exasperating.

"No."

"Then, ma'am," he declared, with a quick change of manner, meant, I should judge, to put me in my proper place, "I do not think we can depend upon the accuracy of your memory;" and he made a motion as if to leave.

As I did not know whether his apparent disappointment was real or not, I let him move to the door without a reply. But once there I stopped him.

"Mr. Gryce," said I, "I don't know what you think about this matter, nor whether you even wish my opinion upon it. But I am going to express it, for all that. *I* do not believe that Howard killed his wife with a hat-pin."

"No?" retorted the old gentleman, peering into his hat, with an ironical smile which that inoffensive article of attire had certainly not merited. "And why, Miss Butterworth, why? You must have substantial reasons for any opinion you would form."

"I have an intuition," I responded, "backed by certain reasons. The intuition won't impress you very deeply, but the reasons may not be without some weight, and I am going to confide them to you."

"Do," he entreated in a jocose manner which struck me as inappropriate, but which I was willing to overlook on account of his age and very fatherly manner.

"Well, then," said I, "this is one. If the crime was a premeditated one, if he hated his wife and felt it for his interest to have her out of the way, a man of Mr. Van Burnam's good sense would have chosen any other spot than his father's house to kill her in, knowing that her identity could not be hidden if once she was associated with the Van Burnam name. If, on the contrary, he took her there in good faith, and her death was the unexpected result of a quarrel between them, then the means employed would have been simpler. An angry man does not stop to perform a delicate surgical operation when moved to the point of murder, but uses his hands or his fists, just as Mr. Van Burnam himself suggested."

"Humph!" grunted the detective, staring very hard indeed into his hat.

"You must not think me this young man's friend," I went on, with a well meant desire to impress him with the impartiality of my attitude. "I never have spoken to him nor he to me, but I am the friend of justice, and I must declare that there was a note of surprise in the emotion he showed at sight of his wife's hat, that was far too natural to be assumed."

The detective failed to be impressed. I might have expected this, knowing his sex and the reliance such a man is apt to place upon his own powers.

"Acting, ma'am, acting!" was his laconic comment. "A very uncommon character, that of Mr. Howard Van Burnam. I do not think you do it full justice."

"Perhaps not, but see that you don't slight mine. I do not expect you to heed these suggestions any more than you did those I offered you in connection with Mrs. Boppert, the scrub-woman; but my conscience is eased by my communication, and that is much to a solitary woman like myself who is obliged to spend many a long hour alone with no other companion."

"Something has been accomplished, then, by this delay," he observed. Then, as if ashamed of this momentary display of irritation, he added in the genial tones more natural to him: "I don't blame you for your good opinion of this interesting, but by no means reliable, young man, Miss Butterworth. A woman's kind heart stands in the way of her proper judgment of criminals."

"You will not find its instincts fail even if you do its judgment."

His bow was as full of politeness as it was lacking in conviction.

"I hope you won't let your instincts lead you into any unnecessary detective work," he quietly suggested.

"That I cannot promise. If you arrest Howard Van Burnam for murder, I may be tempted to meddle with matters which don't concern me."

An amused smile broke through his simulated seriousness.

"Pray accept my congratulations, then, in advance, ma'am. My health has been such that I have long anticipated giving up my profession; but if I am to have such assistants as you in my work, I shall be inclined to remain in it some time longer."

"When a man as busy as you stops to indulge in sarcasm, he is in more or less good spirits. Such a condition, I am told, only prevails with detectives when they have come to a positive conclusion concerning the case they are engaged upon."

"I see you already understand the members of your future profession."

"As much as is necessary at this juncture," I retorted. Then seeing him about to repeat his bow, I added sharply: "You need not trouble yourself to show me too much politeness. If I meddle in this matter at all it will not be as your coadjutor, but as your rival."

"My rival?"

"Yes, your rival; and rivals are never good friends until one of them is hopelessly defeated."

"Miss Butterworth, I see myself already at your feet."

And with this sally and a short chuckle which did more than anything he had said towards settling me in my half-formed determination to do as I had threatened, he opened the door and quietly disappeared.

XVIII.
THE LITTLE PINCUSHION.

The verdict rendered by the Coroner's jury showed it to be a more discriminating set of men than I had calculated upon. It was murder inflicted by a hand unknown.

I was so gratified by this that I left the court-room in quite an agitated frame of mind, so agitated, indeed, that I walked through one door instead of another, and thus came unexpectedly upon a group formed almost exclusively of the Van Burnam family.

Starting back, for I dislike anything that looks like intrusion, especially when no great end is to be gained by it, I was about to retrace my steps when I felt two soft arms about my neck.

"Oh, Miss Butterworth, isn't it a mercy that this dreadful thing is over! I don't know when I have ever felt anything so keenly."

It was Isabella Van Burnam.

Startled, for the embraces bestowed on me are few, I gave a subdued sort of grunt, which nevertheless did not displease this young lady, for her arms tightened, and she murmured in my ear: "You dear old scul! I like you *so* much."

"We are going to be very good neighbors," cooed a still sweeter voice in my other ear. "Papa says we must call on you soon." And Caroline's demure face looked around into mine in a manner some would have thought exceedingly bewitching.

"Thank you, pretty poppets!" I returned, freeing myself as speedily as possible from embraces the sincerity of which I felt open to question. "My house is always open to you." And with little ceremony, I walked steadily out and betook myself to the carriage awaiting me.

I looked upon this display of feeling as the mere gush of two over-excited young women, and was therefore somewhat astonished when I was interrupted in my afternoon nap by an announcement that the two Misses Van Burnam awaited me in the parlor.

Going down, I saw them standing there hand in hand and both as white as a sheet.

"O Miss Butterworth!" they cried, springing towards me, "Howard has been arrested, and we have no one to say a word of comfort to us."

"Arrested!" I repeated, greatly surprised, for I had not expected it to happen so soon, if it happened at all.

"Yes, and father is just about prostrated. Franklin, too, but he keeps up, while father has shut himself into his room and won't see anybody, not even us. O, I don't know how we are to bear it! Such a disgrace, and such a wicked, wicked shame! For Howard never had anything to do with his wife's death, had he, Miss Butterworth?"

"No," I returned, taking my ground at once, and vigorously, for I really believed what I said. "He is innocent of her death, and I would like the chance of proving it."

They evidently had not expected such an unqualified assertion from me, for they almost smothered me with kisses, and called me *their only friend!* and indeed showed so much real feeling this time that I neither pushed them away nor tried to withdraw myself from their embraces.

When their emotions were a little exhausted I led them to a sofa and sat down before them. They were motherless girls, and my heart, if hard, is not made of adamant or entirely unsusceptible to the calls of pity and friendship.

"Girls," said I, "if you will be calm, I should like to ask you a few questions."

"Ask us anything," returned Isabella; "nobody has more right to our confidence than you."

This was another of their exaggerated expressions, but I was so anxious to hear what they had to tell, I let it pass. So instead of rebuking them, I asked where their brother had been arrested, and found it had been at his rooms and in presence of themselves and Franklin. So I inquired further and learned that, so far as they knew, nothing had been discovered beyond what had come out at the inquest except that Howard's trunks had been found packed, as if he had been making preparations for a journey when interrupted by the dreadful event which had put him into the hands of the police. As there was a certain significance in this, the girls seemed almost as much impressed by it as I was, but we did not discuss it long, for I suddenly changed my manner, and taking them both by the hand, asked if they could keep a secret.

"Secret?" they gasped.

"Yes, a secret. You are not the girls I should confide in ordinarily; but this trouble has sobered you."

"O, we can do anything," began Isabella; and "Only try us," murmured Caroline.

But knowing the volubility of the one and the weakness of the other, I shook my head at their promises, and merely tried to impress them with the fact that their brother's safety depended upon their discretion. At which they looked very determined for poppets, and squeezed my hands so tightly that I wished I had left off some of my rings before engaging in this interview.

When they were quiet again and ready to listen I told them my plans. They were surprised, of course, and wondered how I could do anything towards finding out the real murderer of their sister-in-law; but seeing how resolved I looked, changed their tone and avowed with much feeling their perfect confidence in me and in the success of anything I might undertake.

This was encouraging, and ignoring their momentary distrust, I proceeded to say:

"But for me to be successful in this matter, no one must know my interest in it. You must pay me no visits, give me no confidences, nor, if you can help it, mention my name before *any one*, not even before your father and brother. So much for precautionary measures, my dears; and now for the active ones. I have no curiosity, as I think you must see, but I shall have to ask you a few questions which under other circumstances would savor more or less of impertinence. Had your sister-in-law any special admirers among the other sex?"

"Oh," protested Caroline, shrinking back, while Isabella's eyes grew round as a frightened child's. "None that we ever heard of. She wasn't that kind of a woman, was she, Belle? It wasn't for any such reason papa didn't like her."

"No, no, *that* would have been too dreadful. It was her family we objected to, that's all."

"Well, well," I apologized, tapping their hands reassuringly, "I only asked—let me now say—from curiosity, though I have not a particle of that quality, I assure you."

"Did you think—did you have any idea—" faltered Caroline, "that— —"

"Never mind," I interrupted. "You must let my words go in one ear and out of the other after you have answered them. I wish"—here I assumed a brisk air—"that I could go through your parlors again before every trace of the crime perpetrated there has been removed."

"Why, you can," replied Isabella.

"There is no one in them now," added Caroline, "Franklin went out just before we left."

At which I blandly rose, and following their leadership, soon found myself once again in the Van Burnam mansion.

My first glance upon re-entering the parlors was naturally directed towards the spot where the tragedy had taken place. The cabinet had been replaced and the shelves set back upon it; but the latter were empty, and neither on them nor on the adjacent mantel-piece did I see the clock. This set me thinking, and I made up my mind to have another look at that clock. By dint of judicious questions I found that it had been carried into the third room, where we soon found it lying on a shelf of the same closet where the hat had been discovered by Mr. Gryce. Franklin had put it there, fearing that the sight of it might affect Howard, and from the fact that the hands stood as I had left them, I gathered that neither he nor any of the family had discovered that it was in running condition.

Assured of this, I astonished them by requesting to have it taken down and set up on the table, which they had no sooner done than it started to tick just as it had done under my hand a few nights before.

The girls, greatly startled, surveyed each other wonderingly.

"Why, it's going!" cried Caroline.

"Who could have wound it!" marvelled Isabella.

"Hark!" I cried. The clock had begun to strike.

It gave forth five clear notes.

"Well, it's a mystery!" Isabella exclaimed. Then seeing no astonishment in my face, she added: "Did you know about this, Miss Butterworth?"

"My dear girls," I hastened to say, with all the impressiveness characteristic of me in my more serious moments. "I do not expect you to ask me for any information I do not volunteer. This is hard, I know; but some day I will be perfectly frank with you. Are you willing to accept my aid on these terms?"

"O yes," they gasped, but they looked not a little disappointed.

"And now," said I, "leave the clock where it is, and when your brother comes home, show it to him, and say that having the curiosity to examine it you were surprised to find it going, and that you had left it there for him to see. He will be surprised also, and as a consequence will question first you and then the police to find out who wound it. If they acknowledge having done it, you must notify me at once, for that's what I want to know. Do you understand, Caroline? And, Isabella, do you feel that you can go through all this without dropping a word concerning me and my interest in this matter?"

Of course they answered yes, and of course it was with so much effusiveness that I was obliged to remind them that they must keep a check on their enthusiasm, and also to suggest that they should not come to my house or send me any notes, but simply a blank card, signifying: "No one knows who wound the clock."

"How delightfully mysterious!" cried Isabella. And with this girlish exclamation our talk in regard to the clock closed.

The next object that attracted our attention was a paper-covered novel I discovered on a side-table in the same room.

"Whose is this?" I asked.

"Not mine."

"Not mine."

"Yet it was published this summer," I remarked.

They stared at me astonished, and Isabella caught up the book. It was one of those summer publications intended mainly for railroad distribution, and while neither ragged nor soiled, bore evidence of having been read.

"Let me take it," said I.

Isabella at once passed it into my hands.

"Does your brother smoke?" I asked.

"Which brother?"

"Either of them."

"Franklin sometimes, but Howard, never. It disagrees with him, I believe."

"There is a faint odor of tobacco about these pages. Can it have been brought here by Franklin?"

"O no, he never reads novels, not such novels as this, at all events. He loses a lot of pleasure, we think."

I turned the pages over. The latter ones were so fresh I could almost put my finger on the spot where the reader had left off. Feeling like a bloodhound who has just run upon a trail, I returned the book to Caroline, with the injunction to put it away; adding, as I saw her air of hesitation: "If your brother Franklin misses it, it will show that he brought it here, and then I shall have no further interest in it." Which seemed to satisfy her, for she put it away at once on a high shelf.

Perceiving nothing else in these rooms of a suggestive character, I led the way into the hall. There I had a new idea.

"Which of you was the first to go through the rooms upstairs?" I inquired.

"Both of us," answered Isabella. "We came together. Why do you ask, Miss Butterworth?"

"I was wondering if you found everything in order there?"

"We did not notice anything wrong, did we, Caroline? Do you think that the—the person who committed that awful crime went *up-stairs*? I couldn't sleep a wink if I thought so."

"Nor I," Caroline put in. "O, don't say that he went up-stairs, Miss Butterworth!"

"I do not know it," I rejoined.

"But you asked——"

"And I ask again. Wasn't there some little thing out of its usual place? I was up in your front chamber after water for a minute, but I didn't touch anything but the mug."

"We missed the mug, but—O Caroline, the pin-cushion! Do you suppose Miss Butterworth means the pin-cushion?"

I started. Did she refer to the one I had picked up from the floor and placed on a side-table?

"What about the pin-cushion?" I asked.

"O nothing, but we did not know what to make of its being on the table. You see, we had a little pin-cushion shaped like a tomato which always hung at the side of our bureau. It was tied to one of the brackets and was never taken off; Caroline having a fancy for it because it kept her favorite black pins out of the reach of the neighbor's children when they came here. Well, this cushion, this sacred cushion which none of us dared touch, was found by us on a little table by the door, with the ribbon hanging from it by which it had been tied to the bureau. Some one had pulled it off, and very roughly too, for the ribbon was all ragged and torn. But there is nothing in a little thing like that to interest you, is there, Miss Butterworth?"

"No," said I, not relating my part in the affair; "not if our neighbor's children were the marauders."

"But none of them came in for days before we left."

"Are there pins in the cushion?"

"When we found it, do you mean? No."

I did not remember seeing any, but one cannot always trust to one's memory.

"But you had left pins in it?"

"Possibly, I don't remember. Why should I remember such a thing as that?"

I thought to myself, "I would know whether I left pins on my pin-cushion or not," but every one is not as methodical as I am, more's the pity.

"Have you anywhere about you a pin like those you keep on that cushion?" I inquired of Caroline.

She felt at her belt and neck and shook her head.

"I may have upstairs," she replied.

"Then get me one." But before she could start, I pulled her back. "Did either of you sleep in that room last night?"

"No, we were going to," answered Isabella, "but afterwards Caroline took a freak to sleep in one of the rooms on the third floor. She said she wanted to get away from the parlors as far as possible."

"Then I should like a peep at the one overhead."

The wrenching of the pin-cushion from its place had given me an idea.

They looked at me wistfully as they turned to mount the stairs, but I did not enlighten them further. What would an idea be worth shared by them!

Their father undoubtedly lay in the back room, for they moved very softly around the head of the stairs, but once in front they let their tongues run loose again. I, who cared nothing for their babble when it contained no information, walked slowly about the room and finally stopped before the bed.

It had a fresh look, and I at once asked them if it had been lately made up. They assured me that it had not, saying that they always kept their beds spread during their absence, as they did so hate to enter a room disfigured by bare mattresses.

I could have read them a lecture on the niceties of housekeeping, but I refrained; instead of that I pointed to a little dent in the smooth surface of the bed nearest the door.

"Did either of you two make that?" I asked.

They shook their heads in amazement.

"What is there in that?" began Caroline; but I motioned her to bring me the little cushion, which she no sooner did than I laid it in the little dent, which it fitted to a nicety.

"You wonderful old thing!" exclaimed Caroline. "How ever did you think— —"

But I stopped her enthusiasm with a look. I may be wonderful, but I am not old, and it is time they knew it.

"Mr. *Gryce* is *old*," said I; and lifting the cushion, I placed it on a perfectly smooth portion of the bed. "Now take it up," said I, when, lo! a second dent similar to the first.

"You see where that cushion has lain before being placed on the table," I remarked, and reminding Caroline of the pin I wanted, I took my leave and returned to my own house, leaving behind me two girls as much filled with astonishment as the giddiness of their pates would allow.

XIX.
A DECIDED STEP FORWARD.

I felt that I had made an advance. It was a small one, no doubt, but it was an advance. It would not do to rest there, however, or to draw definite conclusions from what I had seen without further facts to guide me. Mrs. Boppert could supply these facts, or so I believed. Accordingly I decided to visit Mrs. Boppert.

Not knowing whether Mr. Gryce had thought it best to put a watch over my movements, but taking it for granted that it would be like him to do so, I made a couple of formal calls on the avenue before I started eastward. I had learned Mrs. Boppert's address before leaving home, but I did not ride directly to the tenement where she lived. I chose, instead, to get out at a little fancy store I saw in the neighborhood.

It was a curious place. I never saw so many or such variety of things in one small spot in my life, but I did not waste any time upon this quaint interior, but stepped immediately up to the good woman I saw leaning over the counter.

"Do you know a Mrs. Boppert who lives at 803?" I asked.

The woman's look was too quick and suspicious for denial; but she was about to attempt it, when I cut her short by saying:

"I wish to see Mrs. Boppert very much, but not in her own rooms. I will pay any one well who will assist me to five minutes' conversation with her in such a place, say, as that I see behind the glass door at the end of this very shop."

The woman, startled by so unexpected a proposition, drew back a step, and was about to shake her head, when I laid on the counter before her (shall I say how much? Yes, for it was not thrown away) a five-dollar bill, which she no sooner saw than she gave a gasp of delight.

"Will you give me *that*?" she cried.

For answer I pushed it towards her, but before her fingers could clutch it, I resolutely said:

"Mrs. Boppert must not know there is anybody waiting here to see her, or she will not come. I have no ill-will towards her, and mean her only good, but she's a timid sort of person, and——"

"I know she's timid," broke in the good woman, eagerly. "And she's had enough to make her so! What with policemen drumming her up at night, and innocent-looking girls and boys luring her into corners to tell them what she saw in that grand house where the murder took place, she's grown that feared of her shadow you can hardly get her out after sundown. But I think I can get her here; and if you mean her no harm, why, ma'am——" Her fingers were on the bill, and charmed with the feel of it, she forgot to finish her sentence.

"Is there any one in the room back there?" I asked, anxious to recall her to herself.

"No, ma'am, no one at all. I am a poor widder, and not used to such company as you; but if you will sit down, I will make myself look more fit and have Mrs. Boppert over here in a minute." And calling to some one of the name of Susie to look after the shop, she led the way towards the glass door I have mentioned.

Relieved to find everything working so smoothly and determined to get the worth of my money out of Mrs. Boppert when I saw her, I followed the woman into the most crowded room I ever entered. The shop was nothing to it; there you could move without hitting anything; here you could not. There were tables against every wall, and chairs where there were no tables. Opposite me was a window-ledge filled with flowering plants, and at my right a grate and mantel-piece covered, that is the latter, with innumerable small articles which had evidently passed a long and forlorn probation on the shop shelves before being brought in here. While I was looking at them and marvelling at the small quantity of dust I found, the woman herself disappeared behind a stack of boxes, for which there was undoubtedly no room in the shop. Could she have gone for Mrs. Boppert already, or had she slipped into another room to hide the money which had come so unexpectedly into her hands?

I was not long left in doubt, for in another moment she returned with a flower-bedecked cap on her smooth gray head, that transformed her into a figure at once so complacent and so ridiculous that, had my nerves not been made of iron, I should certainly have betrayed my amusement. With it she had also put on her company manner, and what with the smiles she bestowed upon me and her perfect satisfaction with her own appearance, I had all I could do to hold my own and keep her to the matter in hand. Finally she managed to take in my anxiety and her own duty, and saying that Mrs. Boppert could never refuse a cup of tea, offered to send her an invitation to supper. As this struck me favorably, I nodded, at which she cocked her head on one side and insinuatingly whispered:

"And would you pay for the tea, ma'am?"

I uttered an indignant "No!" which seemed to surprise her. Immediately becoming humble again, she replied it was no matter, that she had tea enough and that the shop would supply cakes and crackers; to all of which I responded with a look which awed her so completely that she almost dropped the dishes with which she was endeavoring to set one of the tables.

"She does so hate to talk about the murder that it will be a perfect godsend to her to drop into good company like this with no prying neighbors about. Shall I set a chair for you, ma'am?"

I declined the honor, saying that I would remain seated where I was, adding, as I saw her about to go:

"Let her walk straight in, and she will be in the middle of the room before she sees me. That will suit her and me too; for after she has once seen me, she won't be frightened. *But you are not to listen at the door.*"

This I said with great severity, for I saw the woman was becoming very curious, and having said it, I waved her peremptorily away.

She didn't like it, but a thought of the five dollars comforted her. Casting one final look at the table, which was far from uninvitingly set, she slipped out and I was left to contemplate the dozen or so photographs that covered the walls. I found them so atrocious and their arrangement so distracting to my bump of order, which is of a pronounced character, that I finally shut my eyes on the whole scene, and in this attitude began to piece my thoughts together. But before I had proceeded far, steps were heard in the shop, and the next moment the door flew open and in popped Mrs. Boppert, with a face like a peony in full blossom. She stopped when she saw me and stared.

"Why, if it isn't the lady——"

"Hush! Shut the door. I have something very particular to say to you."

"O," she began, looking as if she wanted to back out. But I was too quick for her. I shut the door myself and, taking her by the arm, seated her in the corner.

"You don't show much gratitude," I remarked.

I did not know what she had to be grateful to me for, but she had so plainly intimated at our first interview that she regarded me as having done her some favor, that I was disposed to make what use of it I could, to gain her confidence.

"I know, ma'am, but if you could see how I've been harried, ma'am. It's the murder, and nothing but the murder all the time; and it was to get away from the talk about it that I came here, ma'am, and now it's you I see, and you'll be talking about it too, or why be in such a place as this, ma'am?"

"And what if I do talk about it? You know I'm your friend, or I never would have done you that good turn the morning we came upon the poor girl's body."

"I know, ma'am, and grateful I am for it, too; but I've never understood it, ma'am. Was it to save me from being blamed by the wicked police, or was it a dream you had, and the gentleman had, for I've heard what he said at the inquest, and it's muddled my head till I don't know where I'm standing."

What I had said and what the gentleman had said! What did the poor thing mean? As I did not dare to show my ignorance, I merely shook my head.

"Never mind what caused us to speak as we did, as long as we helped *you*. And we did help you? The police never found out what you had to do with this woman's death, did they?"

"No, ma'am, O no, ma'am. When such a respectable lady as you said that you saw the young lady come into the house in the middle of the night, how was they to disbelieve it. They never asked me if I knew any different."

"No," said I, almost struck dumb by my success, but letting no hint of my complacency escape me. "And I did not mean they should. You are a decent woman, Mrs. Boppert, and should not be troubled."

"Thank you, ma'am. But how did you know she had come to the house before I left. Did you see her?"

I hate a lie as I do poison, but I had to exercise all my Christian principles not to tell one then.

"No," said I, "I didn't see her, but I don't always have to use my eyes to know what is going on in my neighbor's houses." Which is true enough, if it is somewhat humiliating to confess it.

"O ma'am, how smart you are, ma'am! I wish I had some smartness in me. But my husband had all that. He was a man—O what's that?"

"Nothing but the tea-caddy; I knocked it over with my elbow."

"How I do jump at everything! I'm afraid of my own shadow ever since I saw that poor thing lying under that heap of crockery."

"I don't wonder."

"She must have pulled those things over herself, don't you think so, ma'am? No one went in there to murder her. But how came she to have those clothes on. She was dressed quite different when I let her in. I say it's all a muddle, ma'am, and it will be a smart man as can explain it."

"Or a smart woman," I thought.

"Did I do wrong, ma'am? That's what plagues me. She begged so hard to come in, I didn't know how to shut the door on her. Besides her name was Van Burnam, or so she told me."

Here was a coil. Subduing my surprise, I remarked:

"If she asked you to let her in, I do not see how you could refuse her. Was it in the morning or late in the afternoon she came?"

"Don't you know, ma'am? I thought you knew all about it from the way you talked."

Had I been indiscreet? Could she not bear questioning? Eying her with some severity, I declared in a less familiar tone than any I had yet used:

"Nobody knows more about it than I do, but I do not know just the hour at which this lady came to the house. But I do not ask you to tell me if you do not want to."

"O ma'am," she humbly remonstrated, "I am sure I am willing to tell you everything. It was in the afternoon while I was doing the front basement floor."

"And she came to the basement door?"

"Yes, ma'am."

"And asked to be let in?"

"Yes, ma'am."

"Young Mrs. Van Burnam?"

"Yes, ma'am."

"Dressed in a black and white plaid silk, and wearing a hat covered with flowers?"

"Yes, ma'am, or something like that. I know it was very bright and becoming."

"And why did she come to the basement door—a lady dressed like that?"

"Because she knew I couldn't open the front door; that I hadn't the key. O she talked beautiful, ma'am, and wasn't proud with me a bit. She made me let her stay in the house, and when I said it would be dark after a while and that I hadn't done nothing to the rooms upstairs, she laughed and said she didn't care, that she wasn't afraid of the dark and had just as lieve as not stay in the big house alone all night, for she had a book—Did you say anything, ma'am?"

"No, no, go on, she had a book."

"Which she could read till she got sleepy. I never thought anything would happen to her."

"Of course not, why should you? And so you let her into the house and left her there when you went out of it? Well, I don't wonder you were shocked to see her lying dead on the floor next morning."

"Awful, ma'am. I was afraid they would blame me for what had happened. But I didn't do nothing to make her die. I only let her stay in the house. Do you think they will do anything to me if they know it?"

"No," said I, trying to understand this woman's ignorant fears, "they don't punish such things. More's the pity!"—this in confidence to myself. "How could you know that a piece of furniture would fall on her before morning. Did you lock her in when you left the house?"

"Yes, ma'am. She told me to."

Then she was a prisoner.

Confounded by the mystery of the whole affair, I sat so still the woman looked up in wonder, and I saw I had better continue my questions.

"What reason did she give for wanting to stay in the house all night?"

"What reason, ma'am? I don't know. Something about her having to be there when Mr. Van Burnam came home. I didn't make it out, and I didn't try to. I was too busy wondering what she would have to eat."

"And what did she have?"

"I don't know, ma'am. She said she had something, but I didn't see it."

"Perhaps you were blinded by the money she gave you. She gave you some, of course?"

"O, not much, ma'am, not much. And I wouldn't have taken a cent if it had not seemed to make her so happy to give it. The pretty, pretty thing! A real lady, whatever they say about her!"

"And happy? You said she was happy, cheerful-looking, and pretty."

"O yes, ma'am; *she* didn't know what was going to happen. I even heard her sing after she went up-stairs."

I wished that my ears had been attending to their duty that day, and I might have heard her sing too. But the walls between my house and that of the Van Burnams are very thick, as I have had occasion to observe more than once.

"Then she went up-stairs before you left?"

"To be sure, ma'am; what would she do in the kitchen?"

"And you didn't see her again?"

"No, ma'am; but I heard her walking around."

"In the parlors, you mean?"

"Yes, ma'am, in the parlors."

"You did not go up yourself?"

"No, ma'am, I had enough to do below."

"Didn't you go up when you went away?"

"No, ma'am; I didn't like to."

"When did you go?"

"At five, ma'am; I always go at five."

"How did you know it was five?"

"The kitchen clock told me; I wound it, ma'am and set it when the whistles blew at twelve."

"Was that the only clock you wound?"

"Only clock? Do you think I'd be going around the house winding any others?"

Her face showed such surprise, and her eyes met mine so frankly, that I was convinced she spoke the truth. Gratified—I don't know why,—I bestowed upon her my first smile, which seemed to affect her, for her face softened, and she looked at me quite eagerly for a minute before she said:

"You don't think so very bad of me, do you, ma'am?"

But I had been struck by a thought which made me for the moment oblivious to her question. She had wound the clock in the kitchen for her own uses, and why may not the lady above have wound the one in the parlor for hers? Filled with this startling idea, I remarked:

"The young lady wore a watch, of course?"

But the suggestion passed unheeded. Mrs. Boppert was as much absorbed in her own thoughts as I was.

"Did young Mrs. Van Burnam wear a watch?" I persisted.

Mrs. Boppert's face remained a blank.

Provoked at her impassibility, I shook her with an angry hand, imperatively demanding:

"What are you thinking of? Why don't you answer my questions?"

She was herself again in an instant.

"O ma'am, I beg your pardon. I was wondering if you meant the parlor clock."

I calmed myself, looked severe to hide my more than eager interest, and sharply cried:

"Of course I mean the parlor clock. Did you wind it?"

"O no, no, no, I would as soon think of touching gold or silver. But the young lady did, I'm sure, ma'am, for I heard it strike when she was setting of it."

Ah! If my nature had not been an undemonstrative one, and if I had not been bred to a strong sense of social distinctions, I might have betrayed my satisfaction at this announcement in a way that would have made this homely German woman start. As it was I sat stock-still, and even made her think I had not heard her. Venturing to rouse *me* a bit, she spoke again after a minute's silence.

"She might have been lonely, you know, ma'am; and the ticking of a clock is such company."

"Yes," I answered with more than my accustomed vivacity, for she jumped as if I had struck her. "You have hit the nail on the head, Mrs. Boppert, and are a much smarter woman than I thought. But when did she wind the clock?"

"At five o'clock, ma'am; just before I left the house."

"O, and did she know you were going?"

"I think so, ma'am, for I called up, just before I put on my bonnet, that it was five o'clock and that I was going."

"O, you did. And did she answer back?"

"Yes, ma'am. I heard her step in the hall and then her voice. She asked if I was sure it was five, and I told her yes, because I had set the kitchen clock at twelve. She didn't say any more, but just after that I heard the parlor clock begin to strike."

O, thought I, what cannot be got out of the most stupid and unwilling witness by patience and a judicious use of questions. To know that this clock was started after five o'clock, that is, after the hour at which the hands pointed when it fell, and that it was set correctly in starting, and so would give indisputable testimony of the hour when the shelves fell, were points of the greatest importance. I was so pleased I gave the woman another smile.

Instantly she cried:

"But you won't say anything about it, will you, ma'am? They might make me pay for all the things that were broke."

My smile this time was not one of encouragement simply. But it might have been anything for all effect it had on her. The intricacies of the affair had disturbed her poor brain again, and all her powers of mind were given up to lament.

"O," she bemoaned, "I wish I had never seen her! My head wouldn't ache so with the muddle of it. Why, ma'am, her husband said he came to the house at midnight with his wife! How could he when she was inside of it all the time. But then perhaps he said that, just as you did, to save me blame. But why should a gentleman like him do that?"

"It isn't worth while for you to bother your head about it," I expostulated. "It is enough that *my* head aches over it."

I don't suppose she understood me or tried to. Her wits had been sorely tried and my rather severe questioning had not tended to clear them. At all events she went on in another moment as if I had not spoken:

"But what became of her pretty dress? I was never so astonished in my life as when I saw that dark skirt on her."

"She might have left her fine gown upstairs," I ventured, not wishing to go into the niceties of evidence with this woman.

"So she might, so she might, and that may have been her petticoat we saw." But in another moment she saw the impossibility of this, for she added: "But I saw her petticoat, and it was a brown silk one. She showed it when she lifted her skirt to get at her purse. I don't understand it, ma'am."

As her face by this time was almost purple, I thought it a mercy to close the interview; so I uttered some few words of a soothing and encouraging nature, and then seeing that something more tangible was necessary to restore her to any proper condition of spirits, I took out my pocket-book and bestowed on her some of my loose silver.

This was something she *could* understand. She brightened immediately, and before she was well through her expressions of delight, I had quitted the room and in a few minutes later the shop.

I hope the two women had their cup of tea after that.

XX.
MISS BUTTERWORTH'S THEORY.

I was so excited when I entered my carriage that I rode all the way home with my bonnet askew and never knew it. When I reached my room and saw myself in the glass, I was shocked, and stole a glance at Lena, who was setting out my little tea-table, to see if she noticed what a ridiculous figure I cut. But she is discretion itself, and for a girl with two undeniable dimples in her cheeks, smiles seldom—at least when I am looking at her. She was not smiling now, and though, for the reason given above, this was not as comforting as it may appear, I chose not to worry myself any longer about such a trifle when I had matters of so much importance on my mind.

Taking off my bonnet, whose rakish appearance had given me such a shock, I sat down, and for half an hour neither moved nor spoke. I was thinking. A theory which had faintly suggested itself to me at the inquest was taking on body with these later developments. Two hats had been found on the scene of the tragedy, and two pairs of gloves, and now I had learned that there had been two women there, the one whom Mrs. Boppert had locked into the house on leaving it, and the one whom I had seen enter at midnight with Mr. Van Burnam. Which of the two had perished? We had been led to think, and Mr. Van Burnam had himself acknowledged, that it was his wife; but his wife had been dressed quite differently from the murdered woman, and was, as I soon began to see, much more likely to have been the assassin than the victim. Would you like to know my reasons for this extraordinary statement? If so, they are these:

I had always seen a woman's hand in this work, but having no reason to believe in the presence of any other woman on the scene of crime than the victim, I had put this suspicion aside as untenable. But now that I had found the second woman, I returned to it.

But how connect her with the murder? It seemed easy enough to do so if this other woman was her rival. We have heard of no rival, but she may have known of one, and this knowledge may have been at the bottom of her disagreement with her husband and the half-crazy determination she evinced to win his family over to her side. Let us say, then, that the second woman was Mrs. Van Burnam's rival. That he brought her there not knowing that his wife had effected an entrance into the house; brought her there after an afternoon spent at the Hotel D— —, during which he had furnished her with a new outfit of less pronounced type, perhaps, than that she had previously worn. The use of the two carriages and the care they took to throw suspicion off their track, may have been part of a scheme of future elopement, for I had no idea they meant to remain in Mr. Van Burnam's house. For what purpose, then, did they go there? To meet Mrs. Van Burnam and kill her, that their way might be clearer for flight? No; I had rather think that they went to the house without a thought of whom they would encounter, and that only after they had entered the parlors did he realize that the two women he least wished to see together had been brought by his folly face to face.

The presence in the third room of Mrs. Van Burnam's hat, gloves, and novel seemed to argue that she had spent the evening in reading by the dining-room table, but whether this was so or not, the stopping of a carriage in front and the opening of the door by an accustomed hand undoubtedly assured her that either the old gentleman or some other member of the family had unexpectedly arrived. She was, therefore, in or near the parlor-door when they entered, and the shock of meeting her hated rival in company with her husband, under the very roof where she had hoped to lay the foundations of her future happiness, must have been great, if not maddening. Accusations, recriminations even, did not satisfy her. She wanted to kill; but she had no weapon. Suddenly her eyes fell on the hat-pin which her more self-possessed rival had drawn from her hat, possibly before their encounter, and she conceived a plan which seemed to promise her the very revenge she sought. How she carried it out; by what means she was enabled to approach her victim and inflict with such certainty the fatal stab which laid her enemy at her feet, can be left to the imagination. But that she, a woman, and not Howard, a man, drove this woman's weapon into the stranger's spine, I will yet prove, or lose all faith in my own intuitions.

But if this theory is true, how about the shelves that fell at daybreak, and how about her escape from the house without detection? A little thought will explain all that. The man, horrified, no doubt, at the result of his imprudence, and execrating the crime to which it had led, left the house almost immediately. But the woman remained there, possibly because she had fainted, possibly because he would have nothing to do with her; and coming to herself, saw her victim's face staring up at her with an accusing beauty she found it impossible to meet. What should she do to escape it? Where should she go? She hated it so she could have trampled on it, but she restrained her passions till daybreak, when in one wild burst of fury and hatred she drew down the cabinet upon it, and then fled the scene of horror she had herself caused. This was at five, or, to be exact, three minutes before that hour, as shown by the clock she had carelessly set in her lighter moments.

She escaped by the front door, which her husband had mercifully forborne to lock; and she had not been discovered by the police, because her appearance did not tally with the description which had been given them. How did I know this? Remember the discoveries I had made in Miss Van Burnam's room, and allow them to assist you in understanding my conclusions.

Some one had gone into that room; some one who wanted pins; and keeping this fact before my eyes, I saw through the motive and actions of the escaping woman. She had on a dress separated at the waist, and finding, perhaps, a spot of blood on the skirt, she conceived the plan of covering it with her petticoat, which was also of silk and undoubtedly as well made as many women's dresses. But the skirt of the gown was longer than the petticoat and she was obliged to pin it up. Having no pins herself, and finding none on the parlor floor, she went up-stairs to get some. The door at the head of the stairs was locked, but the front room was open, so she entered there. Groping her way to the bureau, for the place was very dark, she found a pin-cushion hanging from a bracket. Feeling it to be full of pins, and knowing that she could see nothing where she was, she tore it away and carried it towards the door. Here there was some light from the skylight over the stairs, so setting the cushion down on the bed, she pinned up the skirt of her gown.

When this was done she started away, brushing the cushion off the bed in her excitement, and fearing to be traced by her many-colored hat, or having no courage remaining for facing again the horror in the parlor, she slid out without one and went, God knows whither, in her terror and remorse.

So much for my theory; now for the facts standing in the way of its complete acceptance. They were two: the scar on the ankle of the dead girl, which was a peculiarity of Louise Van Burnam, and the mark of the rings on her fingers. But who had identified the scar? Her husband. No one else. And if the other woman had, by some strange freak of chance, a scar also on her left foot, then the otherwise unaccountable apathy he had shown at being told of this distinctive mark, as well as his temerity in afterwards taking it as a basis for his false identification, becomes equally consistent and natural; and as for the marks of the rings, it would be strange if such a woman did not wear rings and plenty of them.

Howard's conduct under examination and the contradiction between his first assertions and those that followed, all become clear in the light of this new theory. He had seen his wife kill a defenceless woman before his eyes, and whether influenced by his old affection for her or by his pride in her good name, he could not but be anxious to conceal her guilt even at the cost of his own truthfulness. As long then as circumstances permitted, he preserved his indifferent attitude, and denied that the dead woman was his wife. But when driven to the wall by the indisputable proof which was brought forth of his wife having been in the place of murder, he saw, or thought he did, that a continued denial on his part of Louise Van Burnam being the victim might lead sooner or later to the suspicion of her being the murderer, and influenced by this fear, took the sudden resolution of profiting by all the points which the two women had in common by acknowledging, what everybody had expected him to acknowledge from the first, that the woman at the Morgue was his wife. This would exonerate her, rid him of any apprehension he may have entertained of her ever returning to be a disgrace to him, and would (and perhaps this thought influenced him most, for who can understand such men or the passions that sway them) insure the object of his late devotion a decent burial in a Christian cemetery. To be sure, the risk he ran was great, but the emergency was great, and he may not have stopped to count the cost. At all events, the fact is certain that he perjured himself when he said that it was his wife he brought to the house from the Hotel D— —, and if he perjured himself in this regard, he probably perjured himself in others, and his testimony is not at all to be relied upon.

Convinced though I was in my own mind that I had struck a truth which would bear the closest investigation, I was not satisfied to act upon it till I had put it to the test. The means I took to do this were daring, and quite in keeping with the whole desperate affair. They promised, however, a result important enough to make Mr. Gryce blush for the disdain with which he had met my threats of interference.

XXI.
A SHREWD CONJECTURE.

The test of which I speak was as follows:

I would advertise for a person dressed as I believed Mrs. Van Burnam to have been when she left the scene of crime. If I received news of such a person, I might safely consider my theory established.

I accordingly wrote the following advertisement:

"Information wanted of a woman who applied for lodgings on the morning of the eighteenth inst., dressed in a brown silk skirt and a black and white plaid blouse of fashionable cut. She was without a hat, or if a person so dressed wore a hat, then it was bought early in the morning at some store, in which case let shopkeepers take notice. The person answering this description is eagerly sought for by her relatives, and to any one giving positive information of the same, a liberal reward will be paid. Please address, T. W. Alvord, — — Liberty Street."

I purposely did not mention her personal appearance, for fear of attracting the attention of the police.

This done, I wrote the following letter:

"Dear Miss Ferguson:

"One clever woman recognizes another. I am clever and am not ashamed to own it. You are clever and should not be ashamed to be told so. I was a witness at the inquest in which you so notably distinguished yourself, and I said then, 'There is a woman after my own heart!' But a truce to compliments! What I want and ask of you to procure for me is a photograph of Mrs. Van Burnam. I am a friend of the family, and consider them to be in more trouble than they deserve. If I had her picture I would show it to the Misses Van Burnam, who feel great remorse at their treatment of her, and who want to see how she looked. Cannot you find one in their rooms? The one in Mr. Howard's room here has been confiscated by the police.[C]

"Hoping that you will feel disposed to oblige me in this—and I assure you that my motives in making this request are most excellent—I remain,

"Cordially yours,

"Amelia Butterworth.

"P. S.—Address me, if you please, at 564 —— Avenue. Care of J. H. Denham."

This was my grocer, with whom I left word the next morning to deliver this package in the next bushel of potatoes he sent me.

My smart little maid, Lena, carried these two communications to the east side, where she posted the letter herself and entrusted the advertisement to a lover of hers who carried it to the *Herald* office. While she was gone I tried to rest by exercising my mind in other directions. But I could not. I kept going over Howard's testimony in the light of my own theory, and remarking how the difficulty he experienced in maintaining the position he had taken, forced him into inconsistencies and far-fetched explanations. With his wife for a companion at the Hotel D——, his conduct both there and on the road to his father's house was that of a much weaker man than his words and appearance led one to believe; but if, on the contrary, he had with him a woman with whom he was about to elope (and what did the packing up of all his effects mean, if not that?), all the precautions they took seemed reasonable.

Later, my mind fixed itself on one point. If it was his wife who was with him, as he said, then the bundle they dropped at the old woman's feet contained the much-talked of plaid silk. If it was not, then it was a gown of some different material. Now, could this bundle be found? If it could, then why had not Mr. Gryce produced it? The sight of Mrs. Van Burnam's plaid silk spread out on the Coroner's table would have had a great effect in clinching the suspicion against her husband. But no plaid silk had been found (because it was not dropped in the bundle, but worn away on the murderess's back), and no old woman. I thought I knew the reason of this too. There was no old woman to be found, and the bundle they carried had been got rid of some other way. What way? I would take a walk down that same block and see, and I would take it at the midnight hour too, for only so could I judge of the possibilities there offered for concealing or destroying such an article.

Having made this decision, I cast about to see how I could carry it into effect. I am not a coward, but I have a respectability to maintain, and what errand could Miss Butterworth be supposed to have in the streets at twelve o'clock at night! Fortunately, I remembered that my cook had complained of toothache when I gave her my orders for breakfast, and going down at once into the kitchen, where she sat with her cheek propped up in her hand waiting for Lena, I said with an asperity which admitted of no reply:

"You have a dreadful tooth, Sarah, and you must have something done for it at once. When Lena comes home, send her to me. I am going to the drug-store for some drops, and I want Lena to accompany me."

She looked astounded, of course, but I would not let her answer me. "Don't speak a word," I cried, "it will only make your toothache worse; and don't look as if some hobgoblin had jumped up on the kitchen table. I guess I know my duty, and just what kind of a breakfast I will have in the morning, if you sit up all night groaning with the toothache." And I was out of the room before she had more than begun to say that it was not so bad, and that I needn't trouble, and all that, which was true enough, no doubt, but not what I wanted to hear at that moment.

When Lena came in, I saw by the brightness of her face that she had accomplished her double errand. I therefore signified to her that I was satisfied, and asked if she was too tired to go out again, saying quite peremptorily that Sarah was ill, and that I was going to the drug-store for some medicine, and did not wish to go alone.

Lena's round-eyed wonder was amusing; but she is very discreet, as I have said before, and she ventured nothing save a meek, "It's very late, Miss Butterworth," which was an unnecessary remark, as she soon saw.

I do not like to obtrude my aristocratic tendencies too much into this narrative, but when I found myself in the streets alone with Lena, I could not help feeling some secret qualms lest my conduct savored of impropriety. But the thought that I was working in the cause of truth and justice came to sustain me, and before I had gone two blocks, I felt as much at home under the midnight skies as if I were walking home from church on a Sunday afternoon.

There is a certain drug-store on Third Avenue where I like to deal, and towards this I ostensibly directed my steps. But I took pains to go by the way of Lexington Avenue and Twenty-seventh Street, and upon reaching the block where this mysterious couple were seen, gave all my attention to the possible hiding-places it offered.

Lena, who had followed me like my shadow, and who was evidently too dumfounded at my freak to speak, drew up to my side as we were half-way down it and seized me tremblingly by the arm.

"Two men are coming," said she.

"I am not afraid of men," was my sharp rejoinder. But I told a most abominable lie; for I am afraid of them in such places and under such circumstances, though not under ordinary conditions, and never where the tongue is likely to be the only weapon employed.

The couple who were approaching us now seemed to be in a merry mood. But when they saw us keep to our own side of the way, they stopped their chaffing and allowed us to go by, with just a mocking word or two.

"Sarah ought to be very much obliged to you," whispered Lena.

At the corner of Third Avenue I paused. I had seen nothing so far but bare stoops and dark area-ways. Nothing to suggest a place for the disposal of such cumbersome articles as these persons had made way with. Had the avenue anything better to offer? I stopped under the gas-lamp at the corner to consider, notwithstanding Lena's gentle pull towards the drug-store. Looking to left and right and over the muddy crossings, I sought for inspiration. An almost obstinate belief in my own theory led me to insist in my own mind that they had encountered no old woman, and consequently had not dropped their bundles in the open street. I even entered into an argument about it, standing there with the cable cars whistling by me and Lena tugging away at my arm. "If," said I to myself, "the woman with him had been his wife and the whole thing nothing more than a foolish escapade, they might have done this; but she was not his wife, and the game they were playing was serious, if they did laugh over it, and so their disposal of these tell-tale articles would be serious and such as would protect their secret. Where, then, could they have thrust them?"

My eyes, as I muttered this, were on the one shop in my line of vision that was still open and lighted. It was the den of a Chinese laundryman, and through the windows in front I could see him still at work, ironing.

"Ah!" thought I, and made such a start across the street that Lena gasped in dismay and almost fell to the ground in her frightened attempt to follow me.

"Not that way!" she called. "Miss Butterworth, you are going wrong."

But I kept right on, and only stopped when I reached the laundry.

"I have an errand here," I explained. "Wait in the doorway, Lena, and don't act as if you thought me crazy, for I was never saner in my life."

I don't think this reassured her much, lunatics not being supposed to be very good judges of their own mental condition, but she was so accustomed to obey, that she drew back as I opened the door before me and entered. The surprise on the face of the poor Chinaman when he turned and saw before him a lady of years and no ordinary appearance, daunted me for an instant. But another look only showed me that his very surprise was inoffensive, and gathering courage from the unexpectedness of my own position, I inquired with all the politeness I could show one of his abominable nationality:

"Didn't a gentleman and a heavily veiled lady leave a package with you a few days ago at about the same hour of night as this?"

"Some lalee clo' washee? Yes, ma'am. No done. She tellee me no callee for one week."

"Then that's all right; the lady has died very suddenly, and the gentleman gone away; you will have to keep the clothes a long time."

"Me wantee money, no wantee clo'!"

"I'll pay you for them; I don't care about them being ironed."

"Givee tickee, givee clo'! No givee tickee, no givee clo'!"

This was a poser! But as I did not want the clothes so much as a look at them, I soon got the better of this difficulty.

"I don't want them to-night," said I. "I only wanted to make sure you had them. What night were these people here?"

"Tuesday night, velly late; nicee man, nicee lalee. She wantee talk. Nicee man he pullee she; I no hear if muchee stasch. All washee, see!" he went on, dragging a basket out of the corner, "him no ilon."

I was in such a quiver; so struck with amazement at my own perspicacity in surmising that here was a place where a bundle of underclothing could be lost indefinitely, that I just stared while he turned over the clothes in the basket. For by means of the quality of the articles he was preparing to show me, the question which had been agitating me for hours could be definitely decided. If they proved to be fine and of foreign manufacture, then Howard's story was true and all my fine-spun theories must fall to the ground. But if, on the contrary, they were such as are usually worn by American women, then my own idea as to the identity of the woman who left them here was established, and I could safely consider her as the victim and Louise Van Burnam as the murderess, unless further facts came to prove that he was the guilty one, after all.

The sight of Lena's eyes staring at me with great anxiety through the panes of the door distracted my attention for a moment, and when I looked again, he was holding up two or three garments before me. The articles thus revealed told their story in a moment. They were far from fine, and had even less embroidery on them than I expected.

"Are there any marks on them?" I asked.

He showed me two letters stamped in indelible ink on the band of a skirt. I did not have my glasses with me, but the ink was black, and I read O. R. "The minx's initials," thought I.

When I left the place my complacency was such that Lena did not know what to make of me. She has since informed me that I looked as if I wanted to shout Hurrah! but I cannot believe I so far forgot myself as that. But pleased as I was, I had only discovered how one bundle had been disposed of. The dress and outside fixings still had to be accounted for, and I was the woman to do it.

We had mechanically moved in the direction of the drug-store and were near the curb-stone when I reached this point in my meditations. It had rained a little while before, and a small stream was running down the gutter and emptying itself into the sewer opening. The sight of it sharpened my wits.

If I wanted to get rid of anything of a damaging character, I would drop it at the mouth of one of these holes and gently thrust it into the sewer with my foot, thought I. And never doubting that I had found an explanation of the disappearance of the second bundle, I walked on, deciding that if I had the police at my command I would have the sewer searched at those four corners.

We rode home after visiting the drug-store. I was not going to subject Lena or myself to another midnight walk through Twenty-seventh Street.

FOOTNOTES:

[C] This was *so* probable, it cannot be considered an untruth. — A. B.

XXII.
A BLANK CARD.

The next day at noon Lena brought me up a card on her tray. It was a perfectly blank one.

"Miss Van Burnam's maid said you sent for this," was her demure announcement.

"Miss Van Burnam's maid is right," said I, taking the card and with it a fresh installment of courage.

Nothing happened for two days, then there came word from the kitchen that a bushel of potatoes had arrived. Going down to see them, I drew from their midst a large square envelope, which I immediately carried to my room. It failed to contain a photograph; but there was a letter in it couched in these terms:

"Dear Miss Butterworth:

"The esteem which you are good enough to express for me is returned. I regret that I cannot oblige you. There are no photographs to be found in Mrs. Van Burnam's rooms. Perhaps this fact may be accounted for by the curiosity shown in those apartments by a very spruce new boarder we have had from New York. His taste for that particular quarter of the house was such that I could not keep him away from it except by lock and key. If there was a picture there of Mrs. Van Burnam, he took it, for he departed very suddenly one night. I am glad he took nothing more with him. The talks he had with my servant-girl have almost led to my dismissing her.

"Praying your pardon for the disappointment I am forced to give you, I remain,

"Yours sincerely,

"Susan Ferguson."

So! so! balked by an emissary of Mr. Gryce. Well, well, we would do without the photograph! Mr. Gryce might need it, but not Amelia Butterworth.

This was on a Thursday, and on the evening of Saturday the long-desired clue was given me. It came in the shape of a letter brought me by Mr. Alvord.

Our interview was not an agreeable one. Mr. Alvord is a clever man and an adroit one, or I should not persist in employing him as my lawyer; but he never understood *me*. At this time, and with this letter in his hand, he understood me less than ever, which naturally called out my powers of self-assertion and led to some lively conversation between us. But that is neither here nor there. He had brought me an answer to my advertisement and I was presently engrossed by it. It was an uneducated woman's epistle and its chirography and spelling were dreadful; so I will just mention its contents, which were highly interesting in themselves, as I think you will acknowledge.

She, that is, the writer, whose name, as nearly as I could make out, was Bertha Desberger, knew such a person as I described, and could give me news of her if I would come to her house in West Ninth Street at four o'clock Sunday afternoon.

If I would! I think my face must have shown my satisfaction, for Mr. Alvord, who was watching me, sarcastically remarked:

"You don't seem to find any difficulties in that communication. Now, what do you think of this one?"

He held out another letter which had been directed to him, and which he had opened. Its contents called up a shade of color to my cheek, for I did not want to go through the annoyance of explaining myself again:

"Dear Sir:

"From a strange advertisement which has lately appeared in the *Herald*, I gather that information is wanted of a young woman who on the morning of the eighteenth inst. entered my store without any bonnet on her head, and saying she had met with an accident, bought a hat which she immediately put on. She was pale as a girl could be and looked so ill that I asked her if she was well enough to be out alone; but she gave me no reply and left the store as soon as possible. That is all I can tell you about her."

With this was enclosed his card:

PHINEAS COX,

Millinery,

Trimmed and Untrimmed Hats,

— — Sixth Avenue.

"Now, what does this mean?" asked Mr. Alvord. "The morning of the eighteenth was the morning when the murder was discovered in which you have shown such interest."

"It means," I retorted with some spirit, for simple dignity was thrown away on this man, "that I made a mistake in choosing your office as a medium for my business communications."

This was to the point and he said no more, though he eyed the letter in my hand very curiously, and seemed more than tempted to renew the hostilities with which we had opened our interview.

Had it not been Saturday, and late in the day at that, I would have visited Mr. Cox's store before I slept, but as it was I felt obliged to wait till Monday. Meanwhile I had before me the still more important interview with Mrs. Desberger.

As I had no reason to think that my visiting any number in Ninth Street would arouse suspicion in the police, I rode there quite boldly the next day, and with Lena at my side, entered the house of Mrs. Bertha Desberger.

For this trip I had dressed myself plainly, and drawn over my eyes—and the puffs which I still think it becoming in a woman of my age to wear—a dotted veil, thick enough to conceal my features, without robbing me of that aspect of benignity necessary to the success of my mission. Lena wore her usual neat gray dress, and looked the picture of all the virtues.

A large brass door-plate, well rubbed, was the first sign vouchsafed us of the respectability of the house we were about to enter; and the parlor, when we were ushered into it, fully carried out the promise thus held forth on the door-step. It was respectable, but in wretched taste as regards colors. I, who have the nicest taste in such matters, looked about me in dismay as I encountered the greens and blues, the crimsons and the purples which everywhere surrounded me.

But I was not on a visit to a temple of art, and resolutely shutting my eyes to the offending splendor about me—worsted splendor, you understand,—I waited with subdued expectation for the lady of the house.

She came in presently, bedecked in a flowered gown that was an epitome of the blaze of colors everywhere surrounding us; but her face was a good one, and I saw that I had neither guile nor over-much shrewdness to contend with.

She had seen the coach at the door, and she was all smiles and flutter.

"You have come for the poor girl who stopped here a few days ago," she began, glancing from my face to Lena's with an equally inquiring air, which in itself would have shown her utter ignorance of social distinctions if I had not bidden Lena to keep at my side and hold her head up as if she had business there as well as myself.

"Yes," returned I, "we have. Lena here, has lost a relative (which was true), and knowing no other way of finding her, I suggested the insertion of an advertisement in the paper. You read the description given, of course. Has the person answering it been in this house?"

"Yes; she came on the morning of the eighteenth. I remember it because that was the very day my cook left, and I have not got another one yet." She sighed and went on. "I took a great interest in that unhappy young woman — Was she your sister?" This, somewhat doubtfully, to Lena, who perhaps had too few colors on to suit her.

"No," answered Lena, "she wasn't my sister, but——"

I immediately took the words out of her mouth.

"At what time did she come here, and how long did she stay? We want to find her very much. Did she give you any name, or tell where she was going?"

"She said her name was Oliver." (I thought of the O. R. on the clothes at the laundry.) "But I knew this wasn't so; and if she had not looked so very modest, I might have hesitated to take her in. But, lor! I can't resist a girl in trouble, and she was in trouble, if ever a girl was. And then she had money — Do you know what her trouble was?" This again to Lena, and with an air at once suspicious and curious. But Lena has a good face, too, and her frank eyes at once disarmed the weak and good-natured woman before us.

"I thought" — she went on before Lena could answer — "that whatever it was, *you* had nothing to do with it, nor this lady either."

"No," answered Lena, seeing that I wished her to do the talking. "And we don't know" (which was true enough so far as Lena went) "just what her trouble was. Didn't she tell you?"

"She told nothing. When she came she said she wanted to stay with me a little while. I sometimes take boarders——" She had twenty in the house at that minute, if she had one. Did she think I couldn't see the length of her dining-room table through the crack of the parlor door? "'I can pay,' she said, which I had not doubted, for her blouse was a very expensive one; though I thought her skirt looked queer, and her hat—Did I say she had a hat on? You seemed to doubt that fact in your advertisement. Goodness me! if she had had no hat on, she wouldn't have got as far as my parlor mat. But her blouse showed her to be a lady—and then her face—it was as white as your handkerchief there, madam, but so sweet—I thought of the Madonna faces I had seen in Catholic churches."

I started; inwardly commenting: "Madonna-like, *that* woman!" But a glance at the room about me reassured me. The owner of such hideous sofas and chairs and of the many pictures effacing or rather defacing the paper on the walls, could not be a judge of Madonna faces.

"You admire everything that is good and lovely," I suggested, for Mrs. Desberger had paused at the movement I made.

"Yes, it is my nature to do so, ma'am. I love the beautiful," and she cast a half-apologetic, half-proud look about her. "So I listened to the girl and let her sit down in my parlor. She had had nothing to eat that morning, and though she didn't ask for it, I went to order her a cup of tea, for I knew she couldn't get up-stairs without it. Her eyes followed me when I went out of the room in a way that haunted me, and when I came back—I shall never forget it, ma'am—there she lay stretched out on the floor with her face on the ground and her hands thrown out. Wasn't it horrible, ma'am? I don't wonder you shudder."

Did I shudder? If I did, it was because I was thinking of that other woman, the victim of this one, whom I had seen, with her face turned upward and her arms outstretched, in the gloom of Mr. Van Burnam's half-closed parlor.

"She looked as if she was dead," the good woman continued, "but just as I was about to call for help, her fingers moved and I rushed to lift her. She was neither dead nor had she fainted; she was simply dumb with misery. What could have happened to her? I have asked myself a hundred times."

My mouth was shut very tight, but I shut it still tighter, for the temptation was great to cry: "She had just committed murder!" As it was, no sound whatever left my lips, and the good woman doubtless thought me no better than a stone, for she turned with a shrug to Lena, repeating still more wistfully than before:

"*Don't* you know what her trouble was?"

But, of course, poor Lena had nothing to say, and the woman went on with a sigh:

"Well, I suppose I shall never know what had used that poor creature up so completely. But whatever it was, it gave me enough trouble, though I do not want to complain of it, for why are we here, if not to help and comfort the miserable. It was an hour, ma'am; it was an hour, miss, before I could get that poor girl to speak; but when I did succeed, and had got her to drink the tea and eat a bit of toast, then I felt quite repaid by the look of gratitude she gave me and the way she clung to my sleeve when I tried to leave her for a minute. It was this sleeve, ma'am," she explained, lifting a cluster of rainbow flounces and ribbons which but a minute before had looked little short of ridiculous in my eyes, but which in the light of the wearer's kind-heartedness had lost some of their offensive appearance.

"Poor Mary!" murmured Lena, with what I considered most admirable presence of mind.

"What name did you say?" cried Mrs. Desberger, eager enough to learn all she could of her late mysterious lodger.

"I had rather not tell her name," protested Lena, with a timid air that admirably fitted her rather doll-like prettiness. "*She* didn't tell you what it was, and *I* don't think I ought to."

Good for little Lena! And she did not even know for whom or what she was playing the *rôle* I had set her. "I thought you said Mary. But I won't be inquisitive with you. I wasn't so with her. But where was I in my story? Oh, I got her so she could speak, and afterwards I helped her up-stairs; but she didn't stay there long. When I came back at lunch time—I have to do my marketing no matter what happens—I found her sitting before a table with her head on her hands. She had been weeping, but her face was quite composed now and almost hard.

"'O you good woman!' she cried as I came in. 'I want to thank you.' But I wouldn't let her go on wasting words like that, and presently she was saying quite wildly: 'I want to begin a new life. I want to act as if I had never had a yesterday. I have had trouble, overwhelming trouble, but I will get something out of existence yet. I *will* live, and in order to do so, I will work. Have you a paper, Mrs. Desberger, I want to look at the advertisements?' I brought her a *Herald* and went to preside at my lunch table. When I saw her again she looked almost cheerful. 'I have found just what I want,' she cried, 'a companion's place. But I cannot apply in this dress,' and she looked at the great puffs of her silk blouse as if they gave her the horrors, though why, I cannot imagine, for they were in the latest style and rich enough for a millionaire's daughter, though as to colors I like brighter ones myself. 'Would you'—she was very timid about it—'buy me some things if I gave you the money?'

"If there is one thing more than another that I like, it is to shop, so I expressed my willingness to oblige her, and that afternoon I set out with a nice little sum of money to buy her some clothes. I should have enjoyed it more if she had let me do my own choosing—I saw the loveliest pink and green blouse—but she was very set about what she wanted, and so I just got her some plain things which I think even you, ma'am, would have approved of. I brought them home myself, for she wanted to apply immediately for the place she had seen advertised, but, O dear, when I went up to her room——"

"Was she gone?" burst in Lena.

"O no, but there was such a smudge in it, and—and I could cry when I think of it—there in the grate were the remains of her beautiful silk blouse, all smoking and ruined. She had tried to burn it, and she had succeeded too. I could not get a piece out as big as my hand."

"But you got some of it!" blurted out Lena, guided by a look which I gave her.

"Yes, scraps, it was so handsome. I think I have a bit in my work-basket now."

"O get it for me," urged Lena. "I want it to remember her by."

"My work-basket is here." And going to a sort of *etagère* covered with a thousand knick-knacks picked up at bargain counters, she opened a little cupboard and brought out a basket, from which she presently pulled a small square of silk. It was, as she said, of the richest weaving, and was, as I had not the least doubt, a portion of the dress worn by Mrs. Van Burnam from Haddam.

"Yes, it was hers," said Lena, reading the expression of my face, and putting the scrap away very carefully in her pocket.

"Well, I would have given her five dollars for that blouse," murmured Mrs. Desberger, regretfully. "But girls like her are so improvident."

"And did she leave that day?" I asked, seeing that it was hard for this woman to tear her thoughts away from this coveted article.

"Yes, ma'am. It was late, and I had but little hopes of her getting the situation she was after. But she promised to come back if she didn't; and as she did not come back I decided that she was more successful than I had anticipated."

"And don't you know where she went? Didn't she confide in you at all?"

"No; but as there were but three advertisements for a lady-companion in the *Herald* that day, it will be easy to find her. Would you like to see those advertisements? I saved them out of curiosity."

I assented, as you may believe, and she brought us the clippings at once. Two of them I read without emotion, but the third almost took my breath away. It was an advertisement for a lady-companion accustomed to the typewriter and of some taste in dressmaking, and the address given was that of Miss Althorpe.

If this woman, steeped in misery and darkened by crime, should be there!

As I shall not mention Mrs. Desberger again for some time, I will here say that at the first opportunity which presented itself I sent Lena to the shops with orders to buy and have sent to Mrs. Desberger the ugliest and most flaunting of silk blouses that could be found on Sixth Avenue; and as Lena's dimples were more than usually pronounced on her return, I have no doubt she chose one to suit the taste and warm the body of the estimable woman, whose kindly nature had made such a favorable impression upon me.

XXIII.
RUTH OLIVER.

From Mrs. Desberger's I rode immediately to Miss Althorpe's, for the purpose of satisfying myself at once as to the presence there of the unhappy fugitive I was tracing.

Six o'clock Sunday night is not a favorable hour for calling at a young lady's house, especially when that lady has a lover who is in the habit of taking tea with the family. But I was in a mood to transgress all rules and even to forget the rights of lovers. Besides, much is forgiven a woman of my stamp, especially by a person of the good sense and amiability of Miss Althorpe.

That I was not mistaken in my calculations was evident from the greeting I received. Miss Althorpe came forward as graciously and with as little surprise in her manner as any one could expect under the circumstances, and for a moment I was so touched by her beauty and the unaffected charm of her manners that I forgot my errand and only thought of the pleasure of meeting a lady who fairly comes up to the standard one has secretly set for one's self. Of course she is much younger than I—some say she is only twenty-three; but a lady is a lady at any age, and Ella Althorpe might be a model for a much older woman than myself.

The room in which we were seated was a large one, and though I could hear Mr. Stone's voice in the adjoining apartment, I did not fear to broach the subject I had come to discuss.

"You may think this intrusion an odd one," I began, "but I believe you advertised a few days ago for a young lady-companion. Have you been suited, Miss Althorpe?"

"O yes; I have a young person with me whom I like very much."

"Ah, you are supplied! Is she any one you know?"

"No, she is a stranger, and what is more, she brought no recommendations with her. But her appearance is so attractive and her desire for the place was so great, that I consented to try her. And she is very satisfactory, poor girl! very satisfactory indeed!"

Ah, here was an opportunity for questions. Without showing too much eagerness and yet with a proper show of interest, I smilingly remarked:

"No one can be called poor long who remains under your roof, Miss Althorpe. But perhaps she has lost friends; so many nice girls are thrown upon their own resources by the death of relatives?"

"She does not wear mourning; but she is in some great trouble for all that. But this cannot interest you, Miss Butterworth; have you some *protégé* whom you wished to recommend for the position?"

I heard her, but did not answer at once. In fact, I was thinking how to proceed. Should I take her into my confidence, or should I continue in the ambiguous manner in which I had begun. Seeing her smile, I became conscious of the awkward silence.

"Pardon me," said I, resuming my best manner, "but there is something I want to say which may strike you as peculiar."

"O no," said she.

"I *am* interested in the girl you have befriended, and for very different reasons from those you suppose. I fear—I have great reason to fear—that she is not just the person you would like to harbor under your roof."

"Indeed! Why, what do you know about her? Anything bad, Miss Butterworth?"

I shook my head, and prayed her first to tell me how the girl looked and under what circumstances she came to her; for I was desirous of making no mistake concerning her identity with the person of whom I was in search.

"She is a sweet-looking girl," was the answer I received; "not beautiful, but interesting in expression and manner. She has brown hair,"—I shuddered,—"brown eyes, and a mouth that would be lovely if it ever smiled. In fact, she is very attractive and so lady-like that I have desired to make a companion of her. But while attentive to all her duties, and manifestly grateful to me for the home I have given her, she shows so little desire for company or conversation that I have desisted for the last day or so from urging her to speak at all. But you asked me under what circumstances she came to me?"

"Yes, on what day, and at what time of day? Was she dressed well, or did her clothes look shabby?"

"She came on the very day I advertised; the eighteenth—yes, it was the eighteenth of this month; and she was dressed, so far as I noticed, very neatly. Indeed, her clothes appeared to be new. They needed to have been, for she brought nothing with her save what was contained in a small hand-bag."

"Also new?" I suggested.

"Very likely; I did not observe."

"O Miss Althorpe!" I exclaimed, this time with considerable vehemence, "I fear, or rather I hope, she is the woman I want."

"*You* want!"

"Yes, *I*; but I cannot tell you for what just yet. I must be sure, for I would not subject an innocent person to suspicion any more than you would."

"Suspicion! She is not honest, then? That would worry me, Miss Butterworth, for the house is full now, as you know, of wedding presents, and—But I cannot believe such a thing of *her*. It is some other fault she has, less despicable and degrading."

"I do not say she has any faults; I only said I feared. What name does she go by?"

"Oliver; Ruth Oliver."

Again I thought of the O. R. on the clothes at the laundry.

"I wish I could see her," I ventured. "I would give anything for a peep at her face unobserved."

"I don't know how I can manage *that*; she is very shy, and never shows herself in the front of the house. She even dines in her own room, having begged for that privilege till after I was married and the household settled on a new basis. But you can go to her room with me. If she is all right, she can have no objection to a visitor; and if she is *not*, it would be well for me to know it at once."

"Certainly," said I, and rose to follow her, turning over in my mind how I should account to this young woman for my intrusion. I had just arrived at what I considered a sensible conclusion, when Miss Althorpe, leaning towards me, said with a whole-souled impetuosity for which I could not but admire her:

"The girl is very nervous, she looks and acts like a person who has had some frightful shock. Don't alarm her, Miss Butterworth, and don't accuse her of anything wrong too suddenly. Perhaps she is innocent, and perhaps if she is not innocent, she has been driven into evil by very great temptations. I am sorry for her, whether she is simply unhappy or deeply remorseful. For I never saw a sweeter face, or eyes with such boundless depths of misery in them."

Just what Mrs. Desberger had said! Strange, but I began to feel a certain sort of sympathy for the wretched being I was hunting down.

"I will be careful," said I. "I merely want to satisfy myself that she is the same girl I heard of last from a Mrs. Desberger."

Miss Althorpe, who was now half-way up the rich staircase which makes her house one of the most remarkable in the city, turned and gave me a quick look over her shoulder.

"I don't know Mrs. Desberger," she remarked.

At which I smiled. Did she think Mrs. Desberger in society?

At the end of an upper passage-way we paused.

"This is the door," whispered Miss Althorpe. "Perhaps I had better go in first and see if she is at all prepared for company."

I was glad to have her do so, for I felt as if I needed to prepare myself for encountering this young girl, over whom, in my mind, hung the dreadful suspicion of murder.

But the time between Miss Althorpe's knock and her entrance, short as it was, was longer than that which elapsed between her going in and her hasty reappearance.

"You can have your wish," said she. "She is lying on her bed asleep, and you can see her without being observed. But," she entreated, with a passionate grip of my arm, which proclaimed her warm nature, "doesn't it seem a little like taking advantage of her?"

"Circumstances justify it in this case," I replied, admiring the consideration of my hostess, but not thinking it worth while to emulate it. And with very little ceremony I pushed open the door and entered the room of the so-called Ruth Oliver.

The hush and quiet which met me, though nothing more than I had reason to expect, gave me my first shock, and the young figure outstretched on a bed of dainty whiteness, my second. Everything about me was so peaceful, and the delicate blue and white of the room so expressive of innocence and repose, that my feet instinctively moved more softly over the polished floor and paused, when they did pause, before that dimly shrouded bed, with something like hesitation in their usually emphatic tread.

The face of that bed's occupant, which I could now plainly see, may have had an influence in producing this effect. It was so rounded with health, and yet so haggard with trouble. Not knowing whether Miss Althorpe was behind me or not, but too intent upon the sleeping girl to care, I bent over the half-averted features and studied them carefully.

They were indeed Madonna-like, something which I had not expected, notwithstanding the assurances I had received to that effect, and while distorted with suffering, amply accounted for the interest shown in her by the good-hearted Mrs. Desberger and the cultured Miss Althorpe.

Resenting this beauty, which so poorly accommodated itself to the character of the woman who possessed it, I leaned nearer, searching for some defect in her loveliness, when I saw that the struggle and anguish visible in her expression were due to some dream she was having.

Moved, even against my will, by the touching sight of her trembling eyelids and working mouth, I was about to wake her when I was stopped by the gentle touch of Miss Althorpe on my shoulder.

"Is she the girl you are looking for?"

I gave one quick glance around the room, and my eyes lighted on the little blue pin-cushion on the satin-wood bureau.

"Did you put those pins there?" I asked, pointing to a dozen or more black pins grouped in one corner.

"*I* did not, no; and I doubt if Crescenze did. Why?"

I drew a small black pin from my belt where I had securely fastened it, and carrying it over to the cushion, compared it with those I saw. They were identical.

"A small matter," I inwardly decided, "but it points in the right direction"; then, in answer to Miss Althorpe, added aloud: "I fear she is. At least I have seen no reason yet for doubting it. But I must make sure. Will you allow me to wake her?"

"O it seems cruel! She is suffering enough already. See how she twists and turns!"

"It will be a mercy, it seems to me, to rouse her from dreams so full of pain and trouble."

"Perhaps, but I will leave you alone to do it. What will you say to her? How account for your intrusion?"

"O I will find means, and they won't be too cruel either. You had better stand back by the bureau and listen. I think I had rather not have the responsibility of doing this thing alone."

Miss Althorpe, not understanding my hesitation, and only half comprehending my errand, gave me a doubtful look but retreated to the spot I had mentioned, and whether it was the rustle of her silk dress or whether the dream of the girl we were watching had reached its climax, a momentary stir took place in the outstretched form before me, and next moment she was flinging up her hands with a cry.

"O how can I touch her! She is dead, and I have never touched a dead body."

I fell back breathing hard, and Miss Althorpe's eyes, meeting mine, grew dark with horror. Indeed she was about to utter a cry herself, but I made an imperative motion, and she merely shrank farther away towards the door.

Meantime I had bent forward and laid my hand on the trembling figure before me.

"Miss Oliver," I said, "rouse yourself, I pray. I have a message for you from Mrs. Desberger."

She turned her head, looked at me like a person in a daze, then slowly moved and sat up.

"Who are you?" she asked, surveying me and the space about her with eyes which seemed to take in nothing till they lit upon Miss Althorpe's figure standing in an attitude of mingled shame and sympathy by the half-open door.

"Oh, Miss Althorpe!" she entreated, "I pray you to excuse me. I did not know you wanted me. I have been asleep."

"It is this lady who wants you," answered Miss Althorpe. "She is a friend of mine and one in whom you can confide."

"Confide!" This was a word to rouse her. She turned livid, and in her eyes as she looked my way both terror and surprise were visible. "Why should you think I had anything to confide? If I had, I should not pass by you, Miss Althorpe, for another."

There were tears in her voice, and I had to remember the victim just laid away in Woodlawn, not to bestow much more compassion on this woman than she rightfully deserved. She had a magnetic voice and a magnetic presence, but that was no reason why I should forget what she had done.

"No one asks for your confidence," I protested, "though it might not hurt you to accept a friend whenever you can get one. I merely wish, as I said before, to give you a message from Mrs. Desberger, under whose roof you stayed before coming here."

"I am obliged to you," she responded, rising to her feet, and trembling very much. "Mrs. Desberger is a kind woman; what does she want of me?"

So I was on the right track; she acknowledged Mrs. Desberger.

"Nothing but to return you this. It fell out of your pocket while you were dressing." And I handed her the little red pin-cushion I had taken from the Van Burnams' front room.

She looked at it, shrunk violently back, and with difficulty prevented herself from showing the full depth of her feelings.

"I don't know anything about it. It is not mine, I don't know it!" And her hair stirred on her forehead as she gazed at the small object lying in the palm of my hand, proving to me that she saw again before her all the horrors of the house from which it had been taken.

"Who are *you*?" she suddenly demanded, tearing her eyes from this simple little cushion and fixing them wildly on my face. "Mrs. Desberger never sent me this. I— —"

"You are right to stop there," I interposed, and then paused, feeling that I had forced a situation which I hardly knew how to handle.

The instant's pause she had given herself seemed to restore her self-possession. Leaving me, she moved towards Miss Althorpe.

"I don't know who this lady is," said she, "or what her errand here with me may mean. But I hope that it is nothing that will force me to leave this house which is my only refuge."

Miss Althorpe, too greatly prejudiced in favor of this girl to hear this appeal unmoved, notwithstanding the show of guilt with which she had met my attack, smiled faintly as she answered:

"Nothing short of the best reasons would make me part from you now. If there are such reasons, you will spare me the pain of making use of them. I think I can so far trust you, Miss Oliver."

No answer; the young girl looked as if she could not speak.

"Are there any reasons why I should not retain you in my house, Miss Oliver?" the gentle mistress of many millions went on. "If there are, you will not wish to stay, I know, when you consider how near my marriage day is, and how undisturbed my mind should be by any cares unattending my wedding."

And still the girl was silent, though her lips moved slightly as if she would have spoken if she could.

"But perhaps you are only unfortunate," suggested Miss Althorpe, with an almost angelic look of pity—I don't often see angels in women. "If that is so, God forbid that you should leave my protection or my house. What do you say, Miss Oliver?"

"That you are God's messenger to me," burst from the other, as if her tongue had been suddenly loosed. "That misfortune, and not wickedness, has driven me to your doors; and that there is no reason why I should leave you unless my secret sufferings make my presence unwelcome to you."

Was this the talk of a frivolous woman caught unawares in the meshes of a fearful crime? If so, she was a more accomplished actress than we had been led to expect even from her own words to her disgusted husband.

"You look like one accustomed to tell the truth," proceeded Miss Althorpe. "Do you not think you have made some mistake, Miss Butterworth?" she asked, approaching me with an ingenuous smile.

I had forgotten to caution her not to make use of my name, and when it fell from her lips I looked to see her unhappy companion recoil from me with a scream.

But strange to say she evinced no emotion, and seeing this, I became more distrustful of her than ever; for, for her to hear without apparent interest the name of the chief witness in the inquest which had been held over the remains of the woman with whose death she had been more or less intimately concerned, argued powers of duplicity such as are only associated with guilt or an extreme simplicity of character. And she was not simple, as the least glance from her deep eyes amply showed.

Recognizing, therefore, that open measures would not do with this woman, I changed my manner at once, and responding to Miss Althorpe, with a gracious smile, remarked with an air of sudden conviction:

"Perhaps I have made some mistake. Miss Oliver's words sound very ingenuous, and I am disposed, if you are, to take her at her word. It is so easy to draw false conclusions in this world." And I put back the pin-cushion into my pocket with an air of being through with the matter, which seemed to impose upon the young woman, for she smiled faintly, showing a row of splendid teeth as she did so.

"Let me apologize," I went on, "if I have intruded upon Miss Oliver against her wishes." And with one comprehensive look about the room which took in all that was visible of her simple wardrobe and humble belongings, I led the way out. Miss Althorpe immediately followed.

"This is a much more serious affair than I have led you to suppose," I confided to her as soon as we were at a suitable distance from Miss Oliver's door. "If she is the person I think her, she is amenable to law, and the police will have to be notified of her whereabouts."

"She *has* stolen, then?"

' "Her fault is a very grave one," I returned.

Miss Althorpe, deeply troubled, looked about her as if for guidance. I, who could have given it to her, made no movement to attract her attention to myself, but waited calmly for her own decision in this matter.

"I wish you would let me consult Mr. Stone," she ventured at last. "I think his judgment might help us."

"I had rather take no one into our confidence,—especially no man. He would consider your welfare only and not hers."

I did not consider myself obliged to acknowledge that the work upon which I was engaged could not be shared by one of the male sex without lessening my triumph over Mr. Gryce.

"Mr. Stone is very just," she remarked, "but he might be biased in a matter of this kind. What way do you see out of the difficulty?"

"Only this. To settle at once and unmistakably, whether she is the person who carried certain articles from the house of a friend of mine. If she is, there will be some evidence of the fact visible in her room or on her person. She has not been out, I believe?"

"Not since she came into the house."

"And has remained for the most part in her own apartment?"

"Always, except when I have summoned her to my assistance."

"Then what I want to know I can learn there. But how can I make my investigations without offence?"

"What do you want to know, Miss Butterworth?"

"Whether she has in her keeping some half dozen rings of considerable value."

"Oh! she could conceal rings so easily."

"She does conceal them; I have no more doubt of it than I have of my standing here; but I must know it before I shall feel ready to call the attention of the police to her."

"Yes, we should both know it. Poor girl! poor girl! to be suspected of a crime! How great must have been her temptation!"

"*I* can manage this matter, Miss Althorpe, if you will entrust it to me."

"How, Miss Butterworth?"

"The girl is ill; let me take care of her."

"Really ill?"

"Yes, or will be so before morning. There is fever in her veins; she has worried herself ill. Oh, I will be good to her."

This in answer to a doubtful look from Miss Althorpe.

"This is a difficult problem you have set me," that lady remarked after a moment's thought. "But anything seems better than sending her away, or sending for the police. But do you suppose she will allow you in her room?"

"I think so; if her fever increases she will not notice much that goes on about her, and I think it will increase; I have seen enough of sickness to be something of a judge."

"And you will search her while she is unconscious?"

"Don't look so horrified, Miss Althorpe. I have promised you I will not worry her. She may need assistance in getting to bed. While I am giving it to her I can judge if there is anything concealed upon her person."

"Yes, perhaps."

"At all events, we shall know more than we do now. Shall I venture, Miss Althorpe?"

"I cannot say no," was the hesitating answer; "you seem so very much in earnest."

"And I am in earnest. I have reasons for being; consideration for you is one of them."

"I do not doubt it. And now will you come down to supper, Miss Butterworth?"

"No," I replied. "My duty is here. Only send word to Lena that she is to drive home and take care of my house in my absence. I shall want nothing, so do not worry about me. Join your lover now, dear; and do not bestow another thought upon this self-styled Miss Oliver or what I am about to do in her room."

XXIV.
A HOUSE OF CARDS.

I did not return immediately to my patient. I waited till her supper came up. Then I took the tray, and assured by the face of the girl who brought it that Miss Althorpe had explained my presence in her house sufficiently for me to feel at my ease before her servants, I carried in the dainty repast she had provided and set it down on the table.

The poor woman was standing where we had left her; but her whole figure showed languor, and she more than leaned against the bedpost behind her. As I looked up from the tray and met her eyes, she shuddered and seemed to be endeavoring to understand who I was and what I was doing in her room. My premonitions in regard to her were well based. She was in a raging fever, and was already more than half oblivious to her surroundings.

Approaching her, I spoke as gently as I could, for her hapless condition appealed to me in spite of my well founded prejudices against her; and seeing she was growing incapable of response, I drew her up on the bed and began to undress her.

I half expected her to recoil at this, or at least to make some show of alarm, but she submitted to my ministrations almost gratefully, and neither shrank nor questioned me till I laid my hands upon her shoes. Then indeed she quivered, and drew her feet away with such an appearance of terror that I was forced to desist from my efforts or drive her into violent delirium.

This satisfied me that Louise Van Burnam lay before me. The scar concerning which so much had been said in the papers would be ever present in the thoughts of this woman as the tell-tale mark by which she might be known, and though at this moment she was on the borders of unconsciousness, the instinct of self-preservation still remained in sufficient force to prompt her to make this effort to protect herself from discovery.

I had told Miss Althorpe that my chief reason for intruding upon Miss Oliver, was to determine if she had in her possession certain rings supposed to have been taken from a friend of mine; and while this was in a measure true—the rings being an important factor in the proof I was accumulating against her,—I was not so anxious to search for them at this time as to find the scar which would settle at once the question of her identity.

When she drew her foot away from me then, so violently, I saw that I needed to search no farther for the evidence required, and could give myself up to making her comfortable. So I bathed her temples, now throbbing with heat, and soon had the satisfaction of seeing her fall into a deep and uneasy slumber. Then I tried again to draw off her shoes, but the start she gave and the smothered cry which escaped her warned me that I must wait yet longer before satisfying my curiosity; so I desisted at once, and out of pure compassion left her to get what good she might from the lethargy into which she had fallen.

Being hungry, or at least feeling the necessity of some slight aliment to help me sustain the fatigues of the night, I sat down now at the table and partook of some of the dainties with which Miss Althorpe had kindly provided me. After which I made out a list of such articles as were necessary to my proper care of the patient who had so strangely fallen into my hands, and then, feeling that I had a right at last to indulge in pure curiosity, I turned my attention to the clothing I had taken from the self-styled Miss Oliver.

The dress was a simple gray one, and the skirts and underclothing all white. But the latter was of the finest texture, and convinced me, before I had given them more than a glance, that they were the property of Howard Van Burnam's wife. For, besides the exquisite quality of the material, there were to be seen, on the edges of the bands and sleeves, the marks of stitches and clinging threads of lace, where the trimming had been torn off, and in one article especially, there were tucks such as you see come from the hands of French needlewomen only.

This, taken with what had gone before, was proof enough to satisfy me that I was on the right track, and after Crescenze had come and gone with the tray and all was quiet in this remote part of the house, I ventured to open a closet door at the foot of the bed. A brown silk skirt was hanging within, and in the pocket of that skirt I found a purse so gay and costly that all doubt vanished as to its being the property of Howard's luxurious wife.

There were several bills in this purse, amounting to about fifteen dollars in money, but no change and no memoranda, which latter seemed a pity. Restoring the purse to its place and the skirt to its peg, I came softly back to the bedside and examined my patient still more carefully than I had done before. She was asleep and breathing heavily, but even with this disadvantage her face had its own attraction, an attraction which evidently had more or less influenced men, and which, for the reason perhaps that I have something masculine in my nature, I discovered to be more or less influencing me, notwithstanding my hatred of an intriguing character.

However, it was not her beauty I came to study, but her hair, her complexion, and her hands. The former was brown, the brown of that same lock I remembered to have seen in the jury's hands at the inquest; and her skin, where fever had not flushed it, was white and smooth. So were her hands, and yet they were not a lady's hands. That I noticed when I first saw her. The marks of the rings she no longer wore, were not enough to blind me to the fact that her fingers lacked the distinctive shape and nicety of Miss Althorpe's, say, or even of the Misses Van Burnam; and though I do not object to this, for I like strong-looking, capable hands myself, they served to help me understand the face, which otherwise would have looked too spiritual for a woman of the peevish and self-satisfied character of Louise Van Burnam. On this innocent and appealing expression she had traded in her short and none too happy career. And as I noted it, I recalled a sentence in Miss Ferguson's testimony, in which she alluded to Mrs. Van Burnam's confidential remark to her husband upon the power she exercised over people when she raised her eyes in entreaty towards them. "Am I not pretty," she had said, "when I am in distress and looking up in this way?" It was the suggestion of a scheming woman, but from what I had seen and was seeing of the woman before me, I could imagine the picture she would thus make, and I do not think she overrated its effects.

Withdrawing from her side once more, I made a tour of the room. Nothing escaped my eyes; nothing was too small to engage my attention. But while I failed to see anything calculated to shake my confidence in the conclusions I had come to, I saw but little to confirm them. This was not strange; for, apart from a few toilet articles and some knitting-work on a shelf, she appeared to have no belongings; everything else in sight being manifestly the property of Miss Althorpe. Even the bureau drawers were empty, and her bag, found under a small table, had not so much in it as a hair-pin, though I searched it inside and out for her rings, which I was positive she had with her, even if she dared not wear them.

When every spot was exhausted I sat down and began to brood over what lay before this poor being, whose flight and the great efforts she made at concealment proved only too conclusively the fatal part she had played in the crime for which her husband had been arrested. I had reached her arraignment before a magistrate, and was already imagining her face with the appeal in it which such an occasion would call forth, when there came a low knock at the door, and Miss Althorpe re-entered.

She had just said good-night to her lover, and her face recalled to me a time when my own cheek was round and my eye was bright and—Well! what is the use of dwelling on matters so long buried in oblivion! A maiden-woman, as independent as myself, need not envy any girl the doubtful blessing of a husband. I chose to be independent, and I am, and what more is there to be said about it? Pardon the digression.

"Is Miss Oliver any better?" asked Miss Althorpe; "and have you found— —"

I put up my finger in warning. Of all things, it was most necessary that the sick woman should not know my real reason for being there.

"She is asleep," I answered quietly, "and I *think* I have found out what is the matter with her."

Miss Althorpe seemed to understand. She cast a look of solicitude towards the bed and then turned towards me.

"I cannot rest," said she, "and will sit with you for a little while, if you don't mind."

I felt the implied compliment keenly.

"You can do me no greater favor," I returned.

She drew up an easy-chair. "That is for you," she smiled, and sat down in a little low rocker at my side.

But she did not talk. Her thoughts seemed to have recurred to some very near and sweet memory, for she smiled softly to herself and looked so deeply happy that I could not resist saying:

"These are delightful days for you, Miss Althorpe."

She sighed softly—how much a sigh can reveal!—and looked up at me brightly. I think she was glad I spoke. Even such reserved natures as hers have their moments of weakness, and she had no mother or sister to appeal to.

"Yes," she replied, "I am very happy; happier than most girls are, I think, just before marriage. It is such a revelation to me—this devotion and admiration from one I love. I have had so little of it in my life. My father— —"

She stopped; I knew why she stopped. I gave her a look of encouragement.

"People have always been anxious for my happiness, and have warned me against matrimony since I was old enough to know the difference between poverty and wealth. Before I was out of short dresses I was warned against fortune-seekers. It was not good advice; it has stood in the way of my happiness all my life, made me distrustful and unnaturally reserved. But now—ah, Miss

Butterworth, Mr. Stone is so estimable a man, so brilliant and so universally admired, that all my doubts of manly worth and disinterestedness have disappeared as if by magic. I trust him implicitly, and—Do I talk too freely? Do you object to such confidences as these?"

"On the contrary," I answered. I liked Miss Althorpe so much and agreed with her so thoroughly in her opinion of this man, that it was a real pleasure to me to hear her speak so unreservedly.

"We are not a foolish couple," she went on, warming with the charm of her topic till she looked beautiful in the half light thrown upon her by the shaded lamp. "We are interested in people and things, and get half our delight from the perfect congeniality of our natures. Mr. Stone has given up his club and all his bachelor pursuits since he knew me, and——"

O love, if at any time in my life I have despised thee, I did not despise thee then! The look with which she finished this sentence would have moved a cynic.

"Forgive me," she prayed. "It is the first time I have poured out my heart to any one of my own sex. It must sound strange to you, but it seemed natural while I was doing it, for you looked as if you could understand."

This to me, to *me*, Amelia Butterworth, of whom men have said I had no more sentiment than a wooden image. I looked my appreciation, and she, blushing slightly, whispered in a delicious tone of mingled shyness and pride:

"Only two weeks now, and I shall have some one to stand between me and the world. *You* have never needed any one, Miss Butterworth, for you do not fear the world, but it awes and troubles me, and my whole heart glows with the thought that I shall be no longer alone in my sorrows or my joys, my perplexities or my doubts. Am I to blame for anticipating this with so much happiness?"

I sighed. It was a less eloquent sigh than hers, but it was a distinct one and it had a distinct echo. Lifting my eyes, for I sat so as to face the bed, I was startled to observe my patient leaning towards us from her pillows, and staring upon us with eyes too hollow for tears but filled with unfathomable grief and yearning.

She had heard this talk of love, she, the forsaken and crime-stained one. I shuddered and laid my hand on Miss Althorpe's.

But I did not seek to stop the conversation, for as our looks met, the sick woman fell back and lapsed, or seemed to lapse, into immediate insensibility again.

"Is Miss Oliver worse?" inquired Miss Althorpe.

I rose and went to the bedside, renewed the bandages on my patient's head, and forced a drop or two of medicine between her half-shut lips.

"No," I returned, "I think her fever is abating." And it was, though the suffering on her face was yet heart-rendingly apparent.

"Is she asleep?"

"She seems to be."

Miss Althorpe made an effort.

"I am not going to talk any more about myself." Then as I came back and sat down by her side, she quietly asked:

"What do you think of the Van Burnam murder?"

Dismayed at the introduction of this topic, I was about to put my hand over her mouth, when I noticed that her words had made no evident impression upon my patient, who lay quietly and with a more composed expression than when I left her bedside. This assured me, as nothing else could have done, that she was really asleep, or in that lethargic state which closes the eyes and ears to what is going on.

"I think," said I, "that the young man Howard stands in a very unfortunate position. Circumstances certainly do look very black against him."

"It is dreadful, unprecedently dreadful. I do not know what to think of it all. The Van Burnams have borne so good a name, and Franklin especially is held in such high esteem. I don't think anything more shocking has ever happened in this city, do you, Miss Butterworth? You saw it all, and should know. Poor, poor Mrs. Van Burnam!"

"She is to be pitied!" I remarked, my eyes fixed on the immovable face of my patient.

"When I heard that a young woman had been found dead in the Van Burnam mansion," Miss Althorpe pursued with such evident interest in this new theme that I did not care to interrupt her unless driven to it by some token of consciousness on the part of my patient, "my thoughts flew instinctively to Howard's wife. Though why, I cannot say, for I never had any reason to expect so tragic a termination to their marriage relations. And I cannot believe now that he killed her, can you, Miss Butterworth? Howard has too much of the gentleman in him to do a brutal thing, and there was brutality as well as adroitness in the perpetration of this crime. Have you thought of that, Miss Butterworth?"

"Yes," I nodded, "I have looked at the crime on all sides."

"Mr. Stone," said she, "feels dreadfully over the part he was forced to play at the inquest. But he had no choice, the police would have his testimony."

"That was right," I declared.

"It has made us doubly anxious to have Howard free himself. But he does not seem able to do so. If his wife had only known— —"

Was there a quiver in the lids I was watching? I half raised my hand and then I let it drop again, convinced that I had been mistaken. Miss Althorpe at once continued:

"She was not a bad-hearted woman, only vain and frivolous. She had set her heart on ruling in the great leather-merchant's house, and she did not know how to bear her disappointment. I have sympathy for her myself. When I saw her— —"

Saw her! I started, upsetting a small work-basket at my side which for once I did not stop to pick up.

"You have seen her!" I repeated, dropping my eyes from the patient to fix them in my unbounded astonishment on Miss Althorpe's face.

"Yes, more than once. She was—if she were living I would not repeat this—a nursery governess in a family where I once visited. That was before her marriage; before she had met either Howard or Franklin Van Burnam."

I was so overwhelmed, that for once I found difficulty in speaking. I glanced from her to the white form in the shrouded bed, and back again in ever-growing astonishment and dismay.

"You have seen her!" I at last reiterated in what I meant to be a whisper, but which fell little short of being a cry, "and you took in this girl?"

Her surprise at this burst was almost equal to mine.

"Yes, why not; what have they in common?"

I sank back, my house of cards was trembling to its foundations.

"Do they—do they not look alike?" I gasped. "I thought—I imagined— —"

"Louise Van Burnam look like that girl! O no, they were very different sort of women. What made you think there was any resemblance between them?"

I did not answer her; the structure I had reared with such care and circumspection had fallen about my ears and I lay gasping under the ruins.

XXV.
"THE RINGS! WHERE ARE THE RINGS?"

Had Mr. Gryce been present, I would have instantly triumphed over my disappointment, bottled up my chagrin, and been the inscrutable Amelia Butterworth before he could say, "Something has gone wrong with this woman!" But Mr. Gryce was not present, and though I did not betray the half I felt. I yet showed enough emotion for Miss Althorpe to remark:

"You seemed surprised by what I have told you. Has any one said that these two women were alike?"

Having to speak, I became myself again in a trice, and nodded vigorously.

"Some one was so foolish," I remarked.

Miss Althorpe looked thoughtful. While she was interested she was not so interested as to take the subject in fully. Her own concerns made her abstracted, and I was very glad of it.

"Louise Van Burnam had a sharp chin and a very cold blue eye. Yet her face was a fascinating one to some."

"Well, it was a dreadful tragedy!" I observed, and tried to turn the subject aside, which fortunately I was able to do after a short effort.

Then I picked the basket up, and perceiving the sick woman's lips faintly moving, I went over to her and found her murmuring to herself.

As Miss Althorpe had risen when I did, I did not dare to listen to these murmurs, but when my charming hostess had bidden me good-night, with many injunctions not to tire myself, and to be sure and remember that a decanter and a plate of biscuits stood on a table outside, I hastened back to the bedside, and leaning over my patient, endeavored to catch the words as they fell from her lips.

As they were simple and but the echo of those running at that very moment through my own brain, I had no difficulty in distinguishing them.

"Van Burnam!" she was saying, "Van Burnam!" varied by a short "Howard!" and once by a doubtful "Franklin!"

"Ah," thought I, with a sudden reaction, "she is the woman I seek, if she is not Louise Van Burnam." And unheeding the start she gave, I pulled off the blanket I had spread over her, and willy-nilly drew off her left shoe and stocking.

Her bare ankle showed no scar, and covering it quickly up I took up her shoe. Immediately the trepidation she had shown at the approach of a stranger's hand towards that article of clothing was explained. In the lining around the top were sewn bills of no ordinary amount, and as the other shoe was probably used as a like depository, she naturally felt concern at any approach which might lead to a discovery of her little fortune.

Amazed at a mystery possessing so many points of interest, I tucked the shoe in under the bedclothes and sat down to review the situation.

The mistake I had made was in concluding that because the fugitive whose traces I had followed had worn the clothes of Louise Van Burnam, she must necessarily be that unfortunate lady. Now I saw that the murdered woman was Howard's wife after all, and this patient of mine her probable rival.

But this necessitated an entire change in my whole line of reasoning. If the rival and not the wife lay before me, then which of the two accompanied him to the scene of tragedy? He had said it was his wife; I had proven to myself that it was the rival; was he right, or was I right, or were neither of us right?

Not being able to decide, I fixed my mind upon another query. When did the two women exchange clothes, or rather, when did this woman procure the silk habiliments and elaborate adornments of her more opulent rival? Was it before either of them entered Mr. Van Burnam's house? Or was it after their encounter there?

Running over in my mind certain little facts of which I had hitherto attempted no explanation, I grouped them together and sought amongst them for inspiration.

These are the facts:

1. One of the garments found on the murdered woman had been torn down the back. As it was a new one, it had evidently been subjected to some quick strain, not explainable by any appearance of struggle.

2. The shoes and stockings found on the victim were the only articles she wore which could not be traced back to Altman's. In the re-dressing of the so-called Mrs. James Pope, these articles had not been changed. Could not that fact be explained by the presence of a considerable sum of money in her shoes?

3. The going out bareheaded of a fugitive, anxious to avoid observation, leaving hat and gloves behind her in a dining-room closet.

I had endeavored to explain this last anomalous action by her fear of being traced by so conspicuous an article as this hat; but it was not a satisfactory explanation to me then and much less so now.

4. And last, and most vital of all, the words which I had heard fall from this half-conscious girl: "*O how can I touch her! She is dead, and I have never touched a dead body!*"

Could inspiration fail me before such a list? Was it not evident that the change had been made after death, and by this seemingly sensitive girl's own hands?

It was a horrible thought and led to others more horrible. For the very commission of such a revolting act argued a desire for concealment only to be explained by great guilt. She had been the offender and the wife the victim; and Howard—Well, his actions continued to be a mystery, but I would not admit his guilt even now. On the contrary, I saw his innocence in a still stronger light. For if he had openly or even covertly connived at his wife's death, would he have so immediately forsaken the accomplice of his guilt, to say nothing of leaving to her the dreadful task of concealing the crime? No, I would rather think that the tragedy took place after his departure, and that his action in denying his wife's identity, as long as it was possible to do so, was to be explained by the fact of his ignorance in regard to his wife's presence in the house where he had supposed himself to have simply left her rival. As the exchange made in the clothing worn by the two women could only have taken place later, and as he naturally judged the victim by her clothing, perhaps he was really deceived himself as to her identity. It was certainly not an improbable supposition, and accounted for much that was otherwise inexplicable in Mr. Van Burnam's conduct.

But the rings? Why could I not find the rings? If my present reasoning were correct, this woman should have those evidences of guilt about her. But had I not searched for them in every available place without success? Annoyed at my failure to fix this one irrefutable proof of guilt upon her, I took up the knitting-work I saw in Miss Oliver's basket, and began to ply the needles by way of relief to my thoughts. But I had no sooner got well under way than some movement on the part of my patient drew my attention again to the bed, and I was startled by beholding her sitting up again, but this time with a look of fear rather than of suffering on her features.

"Don't!" she gasped, pointing with an unsteady hand at the work in my hand. "The click, click of the needles is more than I can stand. Put them down, pray; put them down!"

Her agitation was so great and her nervousness so apparent that I complied at once. However much I might be affected by her guilt, I was not willing to do the slightest thing to worry her nerves even at the expense of my own. As the needles fell from my hand, she sank back and a quick, short sigh escaped her lips. Then she was again quiet, and I allowed my thoughts to return to the old theme. The rings! the rings! Where were the rings, and was it impossible for me to find them?

XXVI.
A TILT WITH MR. GRYCE.

At seven o'clock the next morning my patient was resting so quietly that I considered it safe to leave her for a short time. So I informed Miss Althorpe that I was obliged to go down-town on an important errand, and requested Crescenze to watch over the sick girl in my absence. As she agreed to this, I left the house as soon as breakfast was over and went immediately in search of Mr. Gryce. I wished to make sure that he knew nothing about the rings.

It was eleven o'clock before I succeeded in finding him. As I was certain that a direct question would bring no answer, I dissembled my real intention as much as my principles would allow, and accosted him with the eager look of one who has great news to impart.

"O, Mr. Gryce!" I impetuously cried, just as if I were really the weak woman he thought me, "I have found something; something in connection with the Van Burnam murder. You know I promised to busy myself about it if you arrested Howard Van Burnam."

His smile was tantalizing in the extreme. "Found something?" he repeated. "And may I ask if you have been so good as to bring it with you?"

He was playing with me, this aged and reputable detective. I subdued my anger, subdued my indignation even, and smiling much in his own way, answered briefly:

"I never carry valuables on my person. A half-dozen expensive rings stand for too much money for me to run any undue risk with them."

He was caressing his watch-chain as I spoke, and I noticed that he paused in this action for just an infinitesimal length of time as I said the word rings. Then he went on as before, but I knew I had caught his attention.

"Of what rings do you speak, madam? Of those missing from Mrs. Van Burnam's hands?"

I took a leaf from his book, and allowed myself to indulge in a little banter.

"O, no," I remonstrated, "not those rings, of course. The Queen of Siam's rings, any rings but those in which we are specially interested."

This meeting him on his own ground evidently puzzled him.

"You are facetious, madam. What am I to gather from such levity? That success has crowned your efforts, and that you have found a guiltier party than the one now in custody?"

"Possibly," I returned, limiting my advance by his. "But it would be going too fast to mention that yet. What I want to know is whether *you* have found the rings belonging to Mrs. Van Burnam?"

My triumphant tone, the almost mocking accent I purposely gave to the word *you*, accomplished its purpose. He never dreamed I was playing with him; he thought I was bursting with pride; and casting me a sharp glance (the first, by the way, I had received from him), he inquired with perceptible interest:

"Have *you?*"

Instantly convinced that the whereabouts of these jewels was as little known to him as to me, I rose and prepared to leave. But seeing that he was not satisfied, and that he expected an answer, I assumed a mysterious air and quietly remarked:

"If you will come to my house to-morrow I will explain myself. I am not prepared to more than intimate my discoveries to-day."

But he was not the man to let one off so easily.

"Excuse me," said he, "but matters of this kind do not admit of delay. The grand jury sits within the week, and any evidence worth presenting them must be collected at once. I must ask you to be frank with me, Miss Butterworth."

"And I will be, to-morrow."

"To-day," he insisted, "to-day."

Seeing that I should gain nothing by my present course, I reseated myself, bestowing upon him a decidedly ambiguous smile as I did so.

"You acknowledge then," said I, "that the old maid can tell you something after all. I thought you regarded all my efforts in the light of a jest. What has made you change your mind?"

"Madam, I decline to bandy words. Have you found those rings, or have you not?"

"I have *not*," said I, "but neither have you, and as that is what I wanted to make sure of, I will now take my leave without further ceremony."

Mr. Gryce is not a profane man, but he allowed a word to slip from him which was not entirely one of blessing. He made amends for it next moment, however, by remarking:

"Madam, I once said, as you will doubtless remember, that the day would come when I should find myself at your feet. That day has arrived. And now is there any other little cherished fact known to the police which you would like to have imparted to you?"

I took his humiliation seriously.

"You are very good," I rejoined, "but I will not trouble you for any *facts,* — *those* I am enabled to glean for myself; but what I should like you to tell me is this: Whether if you came upon those rings in the possession of a person known to have been on the scene of crime at the time of its perpetration, you would not consider them as an incontrovertible proof of guilt?"

"Undoubtedly," said he, with a sudden alteration in his manner which warned me that I must muster up all my strength if I would keep my secret till I was quite ready to part with it.

"Then," said I, with a resolute movement towards the door, "that's the whole of my business for to-day. Good-morning, Mr. Gryce; to-morrow I shall expect you."

He made me stop though my foot had crossed the threshold; not by word or look but simply by his fatherly manner.

"Miss Butterworth," he observed, "the suspicions which you have entertained from the first have within the last few days assumed a definite form. In what direction do they point? — tell me."

Some men and most women would have yielded to that imperative *tell me!* But there was no yielding in Amelia Butterworth. Instead of that I treated him to a touch of irony.

"Is it possible," I asked, "that you think it worth while to consult *me*? I thought your eyes were too keen to seek assistance from mine. You are as confident as I am that Howard Van Burnam is innocent of the crime for which you have arrested him."

A look that was dangerously insinuating crossed his face at this. He came forward rapidly and, joining me where I stood, said smilingly:

"Let us join forces, Miss Butterworth. You have from the first refused to consider the younger son of Silas Van Burnam as guilty. Your reasons then were slight and hardly worth communicating. Have you any better ones to advance now? It is not too late to mention them, if you have."

"It will not be too late to-morrow," I retorted.

Convinced that I was not to be moved from my position, he gave me one of his low bows.

"I forgot," said he, "that it was as a rival and not as a coadjutor you meddled in this matter." And he bowed again, this time with a sarcastic air I felt too self-satisfied to resent.

"To-morrow, then?" said I.

"To-morrow."

At that I left him.

I did not return immediately to Miss Althorpe. I visited Cox's millinery store, Mrs. Desberger's house, and the offices of the various city railways. But I got no clue to the rings; and finally satisfied that Miss Oliver, as I must now call her, had not lost or disposed of them on her way from Gramercy Park to her present place of refuge, I returned to Miss Althorpe's with even a greater determination than before to search that luxurious home till I found them.

But a decided surprise awaited me. As the door opened I caught a glimpse of the butler's face, and noticing its embarrassed expression, I at once asked what had happened.

His answer showed a strange mixture of hesitation and bravado.

"Not much, ma'am; only Miss Althorpe is afraid you may not be pleased. Miss Oliver is gone, ma'am; she ran away while Crescenze was out of the room."

XXVII.
FOUND.

I gave a low cry and rushed down the steps.

"Don't go!" I called out to the driver. "I shall want you in ten minutes." And hurrying back, I ran up-stairs in a condition of mind such as I have no reason to be proud of. Happily Mr. Gryce was not there to see me.

"Gone? Miss Oliver gone?" I cried to the maid whom I found trembling in a corner of the hall.

"Yes, ma'am; it was my fault, ma'am. She was in bed so quiet, I thought I might step out for a minute, but when I came back her clothes were missing and she was gone. She must have slipped out at the front door while Dan was in the back hall. I don't see how ever she had the strength to do it."

Nor did I. But I did not stop to reason about it; there was too much to be done. Rushing on, I entered the room I had left in such high hopes a few hours before. Emptiness was before me, and I realized what it was to be baffled at the moment of success. But I did not waste an instant in inactivity. I searched the closets and pulled open the drawers; found her coat and hat gone, but not Mrs. Van Burnam's brown skirt, though the purse had been taken out of the pocket.

"Is her bag here?" I asked.

Yes, it was in its old place under the table; and on the wash-stand and bureau were the simple toilet articles I had been told she had brought there. In what haste she must have fled to leave these necessities behind her!

But the greatest shock I received was the sight of the knitting-work, with which I had so inconsiderately meddled the evening before, lying in ravelled heaps on the table, as if torn to bits in a frenzy. This was a proof that the fever was yet on her; and as I contemplated this fact I took courage, thinking that one in her condition would not be allowed to run the streets long, but would be picked up and put in some hospital.

In this hope I began my search. Miss Althorpe, who came in just as I was about to leave the house, consented to telephone to Police Headquarters a description of the girl, with a request to be notified if such a person should be found in the streets or on the docks or at any of the station-houses that night. "Not," I assured her, as we left the telephone and I prepared to say good-bye for the day, "that you need expect her to be brought back to this house, for I do not mean that she shall ever darken your doors again. So let me know if they find her, and I will relieve you of all further responsibility in the matter."

Then I started out.

To name the streets I traversed or the places I visited that day, would take more space than I would like to devote to the subject. Dusk came, and I had failed in obtaining the least clue to her whereabouts; evening followed, and still no trace of the fugitive. What was I to do? Take Mr. Gryce into my confidence after all? That would be galling to my pride, but I began to fear I should have to submit to this humiliation when I happened to think of the Chinaman. To think of him once was to think of him twice, and to think of him twice was to be conscious of an irresistible desire to visit his place and find out if any one but myself had been there to inquire after the lost one's clothes.

Accompanied by Lena, I hurried away to Third Avenue. The laundry was near Twenty-seventh Street. As we approached I grew troubled and unaccountably expectant. When we reached it I understood my excitement and instantly became calm. For there stood Miss Oliver, gazing like one under a spell through the lighted window-panes into the narrow shop where the owner bent over his ironing. She had evidently stood there some time, for a small group of half-grown lads were watching her with every symptom of being about to break into a mischievous display of curiosity. Her hands, which were without gloves, were pressed against the glass, and her whole attitude showed an intensity of fatigue which would have laid her on the ground had she not been sustained by an equal intensity of purpose.

Sending Lena for a carriage, I approached the poor creature and drew her forcibly from the window.

"Do you want anything here?" I asked. "I will go in with you if you do."

She surveyed me with strange apathy, and yet with a certain sort of relief too. Then she slowly shook her head.

"I don't know anything about it. My head swims and everything looks queer, but some one or something sent me to this place."

"Come in," I urged, "come in for a minute." And half supporting her, half dragging her, I managed to get her across the threshold and into the Chinaman's shop.

Immediately a dozen faces were pressed where hers had been.

The Chinaman, a stolid being, turned as he heard the little bell tinkle which announced a customer.

"Is this the lady who left the clothes here a few nights ago?" I asked.

He stopped and stared, recognizing me slowly, and remembering by degrees what had passed between us at our last interview.

"You tellee me lalee die; how him lalee when lalee die?"

"The lady is not dead; I made a mistake. Is this the lady?"

"Lalee talk; I no see face, I hear speak."

"Have you seen this man before?" I inquired of my nearly insensible companion.

"I think so in a dream," she murmured, trying to recall her poor wandering wits back from some region into which they had strayed.

"Him lalee!" cried the Chinaman, overjoyed at the prospect of getting his money. "Pletty speak, I knowee him. Lalee want clo?"

"Not to-night. The lady is sick; see, she can hardly stand." And overjoyed at this seeming evidence that the police had failed to get wind of my interest in this place, I slipped a coin into the Chinaman's hand, and drew Miss Oliver away towards the carriage I now saw drawing up before the shop.

Lena's eyes when she came up to help me were a sight to see. They seemed to ask who this girl was and what I was going to do with her. I answered the look by a very brief and evidently wholly unexpected explanation.

"This is your cousin who ran away," I remarked. "Don't you recognize her?"

Lena gave me up then and there; but she accepted my explanation, and even lied in her desire to carry out my whim.

"Yes, ma'am," said she, "and glad I am to see her again." And with a deft push here and a gentle pull there, she succeeded in getting the sick woman into the carriage.

The crowd, which had considerably increased by this time, was beginning to flock about us with shouts of no little derision. Escaping it as best I could, I took my seat by the poor girl's side, and bade Lena give the order for home. When we left the curb-stone behind, I felt that the last page in my adventures as an amateur detective had closed.

But I counted without my cost. Miss Oliver, who was in an advanced stage of fever, lay like a dead weight on my shoulder during the drive down the avenue, but when we entered the Park and drew near my house, she began to show such signs of violent agitation that it was with difficulty that the united efforts of Lena and myself could prevent her from throwing herself out of the carriage door which she had somehow managed to open.

As the carriage stopped she grew worse, and though she made no further efforts to leave it, I found her present impulses even harder to contend with than the former. For now she would not be pushed out or dragged out, but crouched back moaning and struggling, her eyes fixed on the stoop, which is not unlike that of the adjoining house; till with a sudden realization that the cause of her terror lay in her fear of re-entering the scene of her late terrifying experiences, I bade the coachman drive on, and reluctantly, I own, carried her back to the house she had left in the morning.

And this is how I came to spend a second night in Miss Althorpe's hospitable mansion.

XXVIII.
TAKEN ABACK.

One incident more and this portion of my story is at an end. My poor patient, sicker than she had been the night before, left me but little leisure for thought or action disconnected with my care for her. But towards morning she grew quieter, and finding in an open drawer those tangled threads of yarn of which I have spoken, I began to rewind them, out of a natural desire to see everything neat and orderly about me. I had nearly finished my task when I heard a strange noise from the bed. It was a sort of gurgling cry which I found hard to interpret, but which only stopped when I laid my work down again. Manifestly this sick girl had very nervous fancies.

When I went down to breakfast the next morning, I was in that complacent state of mind natural to a woman who feels that her abilities have asserted themselves and that she would soon receive a recognition of the same at the hands of the one person for whose commendation she had chiefly been working. The identification of Miss Oliver by the Chinaman was the last link in the chain connecting her with the Mrs. James Pope who had accompanied Mr. Van Burnam to his father's house in Gramercy Park, and though I would fain have had the murdered woman's rings to show, I was contented enough with the discoveries I had made to wish for the hour which would bring me face to face with the detective.

But a surprise awaited me at the breakfast table in the shape of a communication from that gentleman. It had just been brought from my house by Lena, and it ran thus:

"Dear Miss Butterworth:

"Pardon our interference. We have found the rings which you think so conclusive an evidence of guilt against the person secreting them; and, *with your permission* [this was basely underlined], Mr. Franklin Van Burnam will be in custody to-day.

"I will wait upon you at ten.

"Respectfully yours,

"Ebenezar Gryce."

Franklin Van Burnam! Was I dreaming? *Franklin* Van Burnam accused of this crime and in custody! What did it mean? I had found no evidence against Franklin Van Burnam.

BOOK III.
THE GIRL IN GRAY.

XXIX.
AMELIA BECOMES PEREMPTORY.

"Madam, I hope I see you satisfied?"

This was Mr. Gryce's greeting as he entered my parlor on that memorable morning.

"Satisfied?" I repeated, rising and facing him with what he afterwards described as a stony glare.

"Pardon me! I suppose you would have been still more satisfied if we had waited for *you* to point out the guilty man to *us*. But you must make some allowances for professional egotism, Miss Butterworth. We really could not allow you to take the initiatory step in a matter of such importance."

"Oh!" was my sole response; but he has since told me that there was a great deal in that *oh*; so much, that even he was startled by it.

"You set to-day for a talk with me," he went on; "probably relying upon what you intended to assure yourself of yesterday. But our discovery at the same time as yourself of the rings in Mr. Van Burnam's office, need not interfere with your giving us your full confidence. The work you have done has been excellent, and we are disposed to give you considerable credit for it."

"Indeed!"

I had no choice but to thus indulge in ejaculations. The communication he had just made was so startling, and his assumption of my complete understanding of and participation in the discovery he professed to have made, so puzzling, that I dared not venture beyond these simple exclamations, lest he should see the state of mind into which he had thrown me, and shut up like an oyster.

"We have kept counsel over what we have found," the wary old detective continued, with a smile, which I wish I could imitate, but which unhappily belongs to him alone. "I hope that you, or your maid, I should say, have been equally discreet."

My maid!

"I see you are touched; but women find it so hard to keep a secret. But it does not matter. To-night the whole town will know that the older and not the younger brother has had these rings in his keeping."

"It will be nuts for the papers," I commented; then making an effort, I remarked: "You are a most judicious man, Mr. Gryce, and must have other reasons than the discovery of these rings for your threatened arrest of a man of such excellent repute as Silas Van Burnam's eldest son. I should like to hear them, Mr. Gryce. I should like to hear them very much."

My attempt to seem at ease under these embarrassing conditions must have given a certain sharpness to my tone; for, instead of replying, he remarked, with well simulated concern and a fatherly humoring of my folly peculiarly exasperating to one of my temperament: "You are displeased, Miss Butterworth, because we did not let *you* find the rings."

"Perhaps; but we were engaged in an open field. I could not expect the police to stand aside for me."

"Exactly! Especially when you have the secret satisfaction of having put the police on the track of these jewels."

"How?"

"We were simply fortunate in laying our hands on them first. You, or your maid rather, showed us where to look for them."

Lena again.

I was so dumfounded by this last assertion, I did not attempt to reply. Fortunately, he misinterpreted my silence and the "stony glare" with which it was accompanied.

"I know that it must seem to you altogether too bad, to be tripped up at the moment of your anticipated triumph. But if apologies will suffice to express our sense of presumption, then I pray you to accept them, Miss Butterworth, both on my own part and on that of the Superintendent of Police."

I did not understand in the least what he was talking about, but I recognized the sarcasm of his final expression, and had spirit enough to reply:

"The subject is too important for any more nonsense. Whereabouts in Franklin Van Burnam's desk were these rings found, and how do you know that his brother did not put them there?"

"Your ignorance is refreshing, Miss Butterworth. If you will ask a certain young girl dressed in gray, upon what object connected with Mr. Van Burnam's desk she laid her hands yesterday morning, you will have an answer to your first question. The second one is still more easily answered. Mr. Howard Van Burnam did not conceal the rings in the Duane Street office for the reason that he has not been in that office since his wife was killed. Regarding this fact we are as well advised as yourself. Now you change color, Miss Butterworth. But there is no necessity. For an amateur you have made less trouble and fewer mistakes than were to be expected."

Worse and worse! He was patronizing me now, and for results I had done nothing to bring about. I surveyed him in absolute amazement. Was he amusing himself with me, or was he himself deceived as to the nature and trend of my late investigations. This was a question to settle, and at once; and as duplicity had hitherto proved my best weapon in dealing with Mr. Gryce, I concluded to resort to it in this emergency. Clearing my brow, I regarded with a more amenable air the little Hungarian vase he had taken up on entering the room, and into which he had been talking ever since he thought it worth while to compliment its owner.

"I do not wish," said I, "to be published to the world as the discoverer of Franklin Van Burnam's guilt. But I do want credit with the police, if only because one of their number has chosen to look upon my efforts with disdain. I mean you, Mr. Gryce; so, if you are in earnest"—he smiled at the vase most genially—"I will accept your apologies just so far as you honor me with your confidence. I know you are anxious to hear what evidence I have collected, or you would not be wasting time on me this busy morning."

"Shrewd!" was the short ejaculation he shot into the mouth of the vase he was handling.

"If that term of admiration is intended for me," I remarked, "I am sure I am only too sensible of the honor. But flattery has never succeeded in making me talk against my better judgment. I may be shrewd, but a fool could see what you are after this morning. Compliment me when I have deserved it. I can wait."

"I begin to think that what you withhold so resolutely has more than common value, Miss Butterworth. If this is so, I must not be the only one to listen to your explanations. Is not that a carriage I hear stopping? I am expecting Inspector Z——. If that is he you have been wise to delay your communications till he came."

A carriage *was* stopping, and it was the Inspector who alighted from it. I began to feel my importance in a way that was truly gratifying, and cast my eyes up at the portrait of my father with a secret longing that its original stood by to witness the verification of his prophecy.

But I was not so distracted by these thoughts as not to make one attempt to get something from Mr. Gryce before the Inspector joined us.

"Why do you speak to me of my maid in one breath and of a girl in gray in another? Did you think Lena——"

"Hush!" he enjoined, "we will have ample opportunities to discuss this subject later."

"Will we?" thought I. "We will discuss nothing till I know more positively what you are aiming at."

But I showed nothing of this determination in my face. On the contrary, I became all affability as the Inspector entered, and I did the honors of the house in a way I hope my father would have approved of, had he been alive and present.

Mr. Gryce continued to stare into the vase.

"Miss Butterworth,"—it was the Inspector who was speaking,—"I have been told that you take great interest in the Van Burnam murder, and that you have even gone so far as to collect some facts in connection with it which you have not as yet given to the police."

"You have heard correctly," I returned. "I have taken a deep interest in this tragedy, and have come into possession of some facts in reference to it which as yet I have imparted to no living soul."

Mr. Gryce's interest in my poor little vase increased marvellously. Seeing this, I complacently continued:

"I could not have accomplished so much had I indulged in a confidant. Such work as I have attempted depends for its success upon the secrecy with which it is carried on. That is why amateur work is sometimes more effective than professional. No one suspected me of making inquiries, unless it was this gentleman, and he was forewarned of my possible interference. I told him that in case Howard Van Burnam was put under arrest, I should take it upon myself to stir up matters; and I have."

"Then you do not believe in Mr. Van Burnam's guilt? Not even in his complicity, I suppose?" ventured the Inspector.

"I do not know anything about his complicity; but I do not believe the stroke given to his wife came from his hand."

"I see, I see. You believe it the work of his brother."

I stole a look at Mr. Gryce before replying. He had turned the vase upside down, and was intently studying its label; but he could not conceal his expectation of an affirmative answer. Greatly relieved, I immediately took the position I had resolved upon, and calmly but vigorously observed:

"What I believe, and what I have learned in support of my belief, will sound as well in your ears ten minutes hence as now. Before I give you the result of such inquiries as I have been enabled to make, I require to know what evidence you have yourself collected against the gentleman you have just named, and in what respect it is as criminating as that against his brother?"

"Is not that peremptory, Miss Butterworth? And do you think us called upon to part with all or any of the secrets of our office? We have informed you that we have new and startling evidence against the older brother; should not that be sufficient for you?"

"Perhaps so if I were an assistant of yours, or even in your employ. But I am neither; I stand alone, and although I am a woman and unused to this business, I have earned, as I think you will acknowledge later, the right to some consideration on your part. I cannot present the facts I have to relate in a proper manner till I know just how the case stands."

"It is not curiosity that troubles Miss Butterworth—Madam, I said it was not curiosity—but a laudable desire to have the whole matter arranged with precision," dropped now in his dryest tones from the detective's lips.

"Mr. Gryce has a most excellent understanding of my character," I gravely observed.

The Inspector looked nonplussed. He glanced at Mr. Gryce and he glanced at me, but the smile of the former was inscrutable, and my expression, if I showed any, must have betrayed but little relenting.

"If called as a witness, Miss Butterworth,"—this was how he sought to manage me,—"you will have no choice in the matter. You will be compelled to speak or show contempt of court."

"That is true," I acknowledged. "But it is not what I might feel myself called upon to say then, but what I can say now, that is of interest to you at this present moment. So be generous, gentlemen, and satisfy my curiosity, for such Mr. Gryce considers it, in spite of his assertions to the contrary. Will it not all come out in the papers a few hours hence, and have I not earned as much at your hands as the reporters?"

"The reporters are our bane. Do not liken yourself to the reporters."

"Yet they sometimes give you a valuable clue."

Mr. Gryce looked as if he would like to disclaim this, but he was a judicious soul, and merely gave a twist to the vase which I thought would cost me that small article of vertu.

"Shall we humor Miss Butterworth?" asked the Inspector.

"We will do better," answered Mr. Gryce, setting the vase down with a precision that made me jump; for I am a worshipper of *bric-à-brac*, and prize the few articles I own, possibly beyond their real value. "We will treat her as a coadjutor, which, by the way, she says she is not, and by the trust we place in her, secure that discretionary use of our confidence which she shows with so much spirit in regard to her own."

"Begin then," said I.

"I will," said he, "but first allow me to acknowledge that you are the person who first put us on the track of Franklin Van Burnam."

XXX.
THE MATTER AS STATED BY MR. GRYCE.

I had exhausted my wonder, so I accepted this statement with no more display of surprise than a grim smile.

"When you failed to identify Howard Van Burnam as the man who accompanied his wife into the adjacent house, I realized that I must look elsewhere for the murderer of Louise Van Burnam. You see I had more confidence in the excellence of your memory than you had yourself, so much indeed that I gave you more than one chance to exercise it, having, by certain little methods I sometimes employ, induced different moods in Mr. Van Burnam at the time of his several visits, so that his bearing might vary, and you have every opportunity to recognize him for the man you had seen on that fatal night."

"Then it was he you brought here each time?" I broke in.

"It was he."

"Well!" I ejaculated.

"The Superintendent and some others whom I need not mention,"—here Mr. Gryce took up another small object from the table,—"believed implicitly in his guilt; conjugal murder is so common and the causes which lead to it so frequently puerile. Therefore I had to work alone. But this did not cause me any concern. *Your* doubts emphasized mine, and when you confided to me that you had seen a figure similar to the one we were trying to identify, enter the adjoining house on the evening of the funeral, I made immediate inquiries and discovered that the gentleman who had entered the house right after the four persons described by you was *Franklin Van Burnam*. This gave me a definite clue, and this is why I say that it was you who gave me my first start in this matter."

"Humph!" thought I to myself, as with a sudden shock I remembered that one of the words which had fallen from Miss Oliver's lips during her delirium had been this very name of Franklin.

"I had had my doubts of this gentleman before," continued the detective, warming gradually with his subject. "A man of my experience doubts every one in a case of this kind, and I had formed at odd times a sort of side theory, so to speak, into which some little matters which came up during the inquest seemed to fit with more or less nicety; but I had no real justification for suspicion till the event of which I speak. That you had evidently formed the same theory as myself and were bound to enter into the lists with me, put me on my mettle, madam, and with your knowledge or without it, the struggle between us began."

"So your disdain of me," I here put in with a triumphant air I could not subdue, "was only simulated? I shall know what to think of you hereafter. But don't stop, go on, this is all deeply interesting to me."

"I can understand that. To proceed then; my first duty, of course, was to watch *you*. You had reasons of your own for suspecting this man, so by watching you I hoped to surprise them."

"Good!" I cried, unable to entirely conceal the astonishment and grim amusement into which his continued misconception of the trend of my suspicions threw me.

"But you led us a chase, madam; I must acknowledge that you led us a chase. Your being an amateur led me to anticipate your using an amateur's methods, but you showed skill, madam, and the man I sent to keep watch over Mrs. Boppert against your looked-for visit there, was foiled by the very simple strategy you used in meeting her at a neighboring shop."

"Good!" I again cried, in my relief that the discovery made at that meeting had not been shared by him.

"We had sounded Mrs. Boppert ourselves, but she had seemed a very hopeless job, and I do not yet see how you got any water out of that stone—if you did."

"No?" I retorted ambiguously, enjoying the Inspector's manifest delight in this scene as much as I did my own secret thoughts and the prospect of the surprise I was holding in store for them.

"But your interference with the clock and the discovery you made that it had been going at the time the shelves fell, was not unknown to us, and we have made use of it, good use as you will hereafter see."

"So! those girls could not keep a secret after all," I muttered; and waited with some anxiety to hear him mention the pin-cushion; but he did not, greatly to my relief.

"Don't blame the girls!" he put in (his ears evidently are as sharp as mine); "the inquiries having proceeded from Franklin, it was only natural for me to suspect that he was trying to mislead us by some hocus-pocus story. So *I* visited the girls. That I had difficulty in getting to the root of the matter is to their credit, Miss Butterworth, seeing that you had made them promise secrecy."

"You are right," I nodded, and forgave them on the spot. If I could not withstand Mr. Gryce's eloquence—and it affected me at times—how could I expect these girls to. Besides, they had not revealed the more important secret I had confided to them, and in consideration of this I was ready to pardon them most anything.

"That the clock was going at the time the shelves fell, and that he should be the one to draw our attention to it would seem to the superficial mind proof positive that he was innocent of the deed with which it was so closely associated," the detective proceeded. "But to one skilled in the subterfuges of criminals, this seemingly conclusive fact in his favor was capable of an explanation so in keeping with the subtlety shown in every other feature of this remarkable crime, that I began to regard it as a point against him rather than in his favor. Of which more hereafter.

"Not allowing myself to be deterred, then, by this momentary set-back, and rejoicing in an affair considered as settled by my superiors, I proceeded to establish Franklin Van Burnam's connection with the crime which had been laid with so much apparent reason at his brother's door.

"The first fact to be settled was, of course, whether your identification of him as the gentleman who accompanied his victim into Mr. Van Burnam's house could be corroborated by any of the many persons who had seen the so-called Mr. James Pope at the Hotel D——.

"As none of the witnesses who attended the inquest had presumed to recognize in either of these sleek and haughty gentlemen the shrinking person just mentioned, I knew that any open attempt on my part to bring about an identification would result disastrously. So I employed strategy— like my betters, Miss Butterworth" (here his bow was overpowering in its mock humility); "and rightly considering that for a person to be satisfactorily identified with another, he must be seen under the same circumstances and in nearly the same place, I sought out Franklin Van Burnam, and with specious promises of some great benefit to be done his brother, induced him to accompany me to the Hotel D——.

"Whether he saw through my plans and thought that a brave front and an assumption of candor would best serve him in this unexpected dilemma, or whether he felt so entrenched behind the precautions he had taken as not to fear discovery under any circumstances, he made but one demur before preparing to accompany me. This demur was significant, however, for it was occasioned by my advice to change his dress for one less conspicuously fashionable, or to hide it under an ulster or mackintosh. And as a proof of his hardihood—remember, madam, that his connection with this crime has been established—he actually did put on the ulster, though he must have known what a difference it would make in his appearance.

"The result was all I could desire. As we entered the hotel, I saw a certain hackman start and lean forward to look after him. It was the one who had driven Mr. and Mrs. Pope away from the hotel. And when we passed the porter, the wink which I gave him was met by a lift of his eyelids which he afterwards interpreted into 'Like! very like!'

"But it was from the clerk I received the most unequivocal proof of his identity. On entering the office I had left Mr. Van Burnam as near as possible to the spot where Mr. Pope had stood while his so-called wife was inscribing their names in the register, and bidding him to remain in the background while I had a few words at the desk, all in his brother's interests of course, I succeeded in secretly directing Mr. Henshaw's attention towards him. The start which he gave and the exclamation he uttered were unequivocal. 'Why, there's the man now!' he cried, happily in a whisper. 'Anxious look, drooping head, brown moustache, everything but the duster.' 'Bah!' said I; 'that's Mr. *Franklin* Van Burnam you are looking at! What are you thinking of?' 'Can't help it,' said he; 'I saw both of the brothers at the inquest, and saw nothing in them then to remind me of our late mysterious guest. But as he stands there, he's a —— sight more like James Pope than the other one is, and don't you forget it.' I shrugged my shoulders, told him he was a fool, and that fools had better keep their follies to themselves, and came away with my man, outwardly disgusted but inwardly in most excellent trim for pursuing an investigation which had opened so auspiciously.

"Whether this man possessed any motive for a crime so seemingly out of accordance with his life and disposition was, of course, the next point to settle. His conduct at the inquest certainly showed no decided animosity toward his brother's wife, nor was there on the surface of affairs any token of the mortal hatred which alone could account for a crime at once so deliberate and so brutal. But we detectives plunge below the surface, and after settling the question of Franklin's identity with the so-called Mr. Pope of the Hotel D——, I left New York and its interests—among which I reckoned your efforts at detective work, Miss Butterworth—to a young man in my office, who, I am afraid, did not quite understand the persistence of your character;

for he had nothing to tell me concerning you on my return, save that you had been cultivating Miss Althorpe, which, of course, was such a natural thing for you to do, I wonder he thought it necessary to mention it.

"My destination was Four Corners, the place where Howard first met his future wife. In relating what I learned there, I shall doubtless repeat facts with which you are acquainted, Miss Butterworth."

"That is of no consequence," I returned, with almost brazen duplicity; for I not only was ignorant of what he was going to say, but had every reason to believe that it would bear as remote a connection as possible to the secret then laboring in my breast. "A statement of the case from your lips," I pursued, "will emphasize what I know. Do not stint any of your disclosures, then, I beg. I have an ear for all." This was truer than my rather sarcastic tone would convey, for might not his story after all prove to have some unexpected relation with the facts I had myself gathered together.

"It is a pleasure," said he, "to think I am capable of giving any information to Miss Butterworth, and as I did not run across you or your very nimble and pert little maid during my stay at Four Corners, I shall take it for granted that you confined your inquiries to the city and the society of which you are such a shining light."

This in reference to my double visit at Miss Althorpe's, no doubt.

"Four Corners is a charming town in Southern Vermont, and here, three years ago, Howard Van Burnam first met Miss Stapleton. She was living in a gentleman's family at that time as travelling companion to his invalid daughter."

Ah, now I could see what explanation this wary old detective gave himself of my visits to Miss Althorpe, and began to hug myself in anticipation of my coming triumph over him.

"The place did not fit her, for Miss Stapleton only shone in the society of men; but Mr. Harrison had not yet discovered this special idiosyncrasy of hers, and as his daughter was able to see a few friends, and in fact needed some diversion, the way was open to her companion for that acquaintance with Mr. Van Burnam which has led to such disastrous results.

"The house at which their meeting took place was a private one, and I soon found out many facts not widely known in this city. First, that she was not so much in love with Howard as he was with her. *He* succumbed to her fascinations at once, and proposed, I believe, within two weeks after seeing her; but though she accepted him, few of those who saw them together thought her affections very much engaged till Franklin suddenly appeared in town, when her whole manner underwent a change, and she became so sparklingly and irresistibly beautiful that her avowed lover became doubly enslaved, and Franklin—Well, there is evidence to prove that he was not insensible to her charms either; that, in spite of her engagement to his brother and the attitude which honor bade him hold towards his prospective sister-in-law, he lost his head for a short time at least, and under her seductions I do not doubt, for she was a double-faced woman according to general repute, went so far as to express his passion in a letter of which I heard much before I was so fortunate as to obtain a sight of it. This was three years ago, and I think Miss Stapleton would have been willing to have broken with Howard and married Franklin if the latter had had the courage to meet his brother's reproaches. But he evidently was deficient in this quality. His very letter, which is a warm one, but which holds out no hope to her of any closer bond between them than that offered by her prospective union with his brother, shows that he still retained some sense of honor, and as he presently left Four Corners and did not appear again where they were till just before their marriage, it is probable that all would have gone well if the woman had shared this sentiment with him. But she was made up of mean materials, and while willing to marry Howard for what he could give her or what she thought he could give her, she yet cherished an implacable grudge against Franklin for his weakness, as she called it, in not following the dictates of his heart. Being sly as well as passionate, she hid her feelings from every one but a venial, though apparently devoted confidante, a young girl named — —"

"Oliver," I finished in my own mind.

But the name he mentioned was quite different.

"Pigot," he said, looking at the filigree basket he held in his hand as if he picked this word out from one of its many interstices. "She was French, and after once finding her, I had but little difficulty in learning all she had to tell. She had been Miss Harrison's maid, but she was not above serving Miss Stapleton in many secret and dishonorable ways. As a consequence, she could give me the details of an interview which that lady had held with Franklin Van Burnam on the evening of her wedding. It took place in Mr. Harrison's garden, and was supposed to be a secret one, but the woman who arranged the meeting was not the person to keep away from it when it occurred, and consequently I have been enabled to learn with more or less accuracy what took place between them. It was not to Miss Stapleton's credit. Mr. Van Burnam merely wanted his letter back, but she refused to return it unless he would promise her a complete recognition by his family of her marriage and ensure her a reception in his father's house as Howard's wife. This was more than he could engage himself to perform. He had already, according to his own story, made every effort possible to influence the old gentleman in her favor, but had only succeeded in irritating him against himself. It was an acknowledgment which would have satisfied most women, but it did not satisfy her. She declared her intention of keeping the letter for fear he would cease his exertions; and heedless of the effect produced upon him by the barefaced threat, proceeded to inveigh against his brother for the very love which made her union with him possible; and as if this was not bad enough, showed at the same time such a disposition to profit by whatever worldly good the match promised, that Franklin lost all regard for her, and began to hate her.

"As he made no effort to conceal his feelings, she must have become immediately aware of the change which had taken place in them. But however affected by this, she gave no sign of relenting in her purpose. On the contrary, she persisted in her determination to retain his letter, and when he remonstrated with her and threatened to leave town before her marriage, she retorted by saying that, if he did so, she would show his letter to his brother as soon as the minister had made them one. This threat seemed to affect Franklin deeply, and while it intensified his feeling of animosity towards her, subjected him for the moment to her whim. He stayed in Four Corners till the ceremony was performed, but was such a gloomy guest that all united in saying that he did the occasion no credit.

"So much for my work in Four Corners."

I had by this time become aware that Mr. Gryce was addressing himself chiefly to the Inspector, being gratified no doubt at this opportunity of presenting his case at length before that gentleman. But true to his special habits, he looked at neither of us, but rather at the fretted basket, upon the handle of which he tapped out his arguments as he quickly proceeded:

"The young couple spent the first months of their married life in Yonkers; so to Yonkers I went next. There I learned that Franklin had visited the place twice; both times, as I judge, upon a peremptory summons from her. The result was mutual fret and heartburning, for she had made no progress in her endeavors to win recognition from the Van Burnams; and even had had occasion to perceive that her husband's love, based as it was upon her physical attributes, had begun to feel the stress of her uneasiness and dissatisfaction. She became more anxious than ever for social recognition and distinction, and when the family went to Europe, consented to accompany her husband into the quiet retreat he thought best calculated to win the approbation of his father, only upon the assurance of better times in the fall and a possible visit to Washington in the winter. But the quiet to which she was subjected had a bad effect upon her. Under it she grew more and more restless, and as the time approached for the family's return, conceived so many plans for conciliating them that her husband could not restrain his disgust. But the worst plan of all and the one which undoubtedly led to her death, he never knew. This was to surprise Franklin at his office and, by renewed threats of showing this old love-letter to his brother, win an absolute promise from him to support her in a fresh endeavor to win his father's favor. You see she did not understand Silas Van Burnam's real character, and persisted in holding the most extravagant views concerning Franklin's ascendancy over him as well as over the rest of the family. She even went so far as to insist in the interview, which Jane Pigot overheard, that it was Franklin himself who stood in the way of her desires, and that if he chose he could obtain for her an invitation to take up her abode with the rest of them in Gramercy Park. To Duane Street she therefore went before making her appearance at Mrs. Parker's; a fact which was not brought out at the inquest; Franklin not disclosing it of course, and the clerk not recognizing her under the false name she chose to give. Of the details of this interview I am ignorant, but as she was closeted with him some time, it is only natural to suppose that conversation of some importance took place between them. The clerk who works in the outer office did not, as I have said, know who she was at the time, but he noticed her face when she came out, and he declares that it was insolent with triumph, while Mr. Franklin, who was polite enough or calculating enough to bow her out of the room, was pale with rage, and acted so unlike himself that everybody observed it. She held his letter in her hand, a letter easily distinguishable by the violet-colored seal on the back, and she filliped with it in a most aggravating way as she crossed the floor, pretending to lay it down on Howard's desk as she went by and then taking it up again with an arch look at Franklin, pretty enough to see but hateful in its effect on him. As he went back to his own room his face was full of anger, and such was the effect of this visit on him that he declined to see any one else that day. She had probably shown such determination to reveal his past perfidy to her husband, that his fears were fully aroused at last, and he saw he was not only likely to lose his good name but the esteem with which he was accustomed to be regarded by this younger and evidently much-loved brother.

"And now, considering his intense pride, as well as his affection for Howard, do you not see the motive which this seemingly good man had for putting his troublesome sister-in-law out of existence? He wanted that letter back, and to obtain it had to resort to crime. Or such is my present theory of this murder, Miss Butterworth. Does it correspond with yours?"

XXXI.
SOME FINE WORK.

"O perfectly!" I assented, with just the shade of irony necessary to rob the assertion of its mendacity. "But go on, go on. You have not begun to satisfy me yet. You did not stop with finding a motive for the crime I am sure."

"Madam, you are a female Shylock; you will have the whole of the bond or none."

"We are not here to draw comparisons," I retorted. "Keep to the subject, Mr. Gryce; keep to the subject."

He laughed; laid down the little basket he held, took it up again, and finally resumed:

"Madam, you are right; we did not stop at finding a motive. Our next step was to collect evidence directly connecting him with the crime."

"And you succeeded in this?"

My tone was unnecessarily eager, this was all so unaccountable to me; but he did not appear to notice it.

"We did. Indeed the evidence against him is stronger than that against his brother. For if we ignore the latter part of Howard's testimony, which was evidently a tissue of lies, what remains against him? Three things: his dogged persistency in not recognizing his wife in the murdered woman; the receiving of the house keys from his brother; and the fact that he was seen on the stoop of his father's house at an unusual hour in the morning following this murder. Now what have we against Franklin? Many things.

"First:

"That he can no more account for the hours between half-past eleven on Tuesday morning and five o'clock on the following Wednesday morning than his brother can. In one breath he declares that he was shut up in his rooms at the hotel, for which no corroborative evidence is forthcoming; and in another that he was on a tramp after his brother, which seems equally improbable and incapable of proof.

"Second:

"That he and not Howard was the man in a linen duster, and that he and not Howard was in possession of the keys that night. As these are serious statements to make, I will give you my reasons for them. They are distinct from the recognition of his person by the inmates of the Hotel D——, and added to that recognition, form a strong case against him. The janitor who has charge of the offices in Duane Street, happening to have a leisure moment on the morning of the day on which Mrs. Van Burnam was murdered, was making the most of it by watching the unloading of a huge boiler some four doors below the Van Burnam warehouse. He was consequently looking intently in that direction when Howard passed him, coming from the interview with his brother in which he had been given the keys. Mr. Van Burnam was walking briskly, but finding the sidewalk blocked by the boiler to which I have alluded, paused for a moment to let it pass, and being greatly heated, took out his handkerchief to wipe his forehead. This done, he moved on, just as a man dressed in a long duster came up behind him, stopping where he stopped and picking up from the ground something which the first gentleman had evidently dropped. This last man's figure looked more or less familiar to the janitor, so did the duster, and later he discovered that the latter was the one which he had seen hanging for so long a time in the little disused closet under the warehouse stairs. Its wearer was Franklin Van Burnam, who, as I took pains to learn, had left the office immediately in the wake of his brother, and the object he picked up was the bunch of keys which the latter had inadvertently dropped. He may have thought he lost them later, but it was then and there they slipped from his pocket. I will here add that the duster found by the hackman in his coach has been identified as the one missing from the closet just mentioned.

"Third:

"The keys with which Mr. Van Burnam's house was unlocked were found hanging in their usual place by noon of the next day. They could not have been taken there by Howard, for he was not seen at the office after the murder. By whom then were they returned, if not by Franklin?

"Fourth:

"The letter, for the possession of which I believe this crime to have been perpetrated, was found by us in a supposedly secret drawer of this gentleman's desk. It was much crumpled, and bore evidences of having been rather rudely dealt with since it was last seen in Mrs. Van Burnam's hand in that very office.

"But the fact which is most convincing, and which will tell most heavily against him, is the unexpected discovery of the murdered lady's rings, also in this same desk. How *you* became aware that anything of such importance could be found there, knowing even the exact place in which they were secreted, I will not stop to ask at this moment. Enough that when your maid entered the Van Burnam offices and insisted with so much ingenuousness that she was expected by Mr. Van Burnam and would wait for his return, the clerk most devoted to my interests became distrustful of her intentions, having been told to be on the look-out for a girl in gray or a lady in black with puffs on each side of two very sharp eyes. You will pardon me, Miss Butterworth. He therefore kept his eyes on the girl and presently espied her stretching out her hand towards a hook at the side of Mr. Franklin Van Burnam's desk. As it is upon this hook this gentleman strings his unanswered letters, the clerk rose from his place as quickly as possible, and coming forward with every appearance of polite solicitude, — did she not say he was polite, Miss Butterworth? — inquired what she wished, thinking she was after some letter, or possibly anxious for a specimen of some one's handwriting. But she gave him no other reply than a blush and a confused look, for which you must rebuke her, Miss Butterworth, if you are going to continue to employ her as your agent in these very delicate affairs. And she made another mistake. She should not have left so abruptly upon detection, for that gave the clerk an opportunity to telephone for me, which he immediately did. I was at liberty, and I came at once, and, after hearing his story, decided that what was of interest to you must be of interest to me, and so took a look at the letters she had handled, and discovered, what she also must have discovered before she let them slip from her hand, that the five missing rings we were all in search of were hanging on this same hook amid the sheets of Franklin's correspondence. You can imagine, madam, my satisfaction, and the gratitude which I felt towards my agent, who by his quickness had retained to me the honors of a discovery which it would have been injurious to my pride to have had confined entirely to yourself."

"I can understand," I repeated, and trusted myself to say no more, hot as my secret felt upon my lips.

"You have read Poe's story of the filigree basket?" he now suggested, running his finger up and down the filigree work he himself held.

I nodded. I saw what he meant at once.

"Well, the principle involved in that story explains the presence of the rings in the midst of this stack of letters. Franklin Van Burnam, if he is the murderer of his sister-in-law, is one of the subtlest villains this city has ever produced, and knowing that, if once suspected, every secret drawer and professed hiding-place within his reach would be searched, he put these dangerous evidences of his guilt in a place so conspicuous, and yet so little likely to attract attention, that even so old a hand as myself did not think of looking for them there."

He had finished, and the look he gave me was for myself alone.

"And now, madam," said he, "that I have stated the facts of the case against Franklin Van Burnam, has not the moment come for you to show your appreciation of my good nature by a corresponding show of confidence on your part?"

I answered with a distinct negative. "There is too much that is unexplained as yet in your case against Franklin," I objected. "You have shown that he had motive for the murder and that he was connected more or less intimately with the crime we are considering, but you have by no means explained all the phenomena accompanying this tragedy. How, for instance, do you account for Mrs. Van Burnam's whim in changing her clothing, if her brother-in-law, instead of her husband, was her companion at the Hotel D— —?"

You see I was determined to know the whole story before introducing Miss Oliver's name into this complication.

He who had seen through the devices of so many women in his day did not see through mine, perhaps because he took a certain professional pleasure in making his views on this subject clear to the attentive Inspector. At all events, this is the way he responded to my half-curious, half-ironical question:

"A crime planned and perpetrated for the purpose I have just mentioned, Miss Butterworth, could not have been a simple one under any circumstances. But conceived as this one was by a man of more than ordinary intelligence, and carried out with a skill and precaution little short of marvellous, the features which it presents are of such a varying and subtle character that only by the exercise of a certain amount of imagination can they be understood at all. Such an imagination I possess, but how can I be sure that you do?"

"By testing it," I suggested.

"Very good, madam, I will. Not from actual knowledge, then, but from a certain insight I have acquired in my long dealing with such matters, I have come to the conclusion that Franklin Van Burnam did not in the beginning plan to kill this woman in his father's house.

"On the contrary, he had fixed upon a hotel room as the scene of the conflict he foresaw between them, and that he might carry it on without endangering their good names, had urged her to meet him the next morning in the semi-disguise of a gossamer over her fine dress and a heavy veil over her striking features; making the pretence, no doubt, of this being the more appropriate costume for her to appear in before the old gentleman should he so far concede to her demands as to take her to the steamer. For himself he had planned the adoption of a disfiguring duster which had been hanging for a long time in a closet on the ground-floor of the building in Duane Street. All this promised well, but when the time came and he was about to leave his office, his brother unexpectedly appeared and asked for the key to their father's house. Disconcerted no doubt by the appearance of the very person he least wished to see, and astonished by a request so out of keeping with all that had hitherto passed between them, he nevertheless was in too much haste to question him, so gave him what he wanted and Howard went away. As soon after as he could lock his desk and don his hat, Franklin followed, and merely stopping to cover his coat with the old duster, he went out and hastened towards the place of meeting. Under most circumstances all this might have happened without the brothers encountering each other again, but a temporary obstruction on the sidewalk having, as we know, detained Howard, Franklin was enabled to approach him sufficiently close to see him draw his pocket-handkerchief out of his pocket, and with it the keys which he had just given him. The latter fell, and as there was a great pounding of iron going on in the building just over their heads, Howard did not perceive his loss but went quickly on. Franklin coming up behind him picked up the keys, and with a thought, or perhaps as yet with no thought, of the use to which they might be applied, put them in his own pocket before proceeding on his way.

"New York is a large place, and much can take place in it without comment. Franklin Van Burnam and his sister-in-law met and went together to the Hotel D—— without being either recognized or suspected till later developments drew attention to them. That *she* should consent to accompany him to this place, and that after she was there should submit, as she did, to taking all the business of the scheme upon herself, would be inconceivable in a woman of a self-respecting character; but Louise Van Burnam cared for little save her own aggrandisement, and rather enjoyed, so far as we can see, this very doubtful escapade, whose real meaning and murderous purpose she was so far from understanding.

"As the steamer, contrary to all expectation, had not yet been sighted off Fire Island, they took a room and prepared to wait for it. That is, *she* prepared to wait. He had no intention of waiting for its arrival or of going to it when it came; he only wanted his letter. But Louise Van Burnam was not the woman to relinquish it till she had obtained the price she had put on it, and he becoming very soon aware of this fact, began to ask himself if he should not be obliged to resort to extreme measures in order to regain it. One chance only remained for avoiding these. He would seem to embrace her later and probably much-talked-of scheme of presenting herself before his father in his own house rather than at the steamer; and by urging her to make its success more certain by a different style of dress from that she wore, induce a change of clothing, during which he might come upon the letter he was more than confident she carried about her person. Had this plan worked; had he been able to seize upon this compromising bit of paper, even at the cost of a scratch or two from her vigorous fingers, we should not be sitting here at this moment trying to account for the most complicated crime on record. But Louise Van Burnam, while weak and volatile enough to enjoy the romantic features of this transformation scene, even going so far as to write out the order herself with the same effort at disguise she had used in registering their assumed names at the desk, was not entirely his dupe, and having hidden the letter in her shoe——"

"What!" I cried.

"*Having hidden the letter in her shoe,*" repeated Mr. Gryce, with his finest smile, "she had but to signify that the boots sent by Altman were a size too small, for her to retain her secret and keep the one article she traded upon from his envious clutch. You seem struck dumb by this, Miss Butterworth. Have I enlightened you on a point that has hitherto troubled you?"

"Don't ask me; don't look at me." As if he ever looked at any one! "Your perspicacity is amazing, but I will try and not show my sense of it, if it is going to make you stop."

He smiled; the Inspector smiled: neither understood me.

"Very well then, I will go on; but the non-change of shoes had to be accounted for, Miss Butterworth."

"You are right; and it *has* been, of course."

"Have you any better explanation to give?"

I had, or thought I had, and the words trembled on my tongue. But I restrained myself under an air of great impatience. "Time is flying!" I urged, with as near a simulation of his own manner in saying the words as I could affect. "Go on, Mr. Gryce."

And he did, though my manner evidently puzzled him.

"Being foiled in this his last attempt, this smooth and diabolical villain hesitated no longer in carrying out the scheme which had doubtless been maturing in his mind ever since he dropped the key of his father's house into his own pocket. His brother's wife must die, but not in a hotel room with him for a companion. Though scorned, detested, and a stumbling-block in the way of the whole family's future happiness and prosperity, she still was a Van Burnam, and no shadow must fall upon her reputation. Further than this, for he loved life and his own reputation also, and did not mean to endanger either by this act of self-preservation, she must perish as if from accident, or by some blow so undiscoverable that it would be laid to natural causes. He thought he knew how this might be brought about. He had seen her put on her hat with a very thin and sharp pin, and he had heard how one thrust into a certain spot in the spine would effect death without a struggle. A wound like that would be small; almost indiscernible. True it would take skill to inflict it, and it would require dissimulation to bring her into the proper position for the contemplated thrust; but he was not lacking in either of these characteristics; and so he set himself to the task he had promised himself, and with such success that ere long the two left the hotel and proceeded to the house in Gramercy Park with all the caution necessary for preserving a secret which meant reputation to the one, and liberty, if not life, to the other. That he and not she felt the greater need of secrecy, witness their whole conduct, and when, their goal reached, she and not he put the money into the driver's hand, the last act of this curious drama of opposing motives was reached, and only the final catastrophe was wanting.

"With what arts he procured her hat-pin, and by what show of simulated passion he was able to approach near enough to her to inflict that cool and calculating thrust which resulted in her immediate death, I leave to *your* imagination. Enough that he compassed his ends, killing her and regaining the letter for the possession of which he had been willing to take a life. Afterwards— —"

"Well, afterwards?"

"The deed he had thought so complete began to assume a different aspect. The pin had broken in the wound, and, knowing the scrutiny which the body would receive at the hands of a Coroner's jury, he began to see what consequences might follow its discovery. So to hide that wound and give to her death the wished-for appearance of accident, he went back and drew down the cabinet under which she was found. Had he done this at once his hand in the tragedy might have escaped detection, but he waited, and by waiting allowed the blood-vessels to stiffen and all that phenomena to become apparent by means of which the eyes of the physicians were opened to the fact that they must search deeper for the cause of death than the bruises she had received. Thus it is that Justice opens loop-holes in the finest web a criminal can weave."

"A just remark, Mr. Gryce, but in this fine-spun web of *your* weaving, you have not explained how the clock came to be running and to stop at five."

"Cannot you see? A man capable of such a crime would not forget to provide himself with an alibi. He expected to be in his rooms at five, so before pulling down the shelves at three or four, he wound the clock and set it at an hour when he could bring forward testimony to his being in another place. Is not such a theory consistent with his character and with the skill he has displayed from the beginning to the end of this woful affair?"

Aghast at the deftness with which this able detective explained every detail of this crime by means of a theory necessarily hypothetical if the discoveries I had made in the matter were true, and for the moment subjected to the overwhelming influence of his enthusiasm, I sat in a maze, asking myself if all the seemingly irrefutable evidence upon which men had been convicted in times gone by was as false as this. To relieve myself and to gain renewed confidence in my own views and the discoveries I had made in this matter, I repeated the name of Howard, and asked how, in case the whole crime was conceived and perpetrated by his brother, he came to utter such equivocations and to assume that position of guilt which had led to his own arrest.

"Do you think," I inquired, "that he was aware of his brother's part in this affair, and that out of compassion for him he endeavored to take the crime upon his own shoulders?"

"No, madam. Men of the world do not carry their disinterestedness so far. He not only did not know the part his brother took in this crime, but did not even suspect it, or why acknowledge that he lost the key by which the house was entered?"

"I do not understand Howard's actions, even under these circumstances. They seem totally inconsistent to me."

"Madam, they are easily explainable to one who knows the character of his mind. He prizes his honor above every consideration, and regarded it as threatened by the suggestion that his wife had entered his father's empty house at midnight with another man. To save himself that shame, he was willing not only to perjure himself, but to take upon himself the consequences of his perjury. Quixotic, certainly, but some men are constituted that way, and he, for all his amiable characteristics, is the most dogged man I ever encountered. That he ran against snags in his attempted explanations, seemed to make no difference to him. He was bound that no one should accuse him of marrying a false woman, even if he must bear the opprobrium of her death. It is hard to understand such a nature, but re-read his testimony, and see if this explanation of his conduct is not correct."

And still I mechanically repeated: "I do not understand."

Mr. Gryce may not have been a patient man under all circumstances, but he was patient with me that day.

"It was his ignorance, Miss Butterworth, his total ignorance of the whole affair that led him into the inconsistencies he manifested. Let me present his case as I already have his brother's. He knew that his wife had come to New York to appeal to his father, and he gathered from what she said that she intended to do this either in his house or on the dock. To cut short any opportunity she might have for committing the first folly, he begged the key of the house from his brother, and, supposing that he had it all right, went to his rooms, not to Coney Island as he said, and began to pack up his trunks. For he meant to flee the country if his wife disgraced him. He was tired of her caprices and meant to cut them short as far as he was himself concerned. But the striking of the midnight hour brought better counsel. He began to wonder what she had been doing in his absence. Going out, he haunted the region of Gramercy Park for the better part of the night, and at daybreak actually mounted the steps of his father's house and prepared to enter it by means of the key he had obtained from his brother. But the key was not in his pocket, so he came down again and walked away, attracting the attention of Mr. Stone as he did so. The next day he heard of the tragedy which had taken place within those very walls; and though his first fears led him to believe that the victim was his wife, a sight of her clothes naturally dispelled this apprehension, for he knew nothing of her visit to the Hotel D—— or of the change in her habiliments which had taken place there. His father's persistent fears and the quiet pressure brought to bear upon him by the police only irritated him, and not until confronted by the hat found on the scene of death, an article only too well known as his wife's, did he yield to the accumulated evidence in support of her identity. Immediately he felt the full force of his unkindness towards her, and rushing to the Morgue had her poor body taken to that father's house and afterwards given a decent burial. But he could not accept the shame which this acknowledgment naturally brought with it, and, blind to all consequences, insisted, when brought up again for examination, that he was the man with whom she came to that lonely house. The difficulties into which this plunged him were partly foreseen and partly prepared for, and he showed some skill in surmounting them. But falsehoods never fit like truths, and we all felt the strain on our credulity as he met and attempted to parry the Coroner's questions.

"And now, Miss Butterworth, let me again ask if your turn has not come at last for adding the sum of your evidence to ours against Franklin Van Burnam?"

It had; I could not deny it, and as I realized that with it had also come the opportunity for justifying the pretensions I had made, I raised my head with suitable spirit and, after a momentary pause for the purpose of making my words the more impressive, I asked:

"And what has made you think that *I* was interested in fixing the guilt on Franklin Van Burnam?"

XXXII.
ICONOCLASM.

The surprise which this very simple question occasioned, showed itself differently in the two men who heard it. The Inspector, who had never seen me before, simply stared, while Mr. Gryce, with that admirable command over himself which has helped to make him the most successful man on the force, retained his impassibility, though I noticed a small corner drop from my filigree basket as if crushed off by an inadvertent pressure of his hand.

"I judged," was his calm reply, as he laid down the injured toy with an apologetic grunt, "that the clearing of Howard from suspicion meant the establishment of another man's guilt; and so far as we can see there has been no other party in the case besides these two brothers."

"No? Then I fear a great surprise awaits you, Mr. Gryce. This crime, which you have fixed with such care and seeming probability upon Franklin Van Burnam, was not, in my judgment, perpetrated either by him or any other man. It was the act of a woman."

"A woman?"

Both men spoke: the Inspector, as if he thought me demented; Mr. Gryce, as if he would like to have considered me a fool but dared not.

"Yes, a *woman*," I repeated, dropping a quiet curtsey. It was a proper expression of respect when I was young, and I see no reason why it should not be a proper expression of respect now, except that we have lost our manners in gaining our independence, something which is to be regretted perhaps. "A woman whom I know; a woman whom I can lay my hands on at a half-hour's notice; a young woman, sirs; a pretty woman, the owner of one of the two hats found in the Van Burnam parlors."

Had I exploded a bomb-shell the Inspector could not have looked more astounded. The detective, who was a man of greater self-command, did not betray his feelings so plainly, though he was not entirely without them, for, as I made this statement, he turned and looked at me; *Mr. Gryce* looked at me.

"Both of those hats belonged to Mrs. Van Burnam," he protested; "the one she wore from Haddam; the other was in the order from Altman's."

"She never ordered anything from Altman's," was my uncompromising reply. "The woman whom I saw enter next door, and who was the same who left the Hotel D— — with the man in the linen duster, was not Louise Van Burnam. She was that lady's rival, and let me say it, for I dare to think it, not only her rival but the prospective taker of her life. O you need not shake your heads at each other so significantly, gentlemen. I have been collecting evidence as well as yourselves, and what I have learned is very much to the point; very much, indeed."

"The deuce you have!" muttered the Inspector, turning away from me; but Mr. Gryce continued to eye me like a man fascinated.

"Upon what," said he, "do you base these extraordinary assertions? I should like to hear what that evidence is."

"But first," said I, "I must take a few exceptions to certain points you consider yourself to have made against Franklin Van Burnam. You believe him to have committed this crime because you found in a secret drawer of his desk a letter known to have been in Mrs. Van Burnam's hands the day she was murdered, and which you, naturally enough, I acknowledge, conceive he could only have regained by murdering her. But have you not thought of another way in which he could have obtained it, a perfectly harmless way, involving no one either in deceit or crime? May it not have been in the little hand-bag returned by Mrs. Parker on the morning of the discovery, and may not its crumpled condition be accounted for by the haste with which Franklin might have thrust it into his secret drawer at the untoward entrance of some one into his office?"

"I acknowledge that I have not thought of such a possibility," growled the detective, below his breath, but I saw that his self-satisfaction had been shaken.

"As for any proof of complicity being given by the presence of the rings on the hook attached to his desk, I grieve for your sake to be obliged to dispel that illusion also. Those rings, Mr. Gryce and Mr. Inspector, were not discovered there by the girl in gray, but taken there; and hung there at the very moment your spy saw her hand fumbling with the papers."

"Taken there, and hung there by your maid! By the girl Lena, who has so evidently been working in *your* interests! What sort of a confession are you making, Miss Butterworth?"

"Ah, Mr. Gryce," I gently remonstrated, for I actually pitied the old man in his hour of humiliation, "other girls wear gray besides Lena. It was the woman of the Hotel D— — who played this trick in Mr. Van Burnam's office. Lena was not out of my house that day."

I had never thought Mr. Gryce feeble, though I knew he was over seventy if not very near the octogenarian age. But he drew up a chair at this and hastily sat down.

"Tell me about this other girl," said he.

But before I repeat what I said to him, I must explain by what reasoning I had arrived at the conclusion I have just mentioned. That Ruth Oliver was the visitor in Mr. Van Burnam's office there was but little reason to doubt; that her errand was one in connection with the rings was equally plain. What else would have driven her from her bed when she was hardly able to stand, and sent her in a state of fever, if not delirium, down town to this office?

She feared having these rings found in her possession, and she also cherished a desire to throw whatever suspicion was attached to them upon the man who was already compromised. She may have thought it was Howard's desk she approached, and she may have known it to be Franklin's. On that point I was in doubt, but the rest was clear to me from the moment Mr. Gryce mentioned the girl in gray; and even the spot where she had kept them in the interim since the murder was no longer an unsolved mystery to me. Her emotion when I touched her knitting-work and the shreds of unravelled wool I had found lying about after her departure, had set my wits working, and I comprehended now *that they had been wound up in the ball of yarn I had so carelessly handled.*

But what had I to say to Mr. Gryce in answer to his question. Much; and seeing that further delay was injudicious, I began my story then and there. Prefacing my tale with the suspicions I had always had of Mrs. Boppert, I told them of my interview with that woman and of the valuable clue she had given me by confessing that she had let Mrs. Van Burnam into the house prior to the visit of the couple who entered there at midnight. Knowing what an effect this must produce upon Mr. Gryce, utterly unprepared for it as he was, I looked for some burst of anger on his part, or at least some expression of self-reproach. But he only broke a second piece off my little filigree basket, and, totally unconscious of the demolition he was causing, cried out with true professional delight:

"Well! well! I've always said this was a remarkable case, a very remarkable case; but if we don't look out it will go ahead of that one at Sibley. *Two* women in the affair, and one of them in the house before the arrival of the so-called victim and her murderer! What do you think of that, Inspector? Rather late for us to find out so important a detail, eh?"

"Rather," was the dry reply. At which Mr. Gryce's face grew long and he exclaimed, half shamefacedly, half jocularly:

"Outwitted by a woman! Well, it's a new experience for me, Inspector, and you must not be surprised if it takes me a minute or so to get accustomed to it. A scrub-woman too! It cuts, Inspector, it cuts."

But as I went on, and he learned how I had obtained definite proof of the clock having been not only wound by the lady thus admitted to the house, but set also and that correctly, his face grew even longer, and he gazed quite dolefully at the small figure in the carpet to which he had transferred his attention.

"So! so!" came in almost indistinguishable murmur from his lips. "All my pretty theory in regard to its being set by the criminal for the purpose of confirming his attempt at a false alibi was but a figment of my imagination, eh? Sad! sad! But it was neat enough to have been true, was it not, Inspector?"

"Quite," that gentleman good-humoredly admitted, yet with a shade of irony in his tone that made me suspect that, for all his confidence in and evident admiration for this brilliant old detective, he felt a certain amount of pleasure at seeing him for once at fault. Perhaps it gave him more confidence in his own judgment, seeing that their ideas on this case had been opposed from the start.

"Well! well! I'm getting old; that's what they'll say at Headquarters to-morrow. But go on, Miss Butterworth; let us hear what followed; for I am sure your investigations did not stop there."

I complied with his request with as much modesty as possible. But it was hard to suppress all triumph in face of the unrestrained enthusiasm with which he received my communication. When I told him of the doubts I had formed in regard to the disposal of the packages brought from the Hotel D——, and how to settle those doubts I had taken that midnight walk down Twenty-seventh Street, he looked astonished, his lips worked, and I really expected to see him try to pluck that flower up from the carpet, he ogled it so lovingly. But when I mentioned the lighted laundry and my discoveries there, his admiration burst all bounds, and he cried out, seemingly to the rose in the carpet, really to the Inspector:

"Didn't I tell you she was a woman in a thousand? See now! we ought to have thought of that laundry ourselves; but we didn't, none of us did; we were too credulous and too easily satisfied with the evidence given at the inquest. Well, I'm seventy-seven, but I'm not too old to learn. Proceed, Miss Butterworth."

I admired him and I was sorry for him, but I never enjoyed myself so much in my whole life. How could I help it, or how could I prevent myself from throwing a glance now and then at the picture of my father smiling upon me from the opposite wall?

It was my task now to mention the advertisement I had inserted in the newspapers, and the reflections which had led to my rather daring description of the wandering woman as one dressed thus and so, and *without a hat*. This seemed to strike him—as I had expected it would,—and he interrupted me with a quick slap of his leg, for which only that leg was prepared.

"Good!" he ejaculated; "a fine stroke! The work of a woman of genius! I could not have done better myself, Miss Butterworth. And what came of it? Something, I hope; talent like yours should not go unrewarded."

"Two letters came of it," said I. "One from Cox, the milliner, saying that a bareheaded girl had bought a hat in his shop early on the morning designated; and another from a Mrs. Desberger appointing a meeting at which I obtained a definite clue to this girl, who, notwithstanding she wore Mrs. Van Burnam's clothes from the scene of tragedy, is not Mrs. Van Burnam herself, but a person by the name of Oliver, now to be found at Miss Althorpe's house in Twenty-first Street."

As this was in a measure putting the matter into their hands, I saw them both grow impatient in their anxiety to see this girl for themselves. But I kept them for a few minutes longer while I related my discovery of the money in her shoes, and hinted at the explanation it afforded for her not changing those articles under the influence of the man who accompanied her.

This was the last blow I dealt to the pride of Mr. Gryce. He quivered under it, but soon recovered, and was able to enjoy what he called another fine point in this remarkable case.

But the acme of his delight was reached when I informed him of my ineffectual search for the rings, and my final conclusion that they had been wound up in the ball of yarn attached to her knitting-work.

Whether his pleasure lay chiefly in the talent shown by Miss Oliver in her choice of a hiding-place for these jewels, or in the acumen displayed by myself in discovering it, I do not know; but he evinced an unbounded satisfaction in my words, crying aloud:

"Beautiful! I don't know of anything more interesting! We have not seen the like in years! I can almost congratulate myself upon my mistakes, the features of the case they have brought out are so fine!"

But his satisfaction, great as it was, soon gave way to his anxiety to see this girl who, if not the criminal herself, was so important a factor in this great crime.

I was anxious myself to have him see her, though I feared her condition was not such as to promise him any immediate enlightenment on the doubtful portions of this far from thoroughly mastered problem. And I bade him interview the Chinaman also, and Mrs. Desberger, and even Mrs. Boppert, for I did not wish him to take for granted anything I had said, though I saw he had lost his attitude of disdain and was inclined to accept my opinions quite seriously.

He answered in quite an off-hand manner while the Inspector stood by, but when that gentleman had withdrawn towards the door, Mr. Gryce remarked with more earnestness than he had yet used:

"You have saved me from committing a folly, Miss Butterworth. If I had arrested Franklin Van Burnam to-day, and to-morrow all these facts had come to light, I should never have held up my head again. As it is, there will be numerous insinuations uttered by men on the force, and many a whisper will go about that Gryce is getting old, that Gryce has seen his best days."

"Nonsense!" was my vigorous rejoinder. "You didn't have the clue, that is all. Nor did I get it through any keenness on my part, but from the force of circumstances. Mrs. Boppert thought herself indebted to me, and so gave me her confidence. Your laurels are very safe yet. Besides, there is enough work left on this case to keep more than one great detective like you busy. While the Van Burnams have not been proved guilty, they are not so freed from suspicion that you can regard your task as completed. If Ruth Oliver committed this crime, which of these two brothers was involved in it with her? The facts seem to point towards Franklin, but not so unerringly that no doubt is possible on the subject."

"True, true. The mystery has deepened rather than cleared. Miss Butterworth, you will accompany me to Miss Althorpe's."

XXXIII.
"KNOWN, KNOWN, ALL KNOWN."

Mr. Gryce possesses one faculty for which I envy him, and that is his skill in the management of people. He had not been in Miss Althorpe's house five minutes before he had won her confidence and had everything he wished at his command. *I* had to talk some time before getting so far, but *he*—a word and a look did it.

Miss Oliver, for whom I hesitated to inquire, lest I should again find her gone or in a worse condition than when I left, was in reality better, and as we went up-stairs I allowed myself to hope that the questions which had so troubled us would soon be answered and the mystery ended.

But Mr. Gryce evidently knew better, for when we reached her door he turned and said:

"Our task will not be an easy one. Go in first and attract her attention so that I can enter unobserved. I wish to study her before addressing her; but, mind, no words about the murder; leave that to me."

I nodded, feeling that I was falling back into my own place; and knocking softly entered the room.

A maid was sitting with her. Seeing me, she rose and advanced, saying:

"Miss Oliver is sleeping."

"Then I will relieve you," I returned, beckoning Mr. Gryce to come in.

The girl left us and we two contemplated the sick woman silently. Presently I saw Mr. Gryce shake his head. But he did not tell me what he meant by it.

Following the direction of his finger, I sat down in a chair at the head of the bed; he took his station at the side of it in a large arm-chair he saw there. As he did so I saw how fatherly and kind he really looked, and wondered if he was in the habit of so preparing himself to meet the eye of all the suspected criminals he encountered. The thought made me glance again her way. She lay like a statue, and her face, naturally round but now thinned out and hollow, looked up from the pillow in pitiful quiet, the long lashes accentuating the dark places under her eyes.

A sad face, the saddest I ever saw and one of the most haunting.

He seemed to find it so also, for his expression of benevolent interest deepened with every passing moment, till suddenly she stirred; then he gave me a warning glance, and stooping, took her by the wrist and pulled out his watch.

She was deceived by the action. Opening her eyes, she surveyed him languidly for a moment, then heaving a great sigh, turned aside her head.

"Don't tell me I am better, doctor. I do not want to live."

The plaintive tone, the refined accent, seemed to astonish him. Laying down her hand, he answered gently:

"I do not like to hear that from such young lips, but it assures me that I was correct in my first surmise, that it is not medicine you need but a friend. And I can be that friend if you will but allow me."

Moved, encouraged for the instant, she turned her head from side to side, probably to see if they were alone, and not observing me, answered softly:

"You are very good, very thoughtful, doctor, but"—and here her despair returned again—"it is useless; you can do nothing for me."

"You think so," remonstrated the old detective, "but you do not know me, child. Let me show you that I can be of benefit to you." And he drew from his pocket a little package which he opened before her astonished eyes. "Yesterday, in your delirium, you left these rings in an office down-town. As they are valuable, I have brought them back to you. Wasn't I right, my child?"

"No! no!" She started up, and her accents betrayed terror and anguish, "I do not want them; I cannot bear to see them; they do not belong to *me*; they belong to *them*."

"To *them*? Whom do you mean by them?" queried Mr. Gryce, insinuatingly.

"The—the Van Burnams. Is not that the name? Oh, do not make me talk; I am so weak! Only take the rings back."

"I will, child, I will." Mr. Gryce's voice was more than fatherly now, it was tender, really and sincerely tender. "I will take them back; but to which of the brothers shall I return them? To"—he hesitated softly—"to Franklin or to Howard?"

I expected to hear her respond, his manner was so gentle and apparently sincere. But though feverish and on the verge of wildness, she had still some command over herself, and after giving him a look, the intensity of which called out a corresponding expression on his face, she faltered out:

"I—I don't care; I don't know either of the gentlemen; but to the one you call Howard, I think."

The pause which followed was filled by the tap-tap of Mr. Gryce's fingers on his knee.

"That is the one who is in custody," he observed at last. "The other, that is Franklin, has gone scot-free thus far, I hear."

No answer from her close-shut lips.

He waited.

Still no answer.

"If you do not know either of these gentlemen," he insinuated at last, "how did you come to leave the rings at their office?"

"I knew their names—I inquired my way—It is all a dream now. Please, please do not ask me questions. O doctor! do you not see I cannot bear it?"

He smiled—I never could smile like that under any circumstances—and softly patted her hand.

"I see it makes you suffer," he acknowledged, "but I must make you suffer in order to do you any good. If you would tell me all you know about these rings— —"

She passionately turned away her head.

"I might hope to restore you to health and happiness. You know with what they are associated?"

She made a slight motion.

"And that they are an invaluable clue to the murderer of Mrs. Van Burnam?"

Another motion.

"How then, my child, did *you* come to have them?"

Her head, which was rolling to and fro on the pillow, stopped and she gasped, rather than uttered:

"I was *there*."

He knew this, yet it was terrible to hear it from her lips; she was so young and had such an air of purity and innocence. But more heartrending yet was the groan with which she burst forth in another moment, as if impelled by conscience to unburden herself from some overwhelming load:

"I took them; I could not help it; but I did not keep them; you know that I did not keep them. I am no thief, doctor; whatever I am, I am no thief."

"Yes, yes, I see that. But why take them, child? What were you doing in that house, and whom were you with?"

She threw up her arms, but made no reply.

"Will you not tell?" he urged.

A short silence, then a low "No," evidently wrung from her by the deepest anguish.

Mr. Gryce heaved a sigh; the struggle was likely to be a more serious one than he had anticipated.

"Miss Oliver," said he, "more facts are known in relation to this affair than you imagine. Though unsuspected at first, it has secretly been proven that the man who accompanied the woman into the house where the crime took place, was *Franklin* Van Burnam."

A low gasp from the bed, and that was all.

"You know this to be correct, don't you, Miss Oliver?"

"O must you ask?" She was writhing now, and I thought he must desist out of pure compassion. But detectives are made out of very stern stuff, and though he looked sorry he went inexorably on.

"Justice and a sincere desire to help you, force me, my child. Were you not the woman who entered Mr. Van Burnam's house at midnight with this man?"

"I entered the house."

"At midnight?"

"Yes."

"And with this man?"

Silence.

"You do not speak, Miss Oliver."

Again silence.

"It was Franklin who was with you at the Hotel D——?"

She uttered a cry.

"And it was Franklin who connived at your change of clothing there, and advised or allowed you to dress yourself in a new suit from Altman's?"

"Oh!" she cried again.

"Then why should it not have been he who accompanied you to the Chinaman's, and afterwards took you in a second hack to the house in Gramercy Park?"

"Known, known, all known!" was her moan.

"Sin and crime cannot long remain hidden in this world, Miss Oliver. The police are acquainted with all your movements from the moment you left the Hotel D— —. That is why I have compassion on you. I wish to save you from the consequences of a crime you saw committed, but in which you took no hand."

"O," she exclaimed in one involuntary burst, as she half rose to her knees, "if you could save me from appearing in the matter at all! If you would let me run away— —"

But Mr. Gryce was not the man to give her hope on any such score.

"Impossible, Miss Oliver. You are the only person who can witness for the guilty. If *I* should let you go, the police would not. Then why not tell at once whose hand drew the hat-pin from your hat and— —"

"Stop!" she shrieked; "stop! you kill me! I cannot bear it! If you bring that moment back to my mind I shall go mad! I feel the horror of it rising in me now! Be still! I pray you, for God's sake, to be still!"

This was mortal anguish; there was no acting in this. Even he was startled by the emotion he had raised, and sat for a moment without speaking. Then the necessity of providing against all further mistakes by fixing the guilt where it belonged, drove him on again, and he said:

"Like many another woman before you, you are trying to shield a guilty man at your own expense. But it is useless, Miss Oliver; the truth always comes to light. Be advised, then, and make a confidant of one who understands you better than you think."

But she would not listen to this.

"No one understands me. I do not understand myself. I only know that I shall make a confidant of no one; that I shall never speak." And turning from him, she buried her head in the bedclothes.

To most men her tone and the action which accompanied it would have been final. But Mr. Gryce possessed great patience. Waiting for just a moment till she seemed more composed, he murmured gently:

"Not if you must suffer more from your silence than from speaking? Not if men—I do not mean myself, child, for I am your friend—will think that *you* are to blame for the death of the woman whom you saw fall under a cruel stab, and whose rings you have?"

"*I!*" Her horror was unmistakable; so were her surprise, her terror, and her shame, but she added nothing to the word she had uttered, and he was forced to say again:

"The world, and by that I mean both good people and bad, will believe all this. *He* will let them believe all this. Men have not the devotion of women."

"Alas! alas!" It was a murmur rather than a cry, and she trembled so the bed shook visibly under her. But she made no response to the entreaty in his look and gesture, and he was compelled to draw back unsatisfied.

When a few heavy minutes had passed, he spoke again, this time in a tone of sadness.

"Few men are worth such sacrifices, Miss Oliver, and a criminal never. But a woman is not moved by that thought. She should be moved by this, however. If either of these brothers is to blame in this matter, consideration for the guiltless one should lead you to mention the name of the guilty."

But even this did not visibly affect her.

"I shall mention no names," said she.

"A sign will answer."

"I shall make no sign."

"Then Howard must go to his trial?"

A gasp, but no words.

"And Franklin proceed on his way undisturbed?"

She tried not to answer, but the words would come. Pray God! I may never see such a struggle again.

"That is as God wills. I can do nothing in the matter." And she sank back crushed and wellnigh insensible.

Mr. Gryce made no further effort to influence her.

XXXIV.
EXACTLY HALF-PAST THREE.

"She is more unfortunate than wicked," was Mr. Gryce's comment as we stepped into the hall. "Nevertheless, watch her closely, for she is in just the mood to do herself a mischief. In an hour, or at the most two, I shall have a woman here to help you. You can stay till then?"

"All night, if you say so."

"That you must settle with Miss Althorpe. As soon as Miss Oliver is up I shall have a little scheme to propose, by means of which I hope to arrive at the truth of this affair. I must know which of these two men she is shielding."

"Then you think she did not kill Mrs. Van Burnam herself?"

"I think the whole matter one of the most puzzling mysteries that has ever come to the notice of the New York police. We are sure that the murdered woman was Mrs. Van Burnam, that this girl was present at her death, and that she availed herself of the opportunity afforded by that death to make the exchange of clothing which has given such a complicated twist to the whole affair. But beyond these facts, we know little more than that it was Franklin Van Burnam who took her to the Gramercy Park house, and Howard who was seen in that same vicinity some two or four hours later. But on which of these two to fix the responsibility of Mrs. Van Burnam's death, is the question."

"She had a hand in it herself," I persisted; "though it may have been without evil intent. No man ever carried that thing through without feminine help. To this opinion I shall stick, much as this girl draws upon my sympathies."

"I shall not try to persuade you to the contrary. But the point is to find out how much help, and to whom it was given."

"And your scheme for doing this?"

"Cannot be carried out till she is on her feet again. So cure her, Miss Butterworth, cure her. When she can go down-stairs, Ebenezer Gryce will be on the scene to test his little scheme."

I promised to do what I could, and when he was gone, I set diligently to work to soothe the child, as he had called her, and get her in trim for the delicate meal which had been sent up. And whether it was owing to a change in my own feelings, or whether the talk with Mr. Gryce had so unnerved her that any womanly ministration was welcome, she responded much more readily to my efforts than ever before, and in a little while lay in so calm and grateful a mood that I was actually sorry to see the nurse when she came. Hoping that something might spring from an interview with Miss Althorpe whereby my departure from the house might be delayed, I descended to the library, and was fortunate enough to find the mistress of the house there. She was sorting invitations, and looked anxious and worried.

"You see me in a difficulty, Miss Butterworth. I had relied on Miss Oliver to oversee this work, as well as to assist me in a great many other details, and I don't know of any one whom I can get on short notice to take her place. My own engagements are many and— —"

"Let me help you," I put in, with that cheerfulness her presence invariably inspires. "I have nothing pressing calling me home, and for once in my life I should like to take an active part in wedding festivities. It would make me feel quite young again."

"But— —" she began.

"Oh," I hastened to say, "you think I would be more of a hindrance to you than a help; that I would do the work, perhaps, but in my own way rather than in yours. Well, that would doubtless have been true of me a month since, but I have learned a great deal in the last few weeks,—you will not ask me how,—and now I stand ready to do your work in your way, and to take a great deal of pleasure in it too."

"Ah, Miss Butterworth," she exclaimed, with a burst of genuine feeling which I would not have lost for the world, "I always knew that you had a kind heart; and I am going to accept your offer in the same spirit in which it is made."

So that was settled, and with it the possibility of my spending another night in this house.

At ten o'clock I stole away from the library and the delightful company of Mr. Stone, who had insisted upon sharing my labors, and went up to Miss Oliver's room. I met the nurse at the door.

"You want to see her," said she. "She's asleep, but does not rest very easily. I don't think I ever saw so pitiful a case. She moans continually, but not with physical pain. Yet she seems to have courage too; for now and then she starts up with a loud cry. Listen."

I did so, and this is what I heard:

"I do not want to live; doctor, I do not want to live; why do you try to make me better?"

"That is what she is saying all the time. Sad, isn't it?"

I acknowledged it to be so, but at the same time wondered if the girl were not right in wishing for death as a relief from her troubles.

Early the next morning I inquired at her door again. Miss Oliver was better. Her fever had left her, and she wore a more natural look than at any time since I had seen her. But it was not an untroubled one, and it was with difficulty I met her eyes when she asked if they were coming for her that day, and if she could see Miss Althorpe before she left. As she was not yet able to leave her bed I could easily answer her first question, but I knew too little of Mr. Gryce's intentions to be able to reply to the second. But I was easy with this suffering woman, very easy, more easy than I ever supposed I could be with any one so intimately associated with crime.

She seemed to accept my explanations as readily as she already had my presence, and I was struck again with surprise as I considered that my name had never aroused in her the least emotion.

"Miss Althorpe has been so good to me I should like to thank her; from my despairing heart, I should like to thank her," she said to me as I stood by her side before leaving. "Do you know"—she went on, catching me by the dress as I was turning away—"what kind of a man she is going to marry? She has such a loving heart, and marriage is such a fearful risk."

"Fearful?" I repeated.

"Is it not fearful? To give one's whole soul to a man and be met by—I must not talk of it; I must not think of it—But is he a good man? Does he love Miss Althorpe? Will she be happy? I have no right to ask, perhaps, but my gratitude towards her is such that I wish her every joy and pleasure."

"Miss Althorpe has chosen well," I rejoined. "Mr. Stone is a man in ten thousand."

The sigh that answered me went to my heart.

"I will pray for her," she murmured; "that will be something to live for."

I did not know what reply to make to this. Everything which this girl said and did was so unexpected and so convincing in its sincerity, I felt moved by her even against my better judgment. I pitied her and yet I dared not urge her on to speak, lest I should fail in my task of making her well. I therefore confined myself to a few haphazard expressions of sympathy and encouragement, and left her in the hands of the nurse.

Next day Mr. Gryce called.

"Your patient is better," said he.

"Much better," was my cheerful reply. "This afternoon she will be able to leave the house."

"Very good; have her down at half-past three and I will be in front with a carriage."

"I dread it," I cried; "but I will have her there."

"You are beginning to like her, Miss Butterworth. Take care! You will lose your head if your sympathies become engaged."

"It sits pretty firmly on my shoulders yet," I retorted; "and as for sympathies, you are full of them yourself. I saw how you looked at her yesterday."

"Bah, *my* looks!"

"You cannot deceive me, Mr. Gryce; you are as sorry for the girl as you can be; and so am I too. By the way, I do not think I should speak of her as a girl. From something she said yesterday I am convinced she is a married woman; and that her husband— —"

"Well, madam?"

"I will not give him a name, at least not before your scheme has been carried out. Are you ready for the undertaking?"

"I will be this afternoon. At half-past three she is to leave the house. Not a minute before and not a minute later. Remember."

XXXV.
A RUSE.

It was a new thing for me to enter into any scheme blindfold. But the past few weeks had taught me many lessons and among them to trust a little in the judgment of others.

Accordingly I was on hand with my patient at the hour designated, and, as I supported her trembling steps down the stairs, I endeavored not to betray the intense interest agitating me, or to awaken by my curiosity any further dread in her mind than that involved by her departure from this home of bounty and good feeling, and her entrance upon an unknown and possibly much to be apprehended future.

Mr. Gryce was awaiting us in the lower hall, and as he caught sight of her slender figure and anxious face his whole attitude became at once so protecting and so sympathetic, I did not wonder at her failure to associate him with the police.

As she stepped down to his side he gave her a genial nod.

"I am glad to see you so far on the road to recovery," he remarked. "It shows me that my prophecy is correct and that in a few days you will be quite yourself again."

She looked at him wistfully.

"You seem to know so much about me, doctor, perhaps you can tell me where they are going to take me."

He lifted a tassel from a curtain near by, looked at it, shook his head at it, and inquired quite irrelevantly:

"Have you bidden good-bye to Miss Althorpe?"

Her eyes stole towards the parlors and she whispered as if half in awe of the splendor everywhere surrounding her:

"I have not had the opportunity. But I should be sorry to go without a word of thanks for her goodness. Is she at home?"

The tassel slipped from his hand.

"You will find her in a carriage at the door. She has an engagement out this afternoon, but wishes to say good-bye to you before leaving."

"Oh, how kind she is!" burst from the girl's white lips; and with a hurried gesture she was making for the door when Mr. Gryce stepped before her and opened it.

Two carriages were drawn up in front, neither of which seemed to possess the elegance of so rich a woman's equipage. But Mr. Gryce appeared satisfied, and pointing to the nearest one, observed quietly:

"You are expected. If she does not open the carriage door for you, do not hesitate to do it yourself. She has something of importance to say to you."

Miss Oliver looked surprised, but prepared to obey him. Steadying herself by the stone balustrade, she slowly descended the steps and advanced towards the carriage. I watched her from the doorway and Mr. Gryce from the vestibule. It seemed an ordinary situation, but something in the latter's face convinced me that interests of no small moment depended upon the interview about to take place.

But before I could decide upon their nature or satisfy myself as to the full meaning of Mr. Gryce's manner, she had started back from the carriage door and was saying to him in a tone of modest embarrassment:

"There is a gentleman in the carriage; you must have made some mistake."

Mr. Gryce, who had evidently expected a different result from his stratagem, hesitated for a moment, during which I felt that he read her through and through; then he responded lightly:

"I made a mistake, eh? Oh, possibly. Look in the other carriage, my child."

With an unaffected air of confidence she turned to do so, and I turned to watch her, for I began to understand the "scheme" at which I was assisting, and foresaw that the emotion she had failed to betray at the door of the first carriage might not necessarily be lacking on the opening of the second.

I was all the more assured of this from the fact that Miss Althorpe's stately figure was very plainly to be seen at that moment, not in the coach Miss Oliver was approaching, but in an elegant victoria just turning the corner.

My expectations were realized; for no sooner had the poor girl swung open the door of the second hack, than her whole body succumbed to a shock so great that I expected to see her fall in a heap on the pavement. But she steadied herself up with a determined effort, and with a sudden movement full of subdued fury, jumped into the carriage and violently shut the door just as the first carriage drove off to give place to Miss Althorpe's turn-out.

"Humph!" sprang from Mr. Gryce's lips in a tone so full of varied emotions that it was with difficulty I refrained from rushing down the stoop to see for myself who was the occupant of the coach into which my late patient had so passionately precipitated herself. But the sight of Miss Althorpe being helped to the ground by her attendant lover, recalled me so suddenly to my own anomalous position on her stoop, that I let my first impulse pass and concerned myself instead with the formation of those apologies I thought necessary to the occasion. But those apologies were never uttered. Mr. Gryce, with the infinite tact he displays in all serious emergencies, came to my rescue, and so distracted Miss Althorpe's attention that she failed to observe that she had interrupted a situation of no small moment.

Meanwhile the coach containing Miss Oliver had, at a signal from the wary detective, drawn off in the wake of the first one, and I had the doubtful satisfaction of seeing them both roll down the street without my having penetrated the secret of either.

A glance from Mr. Stone, who had followed Miss Althorpe up the stoop, interrupted Mr. Gryce's flow of eloquence, and a few minutes later I found myself making those adieux which I had hoped to avoid by departing in Miss Althorpe's absence. Another instant and I was hastening down the street in the direction taken by the two carriages, one of which had paused at the corner a few rods off.

But, spry as I am for one of my settled habits and sedate character, I found myself passed by Mr. Gryce; and when I would have accelerated my steps, he darted forward quite like a boy and, without a word of explanation or any acknowledgment of the mutual understanding which certainly existed between us, leaped into the carriage I was endeavoring to reach, and was driven away. But not before I caught a glimpse of Miss Oliver's gray dress inside.

Determined not to be baffled by this man, I turned about and followed the other carriage. It was approaching a crowded part of the avenue, and in a few minutes I had the gratification of seeing it come to a standstill only a few feet from the curb-stone. The opportunity thus afforded me of satisfying my curiosity was not to be slighted. Without pausing to consider consequences or to question the propriety of my conduct, I stepped boldly up in front of its half-lowered window and looked in. There was but one person inside, and that person was Franklin Van Burnam.

What was I to conclude from this? That the occupant of the other carriage was Howard, and that Mr. Gryce now knew with which of the two brothers Miss Oliver's memories were associated.

BOOK IV.
THE END OF A GREAT MYSTERY.

XXXVI.
THE RESULT.

I was as much surprised at this result of Mr. Gryce's scheme as he was, and possibly I was more chagrined. But I shall not enter into my feelings on the subject, or weary you any further with my conjectures. You will be much more interested, I know, in learning what occurred to Mr. Gryce upon entering the carriage holding Miss Oliver.

He had expected, from the intense emotion she displayed at the sight of Howard Van Burnam (for I was not mistaken as to the identity of the person occupying the carriage with her), to find her flushed with the passions incident upon this meeting, and her companion in a condition of mind which would make it no longer possible for him to deny his connection with this woman and his consequently guilty complicity in a murder to which both were linked by so many incriminating circumstances.

But for all his experience, the detective was disappointed in this expectation, as he had been in so many others connected with this case. There was nothing in Miss Oliver's attitude to indicate that she had unburdened herself of any of the emotions with which she was so grievously agitated, nor was there on Mr. Van Burnam's part any deeper manifestation of feeling than a slight glow on his cheek, and even that disappeared under the detective's scrutiny, leaving him as composed and imperturbable as he had been in his memorable inquisition before the Coroner.

Disappointed, and yet in a measure exhilarated by this sudden check in plans he had thought too well laid for failure, Mr. Gryce surveyed the young girl more carefully, and saw that he had not been mistaken in regard to the force or extent of the feelings which had driven her into Mr. Van Burnam's presence; and turning back to that gentleman, was about to give utterance to some very pertinent remarks, when he was forestalled by Mr. Van Burnam inquiring, in his old calm way, which nothing seemed able to disturb:

"Who is this crazy girl you have forced upon me? If I had known I was to be subjected to such companionship I should not have regarded my outing so favorably."

Mr. Gryce, who never allowed himself to be surprised by anything a suspected criminal might do or say, surveyed him quietly for a moment, then turned towards Miss Oliver.

"You hear what this gentleman calls you?" said he.

Her face was hidden by her hands, but she dropped them as the detective addressed her, showing a countenance so distorted by passion that it stopped the current of his thoughts, and made him question whether the epithet bestowed upon her by their somewhat callous companion was entirely unjustified. But soon the something else which was in her face restored his confidence in her sanity, and he saw that while her reason might be shaken it was not yet dethroned, and that he had good cause to expect sooner or later some action from a woman whose misery could wear an aspect of such desperate resolution.

That he was not the only one affected by the force and desperate character of her glance became presently apparent, for Mr. Van Burnam, with a more kindly tone than he had previously used, observed quietly:

"I see the lady is suffering. I beg pardon for my inconsiderate words. I have no wish to insult the unhappy."

Never was Mr. Gryce so nonplussed. There was a mingled courtesy and composure in the speaker's manner which was as far removed as possible from that strained effort at self-possession which marks suppressed passion or secret fear; while in the vacant look with which she met these words there was neither anger nor scorn nor indeed any of the passions one would expect to see there. The detective consequently did not force the situation, but only watched her more and more attentively till her eyes fell and she crouched away from them both. Then he said:

"You can name this gentleman, can you not, Miss Oliver, even if he does not choose to recognize *you?*"

But her answer, if she made one, was inaudible, and the sole result which Mr. Gryce obtained from this venture was a quick look from Mr. Van Burnam and the following uncompromising words from his lips:

"If you think this young girl knows me, or that I know her, you are greatly mistaken. She is as much of a stranger to me as I am to her, and I take this opportunity of saying so. I hope my liberty and good name are not to be made dependent upon the word of a miserable waif like this."

"Your liberty and your good name will depend upon your innocence," retorted Mr. Gryce, and said no more, feeling himself at a disadvantage before the imperturbability of this man and the silent, non-accusing attitude of this woman, from the shock of whose passions he had anticipated so much and obtained so little.

Meantime they were moving rapidly towards Police Headquarters, and fearing that the sight of that place might alarm Miss Oliver more than was well for her, he strove again to rouse her by a kindly word or so. But it was useless. She evidently tried to pay attention and follow the words he used, but her thoughts were too busy over the one great subject that engrossed her.

"A bad case!" murmured Mr. Van Burnam, and with the phrase seemed to dismiss all thought of her.

"A bad case!" echoed Mr. Gryce, "but," seeing how fast the look of resolution was replacing her previous aspect of frenzy, "one that will do mischief yet to the man who has deceived her."

The stopping of the carriage roused her. Looking up, she spoke for the first time.

"I want a police officer," she said.

Mr. Gryce, with all his assurance restored, leaped to the ground and held out his hand.

"I will take you into the presence of one," said he; and she, without a glance at Mr. Van Burnam, whose knee she brushed in passing, leaped to the ground, and turned her face towards Police Headquarters.

XXXVII.
"TWO WEEKS!"

But before she was well in, her countenance changed.

"No," said she, "I want to think first. Give me time to think. I dare not say a word without thinking."

"Truth needs no consideration. If you wish to denounce this man— —"

Her look said she did.

"Then now is the time."

She gave him a sharp glance; the first she had bestowed upon him since leaving Miss Althorpe's.

"You are no doctor," she declared. "Are you a police-officer?"

"I am a detective."

"Oh!" and she hesitated for a moment, shrinking from him with very natural distrust and aversion. "I have been in the toils then without knowing it; no wonder I am caught. But I am no criminal, sir; and if you are the one most in authority here, I beg the privilege of a few words with you before I am put into confinement."

"I will take you before the Superintendent," said Mr. Gryce. "But do you wish to go alone? Shall not Mr. Van Burnam accompany you?"

"Mr. Van Burnam?"

"Is it not he you wish to denounce?"

"I do not wish to denounce any one to-day."

"What do you wish?" asked Mr. Gryce.

"Let me see the man who has power to hold me here or let me go, and I will tell him."

"Very well," said Mr. Gryce, and led her into the presence of the Superintendent.

She was at this moment quite a different person from what she had been in the carriage. All that was girlish in her aspect or appealing in her bearing had faded away, evidently forever, and left in its place something at once so desperate and so deadly, that she seemed not only a woman but one of a very determined and dangerous nature. Her manner, however, was quiet, and it was only in her eye that one could see how near she was to frenzy.

She spoke before the Superintendent could address her.

"Sir," said she, "I have been brought here on account of a fearful crime I was unhappy enough to witness. I myself am innocent of that crime, but, so far as I know, there is no other person living save the guilty man who committed it, who can tell you how or why or by whom it was done. One man has been arrested for it and another has not. If you will give me two weeks of complete freedom, I will point out to you which is the veritable man of blood, and may Heaven have mercy on his soul!"

"She is mad," signified the Superintendent in by-play to Mr. Gryce.

But the latter shook his head; she was not mad yet.

"I know," she continued, without a hint of the timidity which seemed natural to her under other circumstances, "that this must seem a presumptuous request from one like me, but it is only by granting it that you will ever be able to lay your hand on the murderer of Mrs. Van Burnam. For I will never speak if I cannot speak in my own way and at my own time. The agonies I have suffered must have some compensation. Otherwise I should die of horror and my grief."

"And how do you hope to gain compensation by this delay?" expostulated the Superintendent. "Would you not meet with more satisfaction in denouncing him here and now before he can pass another night in fancied security?"

But she only repeated: "I have said two weeks, and two weeks I must have. Two weeks in which to come and go as I please. Two weeks!" And no argument they could advance succeeded in eliciting from her any other response or in altering in any way her air of quiet determination with its underlying suggestion of frenzy.

Acknowledging their mutual defeat by a look, the Superintendent and detective drew off to one side, and something like the following conversation took place between them.

"You think she's sane?"

"I do."

"And will remain so two weeks?"

"If humored."

"You are sure she is implicated in this crime?"

"She was a witness to it."

"And that she speaks the truth when she declares that she is the only person who can point out the criminal?"

"Yes; that is, she is the only one who will do it. The attitude taken by the Van Burnams, especially by Howard just now in the presence of this girl, shows how little we have to expect from them."

"Yet you think they know as much as she does about it?"

"I do not know what to think. For once I am baffled, Superintendent. Every passion which this woman possesses was roused by her unexpected meeting with Howard Van Burnam, and yet their indifference when confronted, as well as her present action, seems to argue a lack of connection between them which overthrows at once the theory of his guilt. Was it the sight of Franklin, then, which really affected her? and was her apparent indifference at meeting him only an evidence of her self-control? It seems an impossible conclusion to draw, and indeed there are nothing but hitches and improbable features in this case. Nothing fits; nothing jibes. I get just so far in it and then I run up against a wall. Either there is a superhuman power of duplicity in the persons who contrived this murder or we are on the wrong tack altogether."

"In other words, you have tried every means known to you to get at the truth of this matter, and failed."

"I have, sir; sorry as I may be to acknowledge it."

"Then we must accept her terms. She can be shadowed?"

"Every moment."

"Very well, then. Extreme cases must be met by extreme measures. We will let her have her swing, and see what comes of it. Revenge is a great weapon in the hands of a determined woman, and from her look I think she will make the most of it."

And returning to where the young girl stood, the Superintendent asked her whether she felt sure the murderer would not escape in the time that must elapse before his apprehension.

Instantly her cheek, which had looked as if it could never show color again, flushed a deep and painful scarlet, and she cried vehemently:

"If any hint of what is here passing should reach him I should be powerless to prevent his flight. Swear, then, that my very existence shall be kept a secret between you two, or I will do nothing towards his apprehension,—no, not even to save the innocent."

"We will not swear, but we will promise," returned the Superintendent. "And now, when may we expect to hear from you again?"

"Two weeks from to-night as the clock strikes eight. Be wherever I may chance to be at that hour, and see on whose arm I lay my hand. It will be that of the man who killed Mrs. Van Burnam."

XXXVIII.
A WHITE SATIN GOWN.

The events just related did not come to my knowledge for some days after they occurred, but I have recorded them at this time that I might in some way prepare you for an interview which shortly after took place between myself and Mr. Gryce.

I had not seen him since our rather unsatisfactory parting in front of Miss Althorpe's house, and the suspense which I had endured in the interim made my greeting unnecessarily warm. But he took it all very naturally.

"You are glad to see me," said he; "been wondering what has become of Miss Oliver. Well, she is in good hands; with Mrs. Desberger, in short; a woman whom I believe you know."

"With Mrs. Desberger?" I *was* surprised. "Why, I have been looking every day in the papers for an account of her arrest."

"No doubt," he answered. "But we police are slow; we are not ready to arrest her yet. Meanwhile you can do us a favor. She wants to see you; are you willing to visit her?"

My answer contained but little of the curiosity and eagerness I really felt.

"I am always at your command. Do you wish me to go now?"

"Miss Oliver is impatient," he admitted. "Her fever is better, but she is in an excited condition of mind which makes her a little unreasonable. To be plain, she is not quite herself, and while we still hope something from her testimony, we are leaving her very much to her own devices, and do not cross her in anything. You will therefore listen to what she says, and, if possible, aid her in anything she may undertake, unless it points directly towards self-destruction. My opinion is that she will surprise you. But you are becoming accustomed to surprises, are you not?"

"Thanks to you, I am."

"Very well, then, I have but one more suggestion to make. You are working for the police now, madam, and nothing that you see or learn in connection with this girl is to be kept back from us. Am I understood?"

"Perfectly; but it is only proper for me to retort that I am not entirely pleased with the part you assign me. Could you not have left thus much to my good sense, and not put it into so many words?"

"Ah, madam, the case at present is too serious for risks of that kind. Mr. Van Burnam's reputation, to say nothing of his life, depends upon our knowledge of this girl's secret; surely you can stretch a point in a matter of so much moment?"

"I have already stretched several, and I can stretch one more, but I hope the girl won't look at me too often with those miserable appealing eyes of hers; they make me feel like a traitor."

"You will not be troubled by any appeal in them. The appeal has vanished; something harder and even more difficult to meet is to be found in them now: wrath, purpose, and a desire for vengeance. She is not the same woman, I assure you."

"Well," I sighed, "I am sorry; there is something about the girl that lays hold of me, and I hate to see such a change in her. Did she ask for me by name?"

"I believe so."

"I cannot understand her wanting me, but I will go; and I won't leave her either till she shows me she is tired of me. I am as anxious to see the end of this matter as you are." Then, with some vague idea that I had earned a right to some show of confidence on his part, I added insinuatingly: "I supposed you would feel the case settled when she almost fainted at the sight of the younger Mr. Van Burnam."

The old ambiguous smile I remembered so well came to modify his brusque rejoinder.

"If she had been a woman like you, I should; but she is a deep one, Miss Butterworth; too deep for the success of a little ruse like mine. Are you ready?"

I was not, but it did not take me long to be so, and before an hour had elapsed I was seated in Mrs. Desberger's parlor in Ninth Street. Miss Oliver was in, and ere long made her appearance. She was dressed in street costume.

I was prepared for a change in her, and yet the shock I felt when I first saw her face must have been apparent, for she immediately remarked:

"You find me quite well, Miss Butterworth. For this I am partially indebted to you. You were very good to nurse me so carefully. Will you be still kinder, and help me in a new matter which I feel quite incompetent to undertake alone?"

Her face was flushed, her manner nervous, but her eyes had an extraordinary look in them which affected me most painfully, notwithstanding the additional effect it gave to her beauty.

"Certainly," said I. "What can I do for you?"

"I wish to buy me a dress," was her unexpected reply. "A handsome dress. Do you object to showing me the best shops? I am a stranger in New York."

More astonished than I can express, but carefully concealing it in remembrance of the caution received from Mr. Gryce, I replied that I would be only too happy to accompany her on such an errand. Upon which she lost her nervousness and prepared at once to go out with me.

"I would have asked Mrs. Desberger," she observed while fitting on her gloves, "but her taste"—here she cast a significant look about the room—"is not quiet enough for me."

"I should think not!" I cried.

"I shall be a trouble to you," the girl went on, with a gleam in her eye that spoke of the restless spirit within. "I have many things to buy, and they must all be rich and handsome."

"If you have money enough, there will be no trouble about that."

"Oh, I have money." She spoke like a millionaire's daughter. "Shall we go to Arnold's?"

As I always traded at Arnold's, I readily acquiesced, and we left the house. But not before she had tied a very thick veil over her face.

"If we meet any one, do not introduce me," she begged. "I cannot talk to people."

"You may rest easy," I assured her.

At the corner she stopped. "Is there any way of getting a carriage?" she asked.

"Do you want one?"

"Yes."

I signalled a hack.

"Now for the dress!" she cried.

We rode at once to Arnold's.

"What kind of a dress do you want?" I inquired as we entered the store.

"An evening one; a white satin, I think."

I could not help the exclamation which escaped me; but I covered it up as quickly as possible by a hurried remark in favor of white, and we proceeded at once to the silk counter.

"I will trust it all to you," she whispered in an odd, choked tone as the clerk approached us. "Get what you would for your daughter—no, no! for Mr. Van Burnam's daughter, if he has one, and do not spare expense. I have five hundred dollars in my pocket."

Mr. Van Burnam's daughter! Well, well! A tragedy of some kind was portending! But I bought the dress.

"Now," said she, "lace, and whatever else I need to make it up suitably. And I must have slippers and gloves. You know what a young girl requires to make her look like a lady. I want to look so well that the most critical eye will detect no fault in my appearance. It can be done, can it not, Miss Butterworth? My face and figure will not spoil the effect, will they?"

"No," said I; "you have a good face and a beautiful figure. You ought to look well. Are you going to a ball, my dear?"

"I am going to a ball," she answered; but her tone was so strange the people passing us turned to look at her.

"Let us have everything sent to the carriage," said she, and went with me from counter to counter with her ready purse in her hand, but not once lifting her veil to look at what was offered us, saying over and over as I sought to consult her in regard to some article: "Buy the richest; I leave it all to you."

Had Mr. Gryce not told me she must be humored, I could never have gone through this ordeal. To see a girl thus expend her hoarded savings on such frivolities was absolutely painful to me, and more than once I was tempted to decline any further participation in such extravagance. But a thought of my obligations to Mr. Gryce restrained me, and I went on spending the poor girl's dollars with more pain to myself than if I had taken them out of my own pocket.

Having purchased all the articles we thought necessary, we were turning towards the door when Miss Oliver whispered:

"Wait for me in the carriage for just a few minutes. I have one more thing to buy, and I must do it alone."

"But——" I began.

"I will do it, and I will not be followed," she insisted, in a shrill tone that made me jump.

And seeing no other way of preventing a scene, I let her leave me, though it cost me an anxious fifteen minutes.

When she rejoined me, as she did at the expiration of that time, I eyed the bundle she held with decided curiosity. But I could make no guess at its contents.

"Now," she cried, as she reseated herself and closed the carriage door, "where shall I find a dressmaker able and willing to make up this satin in five days?"

I could not tell her. But after some little search we succeeded in finding a woman who engaged to make an elegant costume in the time given her. The first measurements were taken, and we drove back to Ninth Street with a lasting memory in my mind of the cold and rigid form of Miss Oliver standing up in Madame's triangular parlor, submitting to the mechanical touches of the modiste with an outward composure, but with a brooding horror in her eyes that bespoke an inward torment.

XXXIX.
THE WATCHFUL EYE.

As I parted with Miss Oliver on Mrs. Desberger's stoop and did not visit her again in that house, I will introduce the report of a person better situated than myself to observe the girl during the next few days. That the person thus alluded to was a woman in the service of the police is evident, and as such may not meet with your approval, but her words are of interest, as witness:

"Fridayp.m.

"Party went out to-day in company with an elderly female of respectable appearance. Said elderly female wears puffs, and moves with great precision. I say this in case her identification should prove necessary.

"I had been warned that Miss O. would probably go out, and as the man set to watch the front door was on duty, I occupied myself during her absence in making a neat little hole in the partitions between our two rooms, so that I should not be obliged to offend my next-door neighbor by too frequent visits to her apartment. This done, I awaited her return, which was delayed till it was almost dark. When she did come in, her arms were full of bundles. These she thrust into a bureau-drawer, with the exception of one, which she laid with great care under her pillow. I wondered what this one could be, but could get no inkling from its size or shape. Her manner when she took off her hat was fiercer than before, and a strange smile, which I had not previously observed on her lips, added force to her expression. But it paled after supper-time, and she had a restless night. I could hear her walk the floor long after I thought it prudent on my part to retire, and at intervals through the night I was disturbed by her moaning, which was not that of a sick person but of one very much afflicted in mind.

"Saturday.

"Party quiet. Sits most of the time with hands clasped on her knee before the fire. Given to quick starts as if suddenly awakened from an absorbing train of thought. A pitiful object, especially when seized by terror as she is at odd times. No walks, no visitors to-day. Once I heard her speak some words in a strange language, and once she drew herself up before the mirror in an attitude of so much dignity I was surprised at the fine appearance she made. The fire of her eyes at this moment was remarkable. I should not be surprised at any move she might make.

"Sunday.

"She has been writing to-day. But when she had filled several pages of letter paper she suddenly tore them all up and threw them into the fire. Time seems to drag with her, for she goes every few minutes to the window from which a distant church clock is visible, and sighs as she turns away. More writing in the evening and some tears. But the writing was burned as before, and the tears stopped by a laugh that augurs little good to the person who called it up. The package has been taken from under her pillow and put in some place not visible from my spy-hole.

"Monday.

"Party out again to-day, gone some two hours or more. When she returned she sat down before the mirror and began dressing her hair. She has fine hair, and she tried arranging it in several ways. None seemed to satisfy her, and she tore it down again and let it hang till supper-time, when she wound it up in its usual simple knot. Mrs. Desberger spent some minutes with her, but their talk was far from confidential, and therefore uninteresting. I wish people would speak louder when they talk to themselves.

"Tuesday.

"Great restlessness on the part of the young person I am watching. No quiet for her, no quiet for me, yet she accomplishes nothing, and as yet has furnished me no clue to her thoughts.

"A huge box was brought into the room to-night. It seemed to cause her dread rather than pleasure, for she shrank at sight of it, and has not yet attempted to open it. But her eyes have never left it since it was set down on the floor. It looks like a dressmaker's box, but why such emotion over a gown?

"Wednesday.

"This morning she opened the box but did not display its contents. I caught one glimpse of a mass of tissue paper, and then she put the cover on again, and for a good half hour sat crouching down beside it, shuddering like one in an ague-fit. I began to feel there was something deadly in the box, her eyes wandered towards it so frequently and with such contradictory looks of dread and savage determination. When she got up it was to see how many more minutes of the wretched day had passed.

"Thursday.

"Party sick; did not try to leave her bed. Breakfast brought up by Mrs. Desberger, who showed her every attention, but could not prevail upon her to eat. Yet she would not let the tray be taken away, and when she was alone again or thought herself alone, she let her eyes rest so long on the knife lying across her plate, that I grew nervous and could hardly restrain myself from rushing into the room. But I remembered my instructions, and kept still even when I saw her hand steal towards this possible weapon, though I kept my own on the bell-rope which fortunately hung at my side. She looked quite capable of wounding herself with the knife, but after balancing it a moment in her hand, she laid it down again and turned with a low moan to the wall. She will not attempt death till she has accomplished what is in her mind.

"Friday.

"All is right in the next room; that is, the young lady is up; but there is another change in her appearance since last night. She has grown contemptuous of herself and indulges less in brooding. But her impatience at the slow passage of time continues, and her interest in the box is even greater than before. She does not open it, however, only looks at it and lays her trembling hand now and then on the cover.

"Saturday.

"A blank day. Party dull and very quiet. Her eyes begin to look like ghastly hollows in her pale face. She talks to herself continually, but in a low mechanical way exceedingly wearing to the listener, especially as no word can be distinguished. Tried to see her in her own room to-day, but she would not admit me.

"Sunday.

"I have noticed from the first a Bible lying on one end of her mantel-shelf. To-day she noticed it also, and impulsively reached out her hand to take it down. But at the first word she read she gave a low cry and hastily closed the book and put it back. Later, however, she took it again and read several chapters. The result was a softening in her manner, but she went to bed as flushed and determined as ever.

"Monday.

"She has walked the floor all day. She has seen no one, and seems scarcely able to contain her impatience. She cannot stand this long.

"Tuesday.

"My surprises began in the morning. As soon as her room had been put in order, Miss O. locked the door and began to open her bundles. First she unrolled a pair of white silk stockings, which she carefully, but without any show of interest, laid on the bed; then she opened a package containing gloves. They were white also, and evidently of the finest quality. Then a lace handkerchief was brought to light, slippers, an evening fan, and a pair of fancy pins, and lastly she opened the mysterious box and took out a dress so rich in quality and of such simple elegance, it almost took my breath away. It was white, and made of the heaviest satin, and it looked as much out of place in that shabby room as its owner did in the moments of exaltation of which I have spoken.

"Though her face was flushed when she lifted out the gown, it became pale again when she saw it lying across her bed. Indeed, a look of passionate abhorrence characterized her features as she contemplated it, and her hands went up before her eyes and she reeled back uttering the first words I have been able to distinguish since I have been on duty. They were violent in character, and seemed to tear their way through her lips almost without her volition. 'It is hate I feel, nothing but hate. Ah, if it were only duty that animated me!'

"Later she grew calmer, and covering up the whole paraphernalia with a stray sheet she had evidently laid by for the purpose, she sent for Mrs. Desberger. When that lady came in she met her with a wan but by no means dubious smile, and ignoring with quiet dignity the very evident curiosity with which that good woman surveyed the bed, she said appealingly:

"'You have been so kind to me, Mrs. Desberger, that I am going to tell you a secret. Will it continue to remain a secret, or shall I see it in the faces of all my fellow-boarders to-morrow?' You can imagine Mrs. Desberger's reply, also the manner in which it was delivered, but not Miss Oliver's secret. She uttered it in these words: 'I am going out to-night, Mrs. Desberger. I am going into great society. I am going to attend Miss Althorpe's wedding.' Then, as the good woman stammered out some words of surprise and pleasure, she went on to say: 'I do not want any one to know it, and I would be so glad if I could slip out of the house without any one seeing me. I shall need a carriage, but you will get one for me, will you not, and let me know the moment it comes. I am shy of what folks say, and besides, as you know, I am neither happy nor well, if I do go to weddings, and have new dresses, and — —' She nearly broke down but collected herself with wonderful promptitude, and with a coaxing look that made her almost ghastly, so much it seemed out of accord with her strained and unnatural manner, she raised a corner of the sheet, saying, 'I will show you my gown, if you will promise to help me quietly out of the house,' which, of course, produced the desired effect upon Mrs. Desberger, that woman's greatest weakness being her love of dress.

"So from that hour I knew what to expect, and after sending precautionary advices to Police Headquarters, I set myself to watch her prepare for the evening. I saw her arrange her hair and put on her elegant gown, and was as much startled by the result as if I had not had the least premonition that she only needed rich clothes to look both beautiful and distinguished. The square parcel she had once hidden under her pillow was brought out and laid on the bed, and when Mrs. Desberger's low knock announced the arrival of the carriage, she caught it up and hid it under the cloak she hastily threw about her. Mrs. Desberger came in and put out the light, but before the room sank into darkness I caught one glimpse of Miss Oliver's face. Its expression was terrible beyond anything I had ever seen on any human countenance."

XL.
AS THE CLOCK STRUCK.

I do not attend weddings in general, but great as my suspense was in reference to Miss Oliver, I felt that I could not miss seeing Miss Althorpe married.

I had ordered a new dress for the occasion, and was in the best of spirits as I rode to the church in which the ceremony was to be performed. The excitement of a great social occasion was for once not disagreeable to me, nor did I mind the crowd, though it pushed me about rather uncomfortably till an usher came to my assistance and seated me in a pew, which I was happy to see commanded a fine view of the chancel.

I was early, but then I always am early, and having ample opportunity for observation, I noted every fine detail of ornamentation with approval, Miss Althorpe's taste being of that fine order which always falls short of ostentation. Her friends are in very many instances my friends, and it was no small part of my pleasure to note their well-known faces among the crowd of those that were strange to me. That the scene was brilliant, and that silks, satins, and diamonds abounded, goes without saying.

At last the church was full, and the hush which usually precedes the coming of the bride was settling over the whole assemblage, when I suddenly observed, in the person of a respectable-looking gentleman seated in a side pew, the form and features of Mr. Gryce, the detective. This was a shock to me, yet what was there in his presence there to alarm me? Might not Miss Althorpe have accorded him this pleasure out of the pure goodness of her heart? I did not look at anybody else, however, after once my eyes fell upon him, but continued to watch his expression, which was non-commital, though a little anxious for one engaged in a purely social function.

The entrance of the clergyman and the sudden peal of the organ in the well-known wedding march recalled my attention to the occasion itself, and as at that moment the bridegroom stepped from the vestry to await his bride at the altar, I was absorbed by his fine appearance and the air of mingled pride and happiness with which he watched the stately approach of the bridal procession.

But suddenly there was a stir through the whole glittering assemblage, and the clergyman made a move and the bridegroom gave a start, and the sound, slight as it was, of moving feet grew still, and I saw advancing from the door on the opposite side of the altar a second bride, clad in white and surrounded by a long veil which completely hid her face. A second bride! and the first was half-way up the aisle, and only one bridegroom stood ready!

The clergyman, who seemed to have as little command of his faculties as the rest of us, tried to speak; but the approaching woman, upon whom every regard was fixed, forestalled him by an authoritative gesture.

Advancing towards the chancel, she took her place on the spot reserved for Miss Althorpe.

Silence had filled the church up to this moment; but at this audacious move, a solitary wailing cry of mingled astonishment and despair went up behind us; but before any of us could turn, and while my own heart stood still, for I thought I recognized this veiled figure, the woman at the altar raised her hand and pointed towards the bridegroom.

"Why does he hesitate?" she cried. "Does he not recognize the only woman with whom he dare face God and man at the altar? Because I am already his wedded wife, and have been so for five long years, does that make my wearing of this veil amiss when he a husband, unreleased by the law, dares enter this sacred place with the hope and expectation of a bridegroom?"

It was Ruth Oliver who spoke. I recognized her voice as I had recognized her apparel; but the emotions aroused in me by her presence and the almost incredible claims she advanced were lost in the horror inspired by the man she thus vehemently accused. No lost spirit from the pit could have shown a more hideous commingling of the most terrible passions known to man than he did in the face of this terrible arraignment; and if Ella Althorpe, cowering in her shame and misery half-way up the aisle, saw him in all his depravity at that instant as I did, nothing could have saved her long-cherished love from immediate death.

Yet he tried to speak.

"It is false!" he cried; "all false! The woman I once called wife is dead."

"Dead, Olive Randolph? Murderer!" she exclaimed. "The blow struck in the dark found another victim!" And pulling the veil from her face, Ruth

Oliver advanced to his side and laid her trembling hand with a firm and decisive movement on his arm.

Was it her words, her touch, or the sound of the clock striking eight in the great tower over our heads, which so totally overwhelmed him? As the last stroke of the hour which was to have seen him united with Miss Althorpe died out in the awed spaces above him, he gave a cry such as I am sure never resounded between those sacred walls before, and sank in a heap on the spot where but a few minutes previous he had lifted his head in all the glow and pride of a prospective bridegroom.

XLI.
SECRET HISTORY.

It was hours before I found myself able to realize that the scene I had just witnessed had a deeper and much more dreadful significance than appeared to the general eye, and that Ruth Oliver, in her desperate interruption of these treacherous nuptials, had not only made good her prior claim to Randolph Stone as her husband, but had pointed him out to all the world as the villainous author of that crime which for so long a time had occupied my own and the public's attention.

Thinking that you may find the same difficulty in grasping this terrible fact, and being anxious to save you from the suspense under which I myself labored for so many hours, I here subjoin a written statement made by this woman some weeks later, in which the whole mystery is explained. It is signed Olive Randolph; the name to which she evidently feels herself best entitled.

"The man known in New York City as Randolph Stone was first seen by me in Michigan five years ago. His name then was John Randolph, and how he has since come to add to this the further appellation of Stone, I must leave to himself to explain.

"I was born in Michigan myself, and till my eighteenth year I lived with my father, who was a widower without any other child, in a little low cottage amid the sand mounds that border the eastern side of the lake.

"I was not pretty, but every man who passed me on the beach or in the streets of the little town where we went to market and to church, stopped to look at me, and this I noticed, and from this perhaps my unhappiness arose.

"For before I was old enough to know the difference between poverty and riches, I began to lose all interest in my simple home duties, and to cast longing looks at the great school building where girls like myself learned to speak like ladies and play the piano. Yet these ambitious promptings might have come to nothing if I had never met *him*. I might have settled down in my own sphere and lived a useful if unsatisfied life like my mother and my mother's mother before her.

"But fate had reserved me for wretchedness, and one day just as I was on the verge of my eighteenth year, I saw John Randolph.

"I was coming out of church when our eyes first met, and I noticed after the first shock my simple heart received from his handsome face and elegant appearance, that he was surveying me with that strange look of admiration I had seen before on so many faces; and the joy this gave me, and the certainty which came with it of my seeing him again, made that moment quite unlike any other in my whole life, and was the beginning of that passion which has undone me, ruined him, and brought death and sorrow to many others of more worth than either of us.

"He was not a resident of the town, but a passing visitor; and his intention had been, as he has since told me, to leave the place on the following day. But the dart which had pierced my breast had not glanced entirely aside from his, and he remained, as he declared, to see what there was in this little country-girl's face to make it so unforgettable. We met first on the beach and afterwards under the strip of pines which separate our cottage from the sand mounds, and though I have no reason to believe he came to these interviews with any honest purpose or deep sincerity of feeling, it is certain he exerted all his powers to make them memorable to me, and that, in doing so, he awoke some of the fire in his own breast which he took such wicked pleasure in arousing in mine.

"In fact he soon showed that this was so, for I could take no step from the house without encountering him; and the one indelible impression remaining to me from those days is the expression his face wore as, one sunny afternoon, he laid my hand on his arm and drew me away to have a look at the lake booming on the beach below us. There was no love in it as I understand love now, but the passion which informed it almost amounted to intoxication, and if such a passion can be understood between a man already cultivated and a girl who hardly knew how to read, it may, in a measure, account for what followed.

"My father, who was no fool, and who saw the selfish quality in this attractive lover of mine, was alarmed by our growing intimacy. Taking an opportunity when we were both in a more sensible mood than common, he put the case before Mr. Randolph in a very decided way. He told him that either he must marry me at once or quit seeing me altogether. No delay was to be considered and no compromise allowed.

"As my father was a man with whom no one ever disputed, John Randolph prepared to leave the town, declaring that he could marry no one at that stage of his career. But before he could carry out his intention, the old intoxication returned, and he came back in a fever of love and impatience to marry me.

"Had I been older or more experienced in the ways of the world, I would have known that such passion as this evinced was short-lived; that there is no witchery in a smile lasting enough to make men like him forget the lack of those social graces to which they are accustomed. But I was mad with happiness, and was unconscious of any cloud lowering upon our future till the day of our first separation came, when an event occurred which showed me what I might expect if I could not speedily raise myself to his level.

"We were out walking, and we met a lady who had known Mr. Randolph elsewhere. She was well dressed, which I was not, though I had not realized it till I saw how attractive she looked in quiet colors and with only a simple ribbon on her hat; and she had, besides, a way of speaking which made my tones sound harsh, and robbed me of that feeling of superiority with which I had hitherto regarded all the girls of my acquaintance.

"But it was not her possession of these advantages, keenly as I felt them, which awakened me to the sense of my position. It was the surprise she showed (a surprise the source of which was not to be mistaken) when he introduced me to her as his wife; and though she recovered herself in a moment, and tried to be kind and gracious, I felt the sting of it and saw that he felt it too, and consequently was not at all astonished when, after she had passed us, he turned and looked at me critically for the first time.

"But his way of showing his dissatisfaction gave me a shock it took me years to recover from. 'Take off that hat,' he cried, and when I had obeyed him, he tore out the spray which to my eyes had been its chief adornment, and threw it into some bushes near by; then he gave me back the hat and asked for the silk neckerchief which I had regarded as the glory of my bridal costume. Giving it to him I saw him put it in his pocket, and understanding now that he was trying to make me look more like the lady we had passed, I cried out passionately: 'It is not these things that make the difference, John, but my voice and way of walking and speaking. Give me money and let me be educated, and then we will see if any other woman can draw your eyes away from me.'

"But he had received a shock that made him cruel. 'You cannot make a silk purse out of a sow's ear,' he sneered, and was silent all the rest of the way home. I was silent too, for I never talk when I am angry, but when we arrived in our own little room I confronted him.

"'Are you going to say any more such cruel things to me?' I asked, 'for if you are, I should like you to say them now and be done with it.'

"He looked desperately angry, but there was yet a little love left in his heart for me, for he laughed after he had looked at me for a minute, and took me in his arms and said some of the fine things with which he had previously won my heart, but not with the old fire and not with the old effect upon me. Yet my love had not grown cold, it had only changed from the unthinking stage to the thinking one, and I was quite in earnest when I said: 'I know I am not as pretty or as nice as the ladies you are accustomed to. But I have a heart that has never known any other passion than its love for you, and from such a heart you ought to expect a lady to grow, and there will. Only give me the chance, John; only let me learn to read and write.'

"But he was in an incredulous state of mind, and it ended in his going away without making any arrangements for my education. He was bound for San Francisco, where he had business to transact, and he promised to be back in four weeks, but before the four weeks elapsed, he wrote me that it would be five, and later on that it would be six, and afterwards that it would be when he had finished a big piece of work he was engaged upon, and which would bring him a large amount of money. I believed him and I doubted him at the same time, but I was not altogether sorry he delayed his return for I had begun school on my own account and was fast laying the foundation of a solid education.

"My means came from my father, who, now it was too late, saw the necessity of my improving myself. The amount of studying I did that first year was amazing, but it was nothing to what I went through the second, for my husband's letters had begun to fail me, and I was forced to work in order to drown grief and keep myself from despair. Finally no letters came at all, and when the second year was over, and I could at least express myself correctly, I woke to the realization that, so far as my husband was concerned, I had gone through all this labor for nothing, and that unless by some fortunate chance I could light upon some clue to his whereabouts in the great world beyond our little town, I would be likely to pass the remainder of my days in widowhood and desolation.

"My father dying at this time and leaving me a thousand dollars, I knew no better way of spending it than in the hopeless search I have just mentioned. Accordingly after his burial I started out on my travels, gaining experience with every mile. I had not been away a week before I realized what a folly I had indulged in in ever hoping to see John Randolph back at my side. I saw the homes in which such men as he lived, and met in cars and on steamboats the kind of people with whom he must associate to be happy, and a gulf seemed to open between us which even such love as mine would be powerless to bridge.

"But though hope thus sank in my breast, I did not lose my old ambition of making myself as worthy of him as circumstances would permit. I read only the best books and I allowed myself to become acquainted with only the best people, and as I saw myself liked by such the awkwardness of my manner gradually disappeared, and I began to feel that the day would come when I should be universally recognized as a lady.

"Meantime I did not advance an iota in the object of my journey; and at last, with every expectation gone of ever seeing my husband again, I made my way to Toledo. Here I speedily found employment, and what was better still to one of my ambitious tendencies, an opportunity to add to the sum of my accomplishments a knowledge of French and music. The French I learned from the family I lived with, and the music from a professor in the same house whose love for his pet art was so great that he found it simple happiness to impart it to one so greedy for improvement as myself.

"Here, in course of time, I also learned type-writing, and it was for the purpose of seeking employment in this capacity that I finally came to New York. This was three months ago.

"I was in complete ignorance of the city when I entered it, and for a day or two I wandered to and fro, searching for a suitable lodging-house. It was while I was on my way to Mrs. Desberger's that I saw advancing towards me a gentleman in whose air and manner I detected a resemblance to the husband who some five years since had deserted me. The shock was too much for my self-control. Quaking in every limb, I stood awaiting his approach, and when he came up to me, and I saw by his startled recognition of me that it was indeed he, I gave a loud cry and threw myself upon his arm. The start he gave was nothing to the frightful expression which crossed his face at this encounter, but I thought both due to his surprise, though now I am convinced they had their origin in the deepest and worst emotions of which a man is capable.

"'John! John!' I cried, and could say no more, for the agitations of five solitary, despairing years were choking me; but he was entirely voiceless, stricken, I have no doubt, beyond any power of mine to realize. How could I dream that in consideration, power, and prestige he had advanced even more rapidly than myself, and that at this very moment he was not only the idol of society, but on the verge of uniting himself to a woman—I will not say of marrying her, for marry her he could not while I lived—who would make him the envied possessor of millions. Such fortune, such daring, yes and such depravity, were beyond the reach of my imagination, and while I thought his pleasure less than mine, I did not dream that my existence was a menace to all his hopes, and that during this moment of speechlessness he was sounding his nature for means to rid himself of me even at the cost of my life.

"His first movement was to push me away, but I clung to him all the harder; at which his whole manner changed and he began to make futile efforts to calm me and lead me away from the spot. Seeing that these attempts were unavailing, he turned pale and raised his arm up passionately, but speedily dropped it again, and casting glances this way and that, broke suddenly into a loud laugh and became, as by the touch of a magician's wand, my old lover again.

"'Why, Olive!' he cried; 'why, Olive! is it you? (Did I say my name was Olive?) Happily met, my dear! I did not know what I had been missing all these years, but now I know it was you. Will you come with me, or shall I go home with you?'

"'I have no home,' said I, 'I have just come into town.'

"'Then I see but one alternative.' He smiled, and what a power there was in his smile when he chose to exert it! 'You must come to my apartments; are you willing?'

"'I am your wife,' I answered.

"He had taken me on his arm by this time and the recoil he made at these words was quite perceptible; but his face still smiled, and I was too mad with joy to be critical.

"'And a very pretty and charming wife you have become,' said he, drawing me on for a few steps. Suddenly he paused, and I felt the old shadow fall between us again. 'But your dress is very shabby,' he remarked.

"It was not; it was not near as shabby as the linen duster he himself wore.

"'Is that rain?' he inquired, looking up as a drop or two fell.

"'Yes, it is raining.'

"'Very well, let us go into this store we are coming to and buy a gossamer. That will cover up your gown. I cannot take you to my house dressed as you are now.'

"Surprised, for I had thought my dress very neat and lady-like, but never dreaming of questioning his taste any more than in the old days in Michigan, I went with him into the shop he had pointed out and bought me a gossamer, for which he paid. When he had helped me to put it on and had tied my veil well over my face, he seemed more at his ease and gave me his arm quite cheerfully.

"'Now,' said he, 'you look well, but how about the time when you will have to take the gossamer off? I tell you what it is, my dear, you will have to refit yourself entirely before I shall be satisfied.' And again I saw him cast about him that furtive and inquiring look which would have awakened more surprise in me than it did had I known that we were in a part of the city where he ran but little chance of meeting any one he knew.

"'This old duster I have on,' he suddenly laughed, 'is a very appropriate companion to your gossamer,' and though I did not agree with him, for my clothes were new, and his old and shabby, I laughed also and never dreamed of evil.

"As this garment which so disfigured him that morning has been the occasion of much false speculation on the part of those whose business it was to inquire into the crime with which it is in a most unhappy way connected, I may as well explain here and now why so fastidious a gentleman as Randolph Stone came to wear it. The gentleman called Howard Van Burnam was not the only person who visited the Van Burnam offices on the morning preceding the murder. Randolph Stone was there also, but he did not see the brothers, for finding them closeted together, he decided not to interrupt them. As he was a frequent visitor there, his presence created no remark nor was his departure noted. Descending the stairs separating the offices from the street, he was about to leave the building, when he noticed that the clouds looked ominous. Being dressed for a luncheon with Miss Althorpe, he felt averse to getting wet, so he stepped back into the adjoining hall and began groping for an umbrella in a little closet under the stairs where he had once before found such an article. While doing this he heard the younger Van Burnam descend and go out, and realizing that he could now see Franklin without difficulty, he was about to return up-stairs when he heard that gentleman also come down and follow his brother into the street.

"His first impulse was to join him, but finding nothing but an old duster in the closet, he gave up this intention, and putting on this shabby but protecting garment, started for his apartments, little realizing into what a course of duplicity and crime it was destined to lead him. For to the wearing of this old duster on this especial morning, innocent as the occasion was, I attribute John Randolph's temptation to murder. Had he gone out without it, he would have taken his usual course up Broadway and never met *me*; or even if he had taken the same roundabout way to his apartments as that which led to our encounter, he would never have dared, in his ordinary fine dress, conspicuous as it made him, to have entered upon those measures, which, as he is clever enough to know, lead to disgrace, if they do not end in a felon's cell. It was John Randolph, then, or Randolph Stone, as he is pleased to call himself in New York, and not Franklin Van Burnam (who had doubtless proceeded in another direction) who came up to where Howard had stood, saw the keys he had dropped, and put them in his own pocket. It was as innocent an action as the donning of the duster, and yet it was fraught with the worst consequences to himself and others.

"Being of the same height and complexion as Franklin Van Burnam, and both gentlemen wearing at that time a moustache (my husband shaved his off after the murder), the mistakes which arose out of this strange equipment were but natural. Seen from the rear or in the semi-darkness of a hotel-office they might look alike, though to me or to any one studying them well, their faces are really very different.

"But to return. Leading me through streets of which I knew nothing, he presently stopped before the entrance of a large hotel.

"'I tell you what, Olive,' said he, 'we had better go in here, take a room, and send for such things as you require to make you look like a lady.'

"As I had no objection to anything which kept me at his side, I told him that whatever suited him suited me, and followed him quite eagerly into the office. I did not know then that this hotel was a second-rate one, not having had experience with the best, but if I had, I should not have wondered at his choice, for there was nothing in his appearance, as I have already intimated, or in his manners up to this point, to lead me to think he was one of the city's great swells, and that it was only in such an unfashionable house as this he would be likely to pass unrecognized. How with his markedly handsome features and distinguished bearing he managed so to carry himself as to look like a man of inferior breeding, I can no more explain than I can the singular change which took place in him when once he found himself in the midst of the crowd which lounged about this office.

"From a man to attract all eyes he became at once a man to attract none, and slouched and looked so ordinary that I stared at him in astonishment, little thinking that he had assumed this manner as a disguise. Seeing me at a loss, he spoke up quite peremptorily:

"'Let us keep our secret, Olive, till you can appear in the world full-fledged. And look here, darling, won't you go to the desk and ask for a room? I am no hand at any such business.'

"Confounded at a proposition so unexpected, but too much under the spell of my feelings to dispute his wishes, I faltered out:

"'But supposing they ask me to register?'

"At which he gave me a look which recalled the old days in Michigan, and quietly sneered:

"'Give them a fictitious name. You have learned to write by this time, have you not?'

"Stung by his taunt, but more in love with him than ever, for his momentary display of passion had made him look both masterful and handsome, I went up to the desk to do his bidding.

"'A room!' said I; and when asked to write our names in the book that lay before me, I put down the first that suggested itself. I wrote with my gloves on, which was why the writing looked so queer that it was taken for a disguised hand.

"This done, he rejoined me, and we went up-stairs, and I was too happy to be in his company again to wonder at his peculiarities or weigh the consequences of the implicit confidence I accorded him. I was desperately in love once more, and entered into every plan he proposed without a thought beyond the joyous present. He was so handsome without his hat; and when after some short delay he threw aside the duster, I felt myself for the first time in my life in the presence of a finished gentleman. Then his manner was so changed. He was so like his oldest and best self, so dangerously like what he was in those long vanished hours under the pines in my sand-swept home on the shores of Lake Michigan. That he faltered at times and sank into strange spells of silence which had something in them that made my breath come fitfully, did not awaken my apprehension or rouse in me more than a passing curiosity. I thought he regretted the past, and when, after one such pause in our conversation, he drew out of his pocket a couple of keys tied together with a string, and surveyed the card attached to them with a strange look, easily enough to be understood by me now, I only laughed at his abstraction, and indulged in a fresh caress to make him more mindful of my presence.

"These keys were the ones which Mrs. Van Burnam's husband had dropped, and which he had picked up before meeting me; and after he had put them back into his pocket he became more talkative than before, and more systematically lover-like. I think he had not seen his way clearly till this moment, the dark and dreadful way which was to end, as he supposed, in my death.

"But I feared nothing, suspected nothing. Such deep and desperate wickedness as he was planning was beyond the wildest flight of my imagination. When he insisted upon sending for a complete set of clothing for me, and when at his dictation I wrote a list of the articles I wanted, I thought he was influenced by his wish as my husband to see me dressed in articles of his own buying. That it was all a plot to rob me of my identity could not strike such a mind as mine, and when the packages came and were received by him in the sly way already known to the public, I saw nothing in his caution but a playful display of mystery that was to end in my romantic establishment in a home of love and luxury.

"Or rather it is thus that I account for my conduct now, and yet the precaution I took not to change the shoes in which my money was hidden, may argue that I was not without some underlying doubt of his complete sincerity. But if so, I hid it from myself, and, as I have every reason to believe, from him also, doubtless excusing my action to myself by considering that I would be none the worse off for a few dollars of my own, even if he was my husband, and had promised me no end of pleasure and comfort.

"That he did intend to make me happy, he had assured me more than once. Indeed, before we had been long in this hotel room, he informed me that great experiences lay before me; that he had prospered much in the last five years and had now a house of his own to offer me and a large circle of friends to make our life in it agreeable.

"'We will go to our house to-night,' said he. 'I have not been living in it lately, and you may find it a little uncomfortable, but we will remedy that to-morrow. Anything is better than staying here under a false name and I cannot take you to my bachelor apartment.'

"I had doubted some of his previous statements, but this one I implicitly believed. Why should not so elegant a man have a house of his own; and if he had told me it was built of marble and hung with Florentine tapestries, I should still have credited it all. I was in fairy-land and he was my knight of romance, even when he again hung his head in leaving the hotel and looked at once so ordinary and uninteresting.

"The ruse he made use of to cut off all connection between ourselves and the Mr. and Mrs. James Pope who had registered at the Hotel D—— was accepted by me with the same lack of suspicion. That he should wish to carry no remembrance of our old life into our new home I thought a delightful piece of folly, and when he proposed that we should bequeath my gossamer and his own disfiguring duster to the coachman in whose hack we were then riding, I laughed gleefully and helped him fold them up and place them under the cushions, though I did wonder why he cut a piece out of the neck of the former, and pouted with the happy freedom of a self-confident woman when he said:

"'It is the first thing I ever bought for you, and I am just foolish enough to wish to preserve this much of it for a keepsake. Do you object, my dear?'

"As I was conscious of cherishing a similar folly in his regard, and could have pressed even that old duster of his to my heart, I offered him a kiss and said 'No,' and he put the scrap away in his pocket. That it was the portion on which was stamped the name of the firm from which it was bought did not occur to me.

"When the coach stopped, he urged me away on foot in a direction entirely strange to me, saying we would take another hack as soon as we had disposed of the bundles we were carrying. How he intended to do this, I did not know. But presently he drew me towards a Chinese laundry, where he bade me leave one of them as washing, and the other he dropped before the opening of a sewer as we stepped up a neighboring curb-stone.

"And still I did not suspect.

"Our ride to Gramercy Park was short, but during it he had time to put a bill in my hand and tell me I was to pay the driver. He had also time to secure the weapon upon which he had probably had his eye fixed from the first. His manner of doing this I can never forgive, for it was a lover's manner, and as such intended to deceive and cajole me. Drawing my head down on his shoulder, he drew off my veil, saying that it was the only article left of my own buying, and that we would leave it behind us in this coach as we had left the gossamer in the other. 'Only I will make sure that no other woman ever wears it,' he laughed, slitting it up and down with his knife. When this was done he kissed me, and then while my heart was tender and the warm tears stood in my eyes, he drew out the pin from my hat, meeting my remonstrances with the assurance that he hated to see my head covered, and that no hat was as pretty as my own brown hair.

"As this was nonsense, and as the coach was beginning to stop, I shook my head at him and put my hat on again, but he had dropped the pin, or so he said, and I had to alight without it.

"When I had paid the driver and the coach had driven off, I had a chance to look up at the house before which we had stopped. Its height and imposing appearance daunted me in spite of the great expectations I had formed, and I ran up the stoop after him in a condition of mingled awe and wild delight that was the poorest preparation possible for what lay before me in the dark interior we were entering.

"He was fumbling nervously in the keyhole with his key, and I heard a whispered oath escape him. But presently the door fell back, and we stepped in to what looked to me like a cavern of darkness.

"'Do not be frightened!' he admonished me. 'I will strike a light in a moment.' And after carefully closing the street door behind us, he stretched out his hand to take mine, or so I judge, for I heard him whisper impatiently, 'Where are you?'

"I was on the threshold of the parlor, to which I had groped my way while he was closing the front door, so I whispered back, 'Here!' but found voice for nothing further, for at that instant I heard a sound proceeding from the depths of darkness in front of me, and was so struck with terror that I fell back against the staircase, just as he passed me and entered the room from which that stealthy noise had issued.

"'Darling!' he whispered, 'darling!' and went stumbling on in the void of darkness before me, till suddenly by some power I cannot explain I seemed to see, faintly but distinctly, and as if with my mind's eye rather than with my bodily one.

"I perceived the shadowy form of a woman standing in the space before him, and beheld him suddenly grasp her with what he meant to be a loving cry, but which to my ears at that moment sounded strangely ferocious, and after holding her a moment suddenly release her, at which she uttered one low, curdling moan and sank at his feet. At the same instant I heard a click, which I did not understand then, but which I now know to have been the head of the hat-pin striking the register.

"Horrified past all power of speech and action, for I saw that he had intended this blow for me, I cowered against the stairs, waiting for him to pass out. This he did not do at once, though the delay must have been short. He stopped long enough by the prostrate form to stir it with his foot, probably to see if life was extinct, but no longer, yet it seemed an eternity before I perceived him groping his way over the threshold; an eternity in which every act of my life passed before me, and every word and every expression with which he had beguiled me came to rack my soul and made the horror of this mad awakening greater.

"No thought of her, or of the guilt with which he had forever damned his soul, came to me in that first moment of misery. *My* loss, *my* escape, and the danger in which I still stood if the least hint reached him of the mistake he had made, filled my mind too entirely for me to dwell on any less impersonal theme. His words, for he muttered several in that short passage out, showed me in what a fools' paradise I had been revelling, and how certainly I had turned his every thought towards murder when I seized him in the street and proclaimed myself his wife. The satisfaction with which he uttered, 'Well struck!' gave little hint of remorse; and the gloating delight with which he added something about the devil having assisted him to make it a safe blow as well as a deadly one, was proof not only of his having used all his cunning in planning this crime, but of his pleasure in its apparent success.

"That he continued in this frame of mind, and that he never lost confidence in the precautions he had taken and in the mystery with which the deed was surrounded, is apparent from the fact that he revisited the Van Burnam office on the following morning, and hung again on its accustomed nail the keys of the Gramercy Park house.

"When the front door had closed, and I knew that he had gone away in the full belief that it was my form he had left lying behind him on that midnight floor, all the accumulated terrors of the situation came to me in full force, and I began to think of her as well as of myself, and longed for courage to approach her or even the daring to call out for help. But the thought that it was my husband who had committed this crime held me tongue-tied, and though I soon began to move inch by inch in her direction, it was some time before I could so far overcome my terror as to enter the room where she lay.

"I had supposed, and still supposed (as was natural after seeing him open the door with the keys he took from his pocket), that the house was his, and the victim a member of his own household. But when, after innumerable hesitations and a bodily shrinking that was little short of torment, I managed to drag myself into the room and light a match which I found on a farther mantel-shelf, I saw enough in the general appearance of the rooms and of the figure at my feet to make me doubt the truth of both these suppositions. Yet no other explanation came to lighten the mystery of the occasion, and dazed as I was by the horror of my position and the mortal dread I felt of the man who in one instant had turned the heaven of my love into a hell of fathomless horrors, I soon had eyes for the one fact only, that the woman lying before me was sufficiently like myself to inspire me with the hope of preserving my secret and keeping from my would-be slayer the knowledge of my having escaped the doom he had prepared for me.

"For ascribe it to what motive you will, that was the one idea now dominating my mind. I wanted him to believe me dead. I wanted to feel that all connection between us was severed forever. He *had* killed me. By killing my love and faith in him he had murdered the better part of myself, and I shrank with inconceivable horror from anything that would bring me again under his eye, or force me to assert claims that it would be the future business of my life to forget.

"When the first match went out I had not courage to light another, so I crept away in the darkness to listen at the foot of the stairs. There was no sound from above, and a terrifying sense began to pervade me that I was in that house alone. Yet there was safety in the thought, and opportunity for what I was planning, and finally, under the stress of the purpose that was every moment developing within me, I went softly up-stairs and listened at all the doors till I was certain that the house was unoccupied. Then I came down and walked resolutely back into the parlor, for I knew if I allowed any time to pass I could never again summon up strength to cross its grisly threshold. Yet I did nothing for hours but crouch in one of its dismal corners, waiting for morning. That I did not go mad in that awful interval is a wonder. I must have been near it more than once.

"I have been asked, and Miss Butterworth has been asked, how in the light of what we now know concerning this poor victim's presence there, we account for her being in the darkness and showing so little terror at our entrance and Mr. Stone's approach. *I* account for it in this way: Two half-burned matches were found in the parlor grate. One I flung there; the other had probably been used by her to light the dining-room gas. If this was still lighted when we drove up, as it may have been, then, alarmed by the sound of the stopping coach, she had put it out, with a vague idea of hiding herself till she knew whether it was the old gentleman who was coming or only her suspicious and unreasonable husband. If it was not lighted then, she was probably aroused from a sleep on the parlor sofa, and was for the moment too dazed to cry out or resent an embrace she had not time to understand before she succumbed to the cruel stab that killed her. Miss Butterworth, however, thinks that the poor creature took the intruder for Franklin till she heard my voice, when she probably became so amazed that she was in a measure paralyzed and found it impossible to move or cry out. As Miss Butterworth is a woman of great discretion I should think her explanation the truest, if I did not consider her a little prejudiced against Mrs. Van Burnam.

"But to return to myself.

"With the first glimmer of light that came through the closed shutters I rose and began my dreadful task. Upheld by a purpose as relentless as that which drove the author of this horror into murder, I stripped the body and put upon it my own clothing, with the one exception of the shoes. Then, when I had re-dressed myself in hers, I steadied up my heart and with one wild pull dragged down the cabinet upon her so that her face might lose its traits and her identification become impossible.

"How I had strength to do this, and how I could contemplate the result without shrieking, I cannot now imagine. Perhaps I was hardly human at this crisis; perhaps something of the demon which had informed him in his awful work had entered into my breast, making this thing possible. I only know that I did what I have said and did it calmly. More than that, that I had mind and judgment left to give to my own appearance. Observing that the dress I had put on was of a conspicuous plaid, I exchanged the skirt portion with the brown silk petticoat under it, and when I observed that it hung below the other, as of course it would, I went through the house till I came upon some pins with which I pinned it up out of sight. Thus equipped, I was still a person to attract attention, especially as I had no hat to put on; my own having fallen from my head and been covered by the dead woman's body, which nothing would induce me to move again.

"But I had confidence in my own powers to escape question, toned up as I was in every nerve by the dreadfulness of my situation, and as soon as I was in decent shape for flight, I opened the front door and prepared to slip out.

"But here the intense dread I felt of my husband, a dread which had actuated all my movements and sustained me in as harrowing a task as ever woman performed, seized me with renewed force, and I quailed at the prospect of entering the streets alone. Supposing he should be on the stoop! Supposing he should be in an opposite window even! Could I encounter him again and live? He was not far away, or so I felt. A murderer, it is said, cannot help haunting the scene of his crime, and if he should see me alive and well, what might I not expect from his astonishment and alarm? I did not dare go out. But neither did I dare remain, so after quaking for a good five minutes on the threshold, I made one wild dash through the door.

"There was no one in sight, and I reached Broadway before I ran across man or woman. Even then I got by without any one speaking to me, and, favored by Providence, found a nook at the end of an alley-way, where I remained undiscovered till it was late enough in the morning for me to enter a shop and buy a hat.

"The rest of my movements are known. I found my way to Mrs. Desberger's, this time without interruption; and from that place sought and found a situation with Miss Althorpe.

"That her fate was in any way connected with mine, or that the Randolph Stone she was engaged to marry was the John Randolph from whose clutches I had just escaped, was, of course, unsuspected by me, and, incredible as it may seem, continued to be unsuspected as long as I remained in the house. There was reason for this. My duties were such as I could well attend to in my own room, and feeling a horror of the world and everything in it, I kept my room as much as possible, and never went out of it when I knew that he was in the house. The very thought of love awakened intolerable emotions in me, and much as I admired and revered Miss Althorpe, I could not bring myself to meet or even talk of the man to whom she was in expectation of being so soon united. There was another thing of which I was ignorant, and that was the circumstances which had invested with so much interest the crime of which I had been witness. I did not know that the victim had been recognized, or that an innocent man had been arrested for her murder. In fact I knew nothing concerning the affair save what I had seen with my own eyes, no one having mentioned the murder in my presence, and I having religiously avoided the very sight of a paper for fear that I should see some account of the horrible affair, and so lose what small remnants of courage I still possessed.

"This apathy concerning a matter so important to myself, or rather this almost frenzied determination to cut myself loose from my dreadful past, may seem strange and unnatural; but it will seem stranger yet when I say that for all these efforts I was haunted night and day by one small fact connected with this past, which made forgetfulness impossible. I had taken the rings from the hands of the dead woman as I had taken away her clothes, and the possession of these valuables, probably because they represented so much money, weighed on my conscience and made me feel like a thief. The purse which I found in a pocket of the skirt I had put on was a trouble to me, but the rings were a source of constant terror and disturbance. I hid them finally in a ball of yarn I was using, but even then I experienced but little peace, for they were not mine, and I lacked the courage to avow it or seek out the person to whom they now rightfully belonged.

"When, therefore, in the intervals of fever which attacked me in Miss Althorpe's house, I overheard enough of a conversation between her and Miss Butterworth to learn that the murdered woman had been a Mrs. Van Burnam, and that her husband or relatives had an office somewhere downtown, I was so seized by the instinct of restitution, that I took the first opportunity that offered to leave my bed and hunt up these people.

"That I would injure them in any way by secretly restoring these jewels, I never dreamed. Indeed, I did not exercise my mind at all on the subject, but only followed the instincts of my delirium; and while to all appearance I showed all the cunning of an insane person, in the pursuit of my purpose, I fail to remember now how I found my way to Duane Street, or by what suggestion of my diseased brain I was induced to slip these rings upon the hook attached to Mr. Van Burnam's desk. Probably the mere utterance of this well-known name into the ears of the passers-by was enough to obtain for me such directions as I needed, but however that may be, the result was misapprehension, and the complications which followed, serious.

"Of the emotion caused in me by the unaccountable discovery of my connection with this crime I need not speak. The love which I at one time felt for John Randolph had turned to gall and bitterness, but enough sense of duty remained in my bruised and broken heart to keep me from denouncing him to the police, till by a sudden stroke of fate or Providence, I saw him in the carriage with Miss Althorpe, and realized that he was not only the man with whom she was upon the point of allying herself, but that it was to preserve his place in her regard and to attain the lofty position promised by this union, he had attempted to murder me, and had murdered another woman only less unfortunate and miserable than myself.

"It was the last and bitterest blow that could come from his hand; and though instinct led me to throw myself into the carriage before which I stood, and thus escape a meeting which I felt I could never survive, I was determined from that moment not only to save Miss Althorpe from an alliance with this villain, but to revenge myself upon him in some never-to-be-forgotten manner.

"That this revenge involved her in a public shame from which her angelic goodness to me should have saved her, I regret now as deeply as even she can wish. But the madness that was upon me made me blind to every other consideration than that of the boundless hatred I bore him; and while I can look for no forgiveness from her on that account, I still hope the day will come when she will see that in spite of my momentary disregard of her feelings, I cherish for her an affection that nothing can efface or make other than the ruling passion of my life."

XLII.
WITH MISS BUTTERWORTH'S COMPLIMENTS.

They tell me that Mr. Gryce has never been quite the same man since the clearing up of this mystery; that his confidence in his own powers is shaken, and that he hints, more often than is agreeable to his superiors, that when a man has passed his seventy-seventh year it is time for him to give up active connection with police matters. *I* do not agree with him. His mistakes, if we may call them such, were not those of failing faculties, but of a man made oversecure in his own conclusions by a series of old successes. Had he listened to *me*—But I will not pursue this suggestion. You will accuse me of egotism, an imputation I cannot bear with equanimity and will not risk; modest depreciation of myself being one of the chief attributes of my character.[D]

Howard Van Burnam bore his release, as he had his arrest, with great outward composure. Mr. Gryce's explanation of his motives in perjuring himself before the Coroner was correct, and while the mass of people wondered at that instinct of pride which led him to risk the imputation of murder sooner than have the world accuse his wife of an unwomanly action, there were others who understood his peculiarities, and thought his conduct quite in keeping with what they knew of his warped and over-sensitive nature.

That he has been greatly moved by the unmerited fate of his weak but unfortunate wife, is evident from the sincerity with which he still mourns her.

I had always understood that Franklin had never been told of the peril in which his good name had stood for a few short hours. But since a certain confidential conversation which took place between us one evening, I have come to the conclusion that the police were not so reticent as they made themselves out to be. In that conversation he professed to thank me for certain good offices I had done him and his, and waxing warm in his gratitude, confessed that without my interference he would have found himself in a strait of no ordinary seriousness; "For," said he, "there has been no over-statement of the feelings I cherished toward my sister-in-law, nor was there any mistake made in thinking that she uttered some very desperate threats against me during the visit she paid me at my office on Monday. But I never thought of ridding myself of her in any way. I only thought of keeping her and my brother apart till I could escape the country. When therefore he came into the office on Tuesday morning for the keys of our father's house, I felt such a dread of the two meeting there, that I left immediately after my brother for the place where she had told me she would await a final message from me. I hoped to move her by one final plea, for I love my brother sincerely, notwithstanding the wrong I once did him. I was therefore with her in another place at the very time I was thought to be with her at the Hotel D— —, a fact which greatly hampered me, as you can see, when I was requested by the police to give an account of how I spent that day. When I left her it was to seek my brother. She had told me of her deliberate intention of spending the night in the Gramercy Park house; and as I saw no way of her doing this without my brother's connivance, I started in search of him, meaning to stick to him when I found him, and keep him away from her till that night was over. I was not successful in my undertaking. He was locked in his rooms it seems, packing up his effects for flight,—we always had the same instincts even when boys,—and receiving no answer to my knock, I hastened away to Gramercy Park to keep a watch over the house against my brother coming there. This was early in the evening, and for hours afterwards I wandered like a restless spirit in and out of those streets, meeting no one I knew, not even my brother, though he was wandering about in very much the same manner, and with very much the same apprehensions.

"The duplicity of the woman became very evident to me the next morning. In my last interview with her she had shown no relenting in her purpose towards me, but when I entered my office after this restless night in the streets, I found lying on my desk her little hand-bag, which had been sent down from Mrs. Parker's. In it was *the letter*, just as you divined, Miss Butterworth. I had hardly got over the shock of this most unexpected good fortune when the news came that a woman had been found dead in my father's house. What was I to think? That it was she, of course, and that my brother had been the man to let her in there. Miss Butterworth," this is how he ended, "I make no demands upon you, as I have made no demands upon the police, to keep the secret contained in that letter from my much-abused brother. Or, rather, it is too late now to keep it, for I have told him all there was to tell, myself, and he has seen fit to overlook my fault, and to regard me with even more affection than he did before this dreadful tragedy came to harrow up our lives."

Do you wonder I like Franklin Van Burnam?

The Misses Van Burnam call upon me regularly, and when they say *"Dear old thing!"* now, they mean it.

Of Miss Althorpe I cannot trust myself to speak. She was, and is, the finest woman I know, and when the great shadow now hanging over her has lost some of its impenetrability, she will be a useful one again, or I do not rightly read the patient smile which makes her face so beautiful in its sadness.

Olive Randolph has, at my request, taken up her abode in my house. The charm which she seems to have exerted over others she has exerted over me, and I doubt if I shall ever wish to part with her again. In return she gives me an affection which I am now getting old enough to appreciate. Her feeling for me and her gratitude to Miss Althorpe are the only treasures left her out of the wreck of her life, and it shall be my business to make them lasting ones.

The fate of Randolph Stone is too well known for me to enlarge upon it. But before I bid farewell to his name, I must say that after that curt confession of his, "Yes, I did it, in the way and for the motive she alleged," I have often tried to imagine the contradictory feelings with which he must have listened to the facts as they came out at the inquest, and convinced, as he had every reason to be, that the victim was his wife, heard his friend Howard not only accept her for his, but insist that he was the man who accompanied her to that house of death. He has never lifted the veil from those hours, and he never will, but I would give much of the peace of mind which has lately come to me, to know what his sensations were, not only at that time, but when, on the evening, after the murder, he opened the papers and read that the woman whom he had left for dead with her brain pierced by a hat-pin, had been found on that same floor crushed under a fallen cabinet; and what explanation he was ever able to make to himself for a fact so inexplicable.

FOOTNOTES:

[D] My attention has been called to the fact that I have not confessed whether it was owing to a mistake made by Mr. Gryce or myself, that Franklin Van Burnam was identified as the man who had entered the adjoining house on the night of the murder. Well, the truth is, neither of us was to blame for that. The man I identified (it was while watching the guests who attended Mrs.

Van Burnam's funeral, you remember) was really Mr. Stone; but owing to the fact that this latter gentleman had lingered in the vestibule till he was joined by Franklin and that they had finally entered together, some confusion was created in the mind of the man on duty in the hall, so that when Mr. Gryce asked him who it was that came in immediately after the four who arrived together, he answered Mr. Franklin Van Burnam; being anxious to win his superior's applause and considering that person much more likely to merit the detective's attention than a mere friend of the family like Mr. Stone. In punishment for this momentary display of egotism, he has been discharged from the force, I believe. — A. B.